1995

HUMAN RESOURCE MANAGEMENT FOR THE HOSPITALITY INDUSTRY

Karen Eich Drummond, M.S., R.D.

VAN NOSTRAND REINHOLD
New York

Library of Congress Catalog Card Number 89-22497
ISBN 0-442-31859-6

I(T)P   Van Nostrand Reinhold is an International Thomson Publishing company.
ITP logo is a trademark under license.

Printed in the United States of America

Van Nostrand Reinhold
115 Fifth Avenue
New York, NY 10003

International Thomson Publishing GmbH
Königswinterer Str. 418
53227 Bonn
Germany

International Thomson Publishing
Berkshire House,168-173
High Holborn, London WC1V 7AA
England

International Thomson Publishing Asia
221 Henderson Bldg. #05-10
Singapore 0315

Thomas Nelson Australia
102 Dodds Street
South Melbourne 3205
Victoria, Australia

International Thomson Publishing Japan
Kyowa Building, 3F
2-2-1 Hirakawacho
Chiyoda-Ku, Tokyo 102
Japan

Nelson Canada
1120 Birchmount Road
Scarborough, Ontario
M1K 5G4, Canada

ARCFF   16   15   14   13   12   11   10   9   8   7   6   5   4   3

Library of Congress Cataloging-in-Publication Data
Drummond, Karen Eich.
    Human resource management for the hospitality industry / Karen
Drummond.
        p.   cm.
    ISBN 0-442-31859-6
    1. Hospitality industry—Personnel management. I. Title.
TX911.3.P4D78   1990
647.94'068'3—dc20   89-22497
                                                          CIP

To ALBERT,
for your love and patience,
and CAITLIN,
for coming into our world.

Contents

Preface

This book has been written for use as a textbook in hospitality management programs, as well as a reference book for practicing and aspiring hospitality managers. It is designed to help hospitality students and managers understand and work with human resource managers and, more important, to deal directly and successfully with human resource issues themselves. Its content focuses on the management of human resources, with particular emphasis on supervision of employees and on traditional functions such as hiring and training.

Up to now, human resource management books have focused on goods-producing industries (manufacturing), rather than service industries such as hospitality. This book puts the spotlight on an industry in which all output—lodging and meals—is consumed when produced, and value is added to the output in intangible ways, such as added convenience. For these and other reasons, the way this industry manages human resources differs from that of companies producing goods.

There are sixteen chapters within two fairly equal sections entitled "Human Resource Functions" and "Managing Staff." Human resource functions discussed include staffing, designing jobs, training, evaluating, working with unions, supplying compensation, and protecting health and safety. The broad function of managing and supervising employees is discussed in chapters on providing management and leadership, communicating, creating a positive and motivating organizational climate, building a team, managing change and resolving conflicts, disciplining employees, and delegating. Two chapters deal with very timely topics: managing a diverse work force and managing service.

Each chapter begins with key questions to highlight the important topics, and key terms and concepts so the student will be able to focus his or her reading. The text contains ample tables and drawings to add to the meaning of the material. Each chapter is then summarized, and study questions are given to review the material and to ask the student to apply the information to hospitality industry situations. All references are listed at the end of each chapter to facilitate further reading.

Human Resource Management for the Hospitality Industry is meant to be both an informative and a practical book. After pertinent facts are presented in each chapter, practical guidelines are given. In an industry beset with labor and service problems, the factual and practical information in this book should help managers administer their most vital resource: their staff.

Acknowledgments

The author would like to thank the following people for their helpful reviews of the proposal and/or manuscript: Walter W. Ashcraft, Florida State University; Kathleen Iverson, Triton College; Carol Kizer, C.C.E., R.D., Columbus Technical Institute; Alan T. Stutts, Ph.D., University of Nevada at Las Vegas.

Introduction

Most people know something about human resources management through applying or being trained for a certain job. For instance, as a job applicant, an individual was probably directed to the company's Personnel Department to fill out an application form and go through an interview. Personnel management includes functions such as selecting, training, and compensating employees, which personnel managers tend to perform separate from each other. Human resource management extends the traditional requirements of personnel management by recognizing the interaction of personnel functions, with each other and with the organization's general objectives. Human resource management also involves an awareness of the economic, social, and legal factors affecting organizations and their employees.

In what activities do human resource managers get involved? Examples are numerous and varied: recruitment and selection of new employees, administration of wages, salaries, and benefits, collective bargaining with unions, job analyses and descriptions, training and development, discipline, performance appraisals, safety and health concerns, Equal Employment Opportunity, and public relations. Such activities all fit within the broadest functional responsibility of human resource managers: the attraction, selection, retention, development, and utilization of employees. Human resource management includes all activities that enhance the effectiveness of employees, such as the development of interpersonal skills.

HUMAN RESOURCES MANAGER

EMPLOYMENT DIVISION

Recruitment
Interviewing
Testing
Placement
Orientation
Reassignments
Terminations
Records

EMPLOYEE DEVELOPMENT DIVISION

Training Program
Training

COMPENSATION DIVISION

Job Analysis
Job Evaluation
Work Standards
Wage Surveys
Employee
   Classification

LABOR RELATIONS DIVISION

Collective
   Bargaining
Legal
Grievances
Suggestion Plans
Bargaining
   Associations

HUMAN RESOURCES PLANNING DIVISION

Forecasting
Personnel
   Inventories
Planning
   Models
Resource
   Information
Career Paths

SAFETY DIVISION

Safety -
   Campaigns
Engineering
Inspections
Education
Accident -
   Investigation
Records
Awards

MEDICAL DIVISION

Examinations
First Aid
Medical Facilities
Health Program
Treatment and
   Services

PERSONNEL RESEARCH DIVISION

Records and Reports
Statistical Analysis
Manuals
Systems and
   Procedures
Policies
Personnel Audits
Opinion Surveys

EMPLOYEE BENEFITS DIVISION

Pensions
Profit Sharing
Savings
Insurance
Cafeteria
Publications
Recreation
Counseling
Parking
Miscellaneous

EQUAL EMPLOYMENT OPPORTUNITY DIV.

Affirmative Action
Planning
Records
Discrimination
Complaints
Counseling and
   Liaison

Figure I-1. Organization of a human resources department.

Human resource managers' responsibilities can be divided into the following four areas:

1. *Policy initiation and formulation:* Human resource managers develop policies in their areas of practice that will ensure consistent guidelines in use throughout the organization.

2. *Advice:* The human resource manager is responsible for advising the other managers in the organization, such as the food and beverage manager, on topics such as disciplinary actions, recruitment, salary administration, and any other problem solving to meet both the employees' and the organization's needs.

3. *Service:* The human resource manager performs an assortment of activities such as those already noted.

4. *Control:* The human resource manager monitors all departments within the organization to be sure they are conforming to established personnel policies.

Figure I-1 shows how a human resource department is organized.

The hospitality industry has only recently given more than casual attention to human resource management, due in part to increased governmental regulations and greater managerial need to attract and retain employees. Some trends affecting this change include the record-keeping requirements of the Equal Employment Opportunity program; the virtual end of the employment-at-will doctrine, resulting in more employers being taken to court for unjustly firing an employee; the increased cost of benefits; and the drying up of the labor market.

It is important to keep in mind that the hospitality manager is also a human resource manager. In smaller hospitality operations, there is likely to be no one whose job is strictly human resource management. Even in larger organizations in which there is a human resource department, the hospitality manager will also function as a human resource manager, but of course within the limits set by the department. Whether the organization is big or small, human resource policies and procedures on topics such as discipline or training are imperative. For a new hospitality manager, it is of first importance to become acquainted with human resource policies and procedures, as well as how closely he or she will need to work with a human resource department or whoever is performing those functions.

Part I

Human Resource Functions

Chapter 1

Staffing

KEY QUESTIONS

1. What are the three basic components of staffing?
2. What is the intent of Equal Employment Opportunity and affirmative action policies, and in which laws are they embodied?
3. How is human resource planning accomplished and why?
4. Why is there a labor shortage for the hospitality industry?
5. What are some industry approaches to the labor shortage?
6. How are applicants recruited?
7. What are the components of the selection process, and how are they used to make appropriate selection decisions?

KEY TERMS AND CONCEPTS

Staffing

Title VII of the Civil Rights Act of 1964

Bona fide occupational qualification (BFOQ)

Equal Employment Opportunity (EEO)

Equal Employment Opportunity Commission (EEOC)

Uniform Guidelines on Employee Selection Procedures

Adverse impact

Age Discrimination in Employment Act

Equal Pay Act

Affirmative action

Fair employment practice acts (FEP)

Human resource planning

Turnover

Retention

Exit interviews

Recruitment

Employment requisition

Promoting from within

Nepotism

Selection

Job specification

Job description

Application

Interview

Preemployment testing

Psychological tests

Performance tests

Polygraph

Background investigation

Can-do factors

Will-do factors

Negligent hiring

Job offer

Staffing is a major function within human resources management and probably the area in which the hospitality manager interacts the most with the human resource department, where one exists. Staffing has three basic components: human resource planning, recruiting, and selecting. Each component warrants separate discussion, along with the laws and guidelines affecting staffing.

The topic of staffing within the hospitality industry has been and will continue to be a hot one. Whereas potential employees were once plentiful, this is no longer the case. The labor shortage has greatly affected how and where the hospitality industry is recruiting employees.

STAFFING AND THE LAW

Employment Discrimination

Table 1-1 lists important federal laws and executive orders regarding employment discrimination. A key piece of legislation, *Title VII of the Civil Rights Act of 1964,* makes it unlawful for an employer to discriminate against applicants or employees with respect to hiring, compensation, or terms or conditions of employment on the basis of race, color, religion, sex, national origin, or pregnancy. The selection of applicants must be based on the person's abilities, experience, and education as they relate to the job standards and requirements. Any criteria used in the selection process must be consistently and directly related to job performance.

The only exception to this law is the case of a *bona fide occupational qualification (BFOQ).* A BFOQ is a job requirement to which the *Equal Employment Opportunity (EEO)* laws do not apply. For example, an attendant in a men's restroom has to be male. In order to meet legal requirements, a BFOQ must be a business necessity; in other words, the business would be negatively affected without such an exemption from the law.

Title VII also created the *Equal Employment Opportunity Commission (EEOC)* to administer and enforce the law. In 1978 the EEOC and three other government agencies—the Civil Service Commission, Department of Labor, and Department of Justice—presented a unified federal position on nondiscriminatory employment practices: the *Uniform Guidelines on Employee Selection Procedures.* This document applies to private employers who employ fifteen or more employees for twenty or more weeks in a calendar year, as well as to federal, state, and local governments. It was designed primarily to show employers how to comply with EEO laws. It also asks employers to be able to demonstrate that selection procedures are job-related and valid—that is, reliable in predicting good job performance. This can be useful if an employer is taken to court and the plaintiff claims there is *adverse impact* (or unequal effect) on a protected group.

Some of the key terms contained in the guidelines are defined below.

Adverse impact: A substantially different rate of selection in hiring, promotion, or other employment decisions that works to the disadvantage of members of a particular race, sex, or religious or ethnic group.

Table 1-1. Important federal laws and executive orders regarding employment discrimination

Federal Laws and Executive Orders	Type of Employment Discrimination Prohibited	Employers Covered
Equal Pay Act of 1963	Sex differences in pay, fringe benefits, and pensions for substantially equal work	Private
Title VII, 1964 Civil Rights Act	Discrimination in all human resource activities based on race, color, sex, religion, or national origin; established Equal Employment Opportunity Commission to administer the law	Private; federal, state, and local governments; unions; employment agencies
Age Discrimination in Employment Act of 1967 (as amended in 1986)	Age discrimination against those forty years of age or older	Private; unions; employment agencies
Executive Order 11478 (1969)	Discrimination based on race, color, religion, sex, national origin, political affiliation, marital status, or physical handicap	Federal government
Equal Employment Opportunity Act of 1972	Amended Title VII, gave EEOC more power to enforce, and extended coverage	Educational institutions; other employers
Rehabilitation Act of 1973, Executive Order 11914 (1974)	Discrimination based on physical or mental handicap	Federal government; federal contractors
Vietnam Era Veterans Readjustment Act of 1974	Discrimination against disabled veterans and Vietnam veterans	Same as above
Pregnancy Discrimination Act of 1978	Discrimination in hiring, promoting, or terminating because of pregnancy; pregnancy to be treated as a medical disability	Same as Title VII

Substantially different rate of selection: The agencies have adopted a rule of thumb under which they will generally consider a selection rate for any race, sex, or ethnic group to be substantially different if it is less than four-fifths, or 80 percent, of the highest selection rate for any other group. This 80 percent rule of thumb is not intended as a legal definition, but rather a practical means of keeping the attention of the enforcement agencies on discrepancies in rates of hiring, promotion, and other selection decisions.

Compliance with these guidelines: Use of a selection procedure is in compliance with these guidelines if it has been validated—if it does not result in adverse impact on any race, sex, or ethnic group—or, in unusual circumstances, if use of the procedure is otherwise justified in accordance with federal law.

The EEOC enforces not only Title VII, but also the *Age Discrimination in Employment Act* and the *Equal Pay Act.* As amended in 1986, the Age Discrimination in Employment Act makes it unlawful to discriminate against anyone over forty years old because of the person's age. The Equal Pay Act requires equal pay, fringe benefits, and pensions for both men and women who do substantially equal work. The intent of Equal Employment Opportunity laws is the employment of individuals in a fair and nondiscriminatory manner.

EEO laws also try to correct special problems of protected groups such as members of minorities, women, older people, and those with physical disabilities. All employers with over 100 employees must submit annually an Equal Employment Opportunity report, referred to as the EEO-1 report. In this report, all employees are first classified into job categories, and each job category is separated into gender and minority status. This form is examined by the EEOC in the event of a discrimination claim, to see if the composition of a specific group in the operator's labor force is at least eighty percent of the normal rate for that area. In order to obtain the data needed for this report, employers are allowed to collect minority group data on job applicants as long as any form requesting such information is kept separate from the application.

To be prepared for possible claims of discrimination and show support of equal employment opportunity, operators should keep records of all recruitment efforts for one year, including advertisements, referral sources, and so on. Title VII requires retention of all employment and personnel records, including applications, for six months, unless the applicant is over 40, in which case it is one year.

Going beyond EEO, *affirmative action* is a policy that requires organizations to correct past discriminatory practices by making extra efforts to recruit, hire, and promote qualified members of protected groups. This is implemented by having organizations set up affirmative action programs to ensure a balanced and representative work force. Affirmative action programs are required for employers with federal contracts over a certain amount, as well as employers who have been found guilty of discriminatory employment practices; such programs are also freely developed by some employers.

In developing an affirmative action program, a company will generally take the following steps (Equal Employment Opportunity Commission 1974):

1. Issue a written equal employment policy and affirmative action commitment.
2. Appoint a top official with responsibility and authority to direct and implement the program.
3. Publicize the policy and affirmative action commitment.
4. Survey present minority and female employment by department and job classification.
5. Develop goals and timetables to improve utilization of minorities, males, and females in each area that has been identified.
6. Develop and implement specific programs to achieve goals.
7. Establish an internal audit and reporting system to monitor and evaluate progress in each aspect of the program.
8. Develop supportive in-house and community programs.

On occasion, the existence of an affirmative action program has led to an accusation of reverse discrimination, which is when an unprotected individual, such as a white male, charges an employer with discrimination because a member of a protected group received preference of some kind.

Besides federal laws, state and local governments also have *fair employment practice acts (FEP)*. They are patterned after federal legislation and often extend antidiscrimination laws to employers with just one or more employees. They might expand the definition of discrimination to include such factors as physical appearance or marital status. State and local agencies such as the Michigan Department of Civil Rights are set up to administer the fair employment practice acts.

Child Labor Provisions of the Fair Labor Standards Act

The Fair Labor Standards Act is a federal law applying to child labor. For minors, there are laws restricting maximum work hours, night work, and jobs involving certain types of equipment and the serving of alcoholic beverages. The federal child labor laws are described below; however, if a state or local law is stricter than the federal one, the state or local law must be followed.

Minimum Employment Age: fourteen years old

Minors fourteen and fifteen years of age may not do any of the following:

Cooking (except at soda fountains, lunch counters, snack bars, or cafeteria serving counters) or baking

Work requiring the use of a ladder

Occupations that involve operating, setting up, adjusting, cleaning, oiling, or repairing power-driven food slicers and grinders, food choppers and cutters, or bakery-type mixers

Work in freezers or meat coolers or in preparation of meats for sale (except wrapping, sealing, labeling, weighing, pricing, or stocking when performed in other areas)

Loading and unloading goods to and from trucks, railroad cars, or conveyors

Work in warehouses, except office or clerical work

Minors sixteen and seventeen years of age may not:

Operate elevators or power-driven hoists

Operate power-driven shearing machines or bakery machinery

Operate circular saws or band saws

Drive certain motor vehicles (without restrictions)

Maximum work hours

Ages fourteen and fifteen: on school days, three hours per day, eighteen hours per week; on nonschool days, eight hours per day, forty hours per week. Also work may not begin before 7 A.M. nor end after 7 P.M., except from June 1 through Labor Day, when evening hours are extended to 9 P.M.

Ages sixteen and over: no restrictions on work hours

Immigration Reform and Control Act (1986)

Under the Immigration Reform and Control Act, employers must verify the identity and employment eligibility of all individuals hired after November 6, 1986, and who continued to be employed after May 31, 1987. This is accomplished by filling out Form I-9, Employment Eligibility Verification. In order for someone who is not a U.S. citizen to work in this country, the employee must have an Alien Registration Receipt Card (frequently referred to as a green card, although it is no longer green).

Form I-9 must be filled out completely by the employer and new employee within three business days of the hire date and kept on file for three years, or one year after an employee is terminated, whichever is later. The new employee must supply documents to establish identity and employment eligibility as listed on Form I-9. Although employers are not required to keep copies of the documentation presented, if documentation is kept for one employee, it should be kept for all employees. If the paperwork is not done correctly, the first-offense maximum fine is $1,000 per instance. In cases where unauthorized aliens have been hired, the first offense has a $2,000 maximum fine, the second offense a $5,000 maximum, and any further offenses a $10,000 maximum.

HUMAN RESOURCE PLANNING

Human resource planning is the process of reviewing personnel to ensure that the appropriate number of employees with the required skills and whatever else is desired are available when needed. When an organization sets long- and short-range plans, it needs to consider personnel. At times a company may have to alter its goals due to the personnel available. For example, some restaurant chains may be unable to open stores in particular areas due to anticipated inadequate staffing.

Human resource planning involves three steps: forecasting needs or demands, analyzing the supply of qualified applicants, and balancing supply and demand. Hospitality managers can begin to forecast labor needs by maintaining a record for each department of the number of budgeted positions by job title, the number of filled and vacant positions, recruiting time required, training time required, and how many people to hire and when. When determining how many people to hire, keep in mind normal turnover rates, peak business months, and anticipated vacancies due to retirement, transfer, termination, promotion, and demotion.

When analyzing the supply of qualified applicants, a good source of information is the local job service or state employment office. It can provide such vital information as the area's unemployment rate, the skill levels of the available work force, the amount of time it usually takes to recruit qualified applicants, the geographic areas from which to draw, the level of competitive wages and benefits for the area, the available transportation, the extent of competition moving into the area, and demographic factors including breakdowns of the age, income, and education level of the local population. Other sources of information include the state department of labor, city or county economic development office, and local Chamber of Commerce and Small Business Administration. Analysis also requires checking out competitors' recruitment strategies, their wages and benefits, and any plans to expand.

The last step in human resources planning involves balancing supply and demand. This is accomplished through recruitment and selection of some personnel and simultaneous reductions in existing staff. Reductions normally occur through resignation, retirement, termination, transfer, layoff, promotion, and demotion. Before discussing recruitment, however, it is necessary to examine in some detail the labor market for the hospitality industry.

THE LABOR MARKET

It is a sad fact that many hotels, motels, and eating establishments are having problems getting qualified employees. For instance, a 1988 study that the National Restaurant Association commissioned found two problems in particular: fewer qualified applicants overall and fewer applicants for hourly jobs. Why is this the case? Table 1-2 describes selected employment characteristics for hotels, motels, and eating and drinking places. Such characteristics lead to several explanations for the current labor shortage:

1. The Bureau of Labor Statistics projected that by 1990 there would be 11 percent fewer workers ages 16 to 24 than there were in 1984. After 1990 the number is expected to continue to decline, but at a lower rate, and in 1995 the number will stabilize. These young people represent an important component of the hospitality job force. The decline in this group has occurred because the post–World War II baby boom ended by the mid-1960s, and the birthrate declined throughout the 1970s.

Table 1-2.   Employment characteristics for hotels, motels, and eating and drinking places

Hotels and Motels	Eating and Drinking Places
In 1986, the average hours worked totaled 30.8 per week.	In 1984, the average work week totaled 26.3 hours, the lowest of any industry.
The average hourly wage was $5.97 in 1986, and it increased with the size of the property.	The average hourly wage was $4.35 (excluding tips) in 1986.
The turnover rate for hourly employees is 105 percent.	The median turnover rate for hourly employees is about 250 percent.
About 44 percent of employees work in food and beverage areas and 20 percent in housekeeping.	Employees are mostly female and younger than in other industries, but are similar in race and ethnic origin.

Sources: Carlino 1988; Hiemstra 1987a; Hiemstra 1987b; National Restaurant Association 1988.

2. Competition for the 16-to-24 age group from retail and other industries is and will continue to be a concern (National Restaurant Association 1988).

3. The average wages paid in the hospitality industry are significantly below the average hourly rate for nonsupervisory jobs (excluding the agricultural sector), which is $8.76 (National Restaurant Association 1988).

4. The high yearly *turnover* rate, especially for eating and drinking places, makes the labor shortage even worse because of the increased frequency of having to find replacements. Turnover refers to the loss of an employee who must be replaced. Turnover, defined as a percentage, is calculated as follows:

$$\text{Turnover Rate} = \frac{\text{Number of Replacements}}{\text{Average Number of Employees}} \times 100\%$$

5. The hospitality industry continues to grow and therefore to have more jobs that need to be filled. Since 1970 the number of jobs in the foodservice industry has more than doubled. Similarly, the demand for lodging has increased, due to overall population growth, business expansion, and rising income (Hiemstra 1987b).

6. Tough new immigration laws have decreased the number of applicants for some operators. The 1986 federal Immigration Reform and Control Act prohibits employers from hiring illegal aliens and fines them heavily for doing so.

7. The unemployment rate is not high in most places, although teenage unemployment, especially for black teenagers, remains high.

8. Last, but not least, is the negative view some people have of working in a hospitality position.

In the restaurant business, about half of all separations—such as resignation or termination—occur within the first thirty days (Carlino 1988). Nationally, the Bureau of National Affairs reports for 1987 that half of all types of employees left their jobs in the first year. As can be seen in Table 1-2, turnover is high in the hospitality industry, and with that comes certain costs. Hiring an unskilled hourly employee who does not work out may cost between $400 and $1,500 per employee, or typically up to about one month's pay. In two surveys of hotels, the cost of hiring and training nonmanagerial employees was between $1,100 to $1,500 each (Bove, 1987). These figures can go up to $2,000 to $3,000 for skilled employees such as line cooks and servers. This basically covers the expenses for recruiting and selecting a new candidate, doing all the necessary paperwork for the new employee such as payroll and benefit records, training the worker, and covering overtime costs incurred while the position is vacant, as well as any severance pay.

It often takes at least five weeks for a position to be filled when taking into account getting the paperwork done, recruiting, interviewing, selecting, and then giving the new employee time to leave the former job and be trained for the new one. The cost of filling positions can go higher the longer the position goes unfilled and the more skill and training are required. And worse than the dollar cost incurred is how high turnover tends to lower both employee morale and quality of service and to cause stress for managers. Unmanaged turnover can cause a significant loss of customers.

Turnover can occur due to either voluntary or involuntary reasons. When an employee leaves a job voluntarily, it may be a blessing, if the worker created problems, or a misfortune, if he or she was a good worker. Good employees might be leaving to make more money elsewhere or to get what they think will be a more interesting and challenging job, perhaps in a better working environment. In many cases, through good selection processes and management, ways can be found to keep desirable employees. Problem employees might also be indicative of poor management procedures, in that frequently they prove to have been hired due to poor selection procedures. Employees also leave jobs involuntarily, due to termination or layoff. Termination, too, can usually be traced to poor selection procedures. Causes of turnover, therefore, may include poor employee selection, wages that are not competitive, few opportunities for advancement, inadequate orientation and training, poor supervision, and unfavorable working environment. Table 1-3 lists related labor trends of interest both in hotels and motels and in eating and drinking places.

What are hospitality operators doing about this situation? Among other things, they are learning that new approaches are needed.

INDUSTRY APPROACHES TO THE LABOR SHORTAGE: RETAINING EMPLOYEES

In order to attract more employees and hold onto them—a decrease in turnover referred to as *retention*—employers are offering better advancement opportunities, higher starting wages, more orientation and training, regular job evaluation, flexible schedules, transportation to work, improved benefits, child care assistance, greater employee involvement in operations, recognition programs, and profit sharing or stock option purchase plans. Other methods being

Table 1-3. Labor trends in hotels and motels and in eating and drinking places

Labor Trends in Hotels and Motels	Labor Trends in Eating and Drinking Places
Larger properties experience the lowest turnover rate for hourly employees.	Labor shortage problems vary by type of establishment and labor market.
Front- and back-office personnel are harder to hire, especially for properties with higher room rates. On the other hand, food and beverage employees are not hard to hire, especially by properties with higher room rates.	Large operations are having more problems with labor shortages than smaller ones are.
Part-time labor is being used more often.	Chain and franchise operations have more problems with labor shortages than independents have.
In the future, the labor supply is expected to meet the demand mostly through the attraction of labor from competing industries, which will mean more wage increases.	Hardest hit are operations in the Northeast, mid-Atlantic, and Midwest regions.
	Labor shortages are worst in areas where unemployment rates are very low.
	It is more difficult to fill back-of-the-house positions, especially cooks and dishwashers.
	There have been increases in the average age of employees and in the employment of blacks, Hispanics, and males.
	Without improving pay and benefits and utilizing new labor sources, there is potential shortfall by 1995 of one million employees.

Sources: Carlino 1988; Hiemstra 1987a; Hiemstra 1987b; National Restaurant Association 1986; National Restaurant Association 1988.

used to reduce turnover include good communication of rules and regulations to employees, accurate job descriptions (listing of job tasks) and job specifications (listing of worker requirements), a process for resolving employee complaints, cross-training or training employees to do more than one job, and effective supervision.

Hospitality operators should conduct *exit interviews* when employees leave, to help determine the reasons for turnover. Be aware, however, that employees are not always honest about why they are leaving a job; they may state they are leaving for a better job, for example, when in reality they are having problems with their supervisor. Figure 1-1 shows an example of an exit interview form.

In addition, some operators are redesigning their facilities and jobs to require less labor. For instance, Dunkin Donuts is emphasizing drive-through instead of sit-down service. Also one fast-food operator is using an automated beverage dispenser that does everything but put lids on the cups. Another fast-food chain is testing a device by which customers enter their own orders at a computer terminal. In the end, however, finding and retaining good employees is crucial.

Name: _____   Department: _____

Today's Date: _____   Supervisor: _____

Hire Date: _____   Termination Date: _____

Starting Position: _____   Ending Position: _____

I. Reasons for Leaving

Please check off the reason for which you are leaving your employment with us. If you are leaving due to resignation, please check off the primary reason why you are resigning.

Voluntary	Involuntary
____ Resignation	____ Temporary position has ended
____ Took another position	____ Laid off
New company: _____	____ Discharged
____ Moving out of town	Reason: _____
____ Going to school	
____ Health reasons	
____ Transportation problems	
____ Home/family/personal reasons	
____ Dissatisfied with type of work	
____ Dissatisfied with advancement	
____ Dissatisfied with salary	
____ Dissatisfied with working conditions	
____ Other (please explain): _____	
____ Retired	
____ Transferring within company	

Figure 1-1. Exit interview form.

II. Employee Comments

1. How would you rate the following within the company? Your responses are strictly confidential.

	Excellent	Good	Average	Below Average	Poor
Compensation					
A. Pay					
B. Amount of vacation and holiday					
C. Amount of paid sick time					
D. Health insurance					
E. Life insurance					
F. Retirement plan					
Working Environment					
G. Physical working conditions					
H. Amount of training					
I. Quality of training					
J. How your job was designed					
K. Performance evaluation system					
L. Disciplinary policies and practices					
M. Recognition for work performance					
N. Amount of communication					
O. Supervisory abilities of your boss					
P. Promotion policies and practices					

Comments:

_____

_____

_____

_____

2. Did you feel a part of the company? ____ Yes ____ No

3. What did you like most about your job and/or the company?

_____

_____

4. What did you like least about your job and/or the company?

_____

_____

5. Please describe any suggestions that you feel would have made your stay with our company more enjoyable and/or of a longer duration.

_____

_____

_____   _____
Signature of Interviewer   Signature of Employee

Figure 1-1. (Continued)

16

RECRUITMENT

Recruitment refers to the search for individuals from both inside and outside an organization in sufficient numbers and with appropriate qualifications to apply for the jobs that need to be filled. Keep in mind that in the 1990's most of the growth in the labor force will consist of females and minorities. In an organization large enough to have its own human resource department, a human resource manager will usually assist by having hopefuls fill out application forms, by advertising for positions, and by posting vacant positions in-house. In the case of a human resource department, the recruiting process is typically started with the hospitality manager filling out and forwarding to it—with the appropriate approvals—an *employment requisition* form (fig. 1-2); this is much like a purchase order and functions as a control mechanism to make sure managers are filling approved positions.

Many organizations have a policy of *promoting from within,* also referred to as internal recruiting, whenever possible. This policy has the advantage of

---

Department: _____   Position to be filled: _____

Position Vacant Due to: ____ Incumbent leaving the company

Name: _____

Separation Date: _____

____ New Position

Is position budgeted? ____ Yes ____ No

Is position temporary ____ or permanent ____ ?

Is position full-time ____ or part-time ____ ?

Hours of position/days off: _____

When needed? _____

Minimum educational and work experience (attach job specification): _____
_____
_____

Critical job duties (attach job description): _____
_____
_____
_____

APPROVALS   Department Head _____ Date _____

General Manager _____ Date _____

Director, Human Resources _____ Date _____

Figure 1-2.   Employment requisition.

rewarding and motivating employees, giving them something to work toward. At times, though, it may be wiser to hire people from the outside who have new ideas and a different perspective. Many employers post vacant positions, meaning that openings are listed in designated locations, such as a bulletin board outside the human resource department. Some companies maintain on computer a complete record of qualifications of every employee so that when a position becomes vacant, the human resource manager can obtain a list of people within the company who could fill the position.

For companies looking outside the organization, there is a wide variety of recruitment methods and sources, including the following:

- Advertising
- In-house publicity
- Employee referrals
- Walk-ins and unsolicited applications
- High schools, vocational-technical schools, colleges and universities
- Job fairs
- Various organizations, agencies, and associations such as those for senior citizens, women, the handicapped, veterans, minorities, and local businesses
- Professional and trade organizations and societies (national, state, and local)
- Branches of the military
- Federal government (veteran and youth training programs)
- State employment service or job service center
- Private Industry Council
- Private employment agencies
- Temporary agencies
- Leasing companies
- Prisons (work-release programs)
- Vendor referrals
- Labor unions (if unionized)

Advertising to fill job openings is often placed in newspapers, usually on Sunday, but also can be done through television, local cable, radio, and professional organizations' publications. Domino's Pizza ran a well-received recruitment advertisement on television, featuring a model store in Plexiglas, upbeat music, and neon signs flashing messages such as ''Earn Cash''—all, of course, targeted to young people. Due to the high cost of advertising and the need for it to be impressive and effective, some operators hire agencies with expertise in recruitment advertising.

When choosing a newspaper, it is important to examine and compare the area where it is distributed, its circulation, characteristics of the readership, and advertising rates. The ad itself should include basic information such as the position title, company name, and location of job. Information to help sell the job includes competitive pay, a complete benefits package, free meals, flexible work hours, or the opportunity for advancement. Be sure to do the following in any advertising: use a company logo when possible, be specific about how people should apply, keep files of all advertising and how many applicants responded to each one, and avoid wording that refers to one sex only, such as busboy or waitress.

In three studies of newspaper recruiting advertisements by Kohl and Stephens in 1984, 1985, and 1986, hospitality firms (along with trade companies) had the highest percentages of questionable or illegal advertisements (Kohl and Stephens 1989). Most were discriminatory in using gender-specific references, such as waiter, busboy, maid, or host. Preferable terms would be server, bus help, housekeeper, and host or hostess.

Jobs can be publicized in many other ways. An in-house publicity program can include a message on place mats, receipts, table tents, and outdoor signs. Notices also can be posted in health clubs, supermarkets, churches, and community centers. Job fairs can be held on or off the company's premises to attract interested possible applicants. Tours can also be offered to potential employees.

Employee referral programs, in which a current employee refers an applicant to the company, are used very successfully by some operators to draw in new workers. Good employees often bring in talented applicants; likewise, poor employees often refer poor applicants. The employee who made the referral is rewarded with a cash bonus or some other type of incentive. When implementing such a program, it is important to include all employees, ask them to fill out a referral or recommendation form, require the referred applicants to undergo and pass the normal selection procedures, and set a period of time for the new employee to work before the other employee receives the entire or partial reward. Rewards vary from a 10-cent hourly raise to a $250 cash bonus, radios, tickets to sports events, or points toward merchandise. The rewards are often given when the new employee completes the time requirement but are sometimes provided in installments. The program may be limited to certain positions and time periods.

Employees can also be recruited through *nepotism*, which refers to hiring relatives of an existing employee. Operations may have policies that either allow this practice or discourage it. Some employers allow relatives to be hired but require them to work in a separate area or department from other relatives.

Educational institutions are an excellent source of potential employees. Many hospitality operators have work-study, co-op, and internship program arrangements with various colleges and other schools. Many also recruit at and send job notices to a school's placement office. Operators can publicize their job openings through career days at local high schools, guest lectures, and posters. Advertising can be done on college campuses through school newspapers, sporting events, or bag stuffers at the bookstore.

Many organizations, associations, and agencies can be a source of potential applicants. Some operators recently have made a lot of effort to attract applicants from women's, senior citizens', handicapped, veteran, minority, fraternal, and business groups, and there are many others. Women's groups include Displaced Homemaker organizations, the National Organization of Women and Weight Watchers, which is predominantly female in membership. Senior citizens' organizations include the American Association for Retired Persons; names of other groups can be obtained through the local Chamber of Commerce or Office on Aging. Sources of handicapped workers include state rehabilitation agencies, job service centers, and nonprofit organizations such as Easter Seals and Goodwill Industries. Sources of veterans include the Veterans Administration and the local Veterans of Foreign Wars and American Legion. Organizations such as the Urban League and state job services are sources of minority employees. Fraternal organizations include the Elks, Girl and Boy Scouts, and church groups. An excellent business group to contact for information on applicants is the local Chamber of Commerce. It is to a hospitality manager's advantage to network with local businesspeople who may be able to help with recruitment and other problems.

Among these groups, hiring retirees is becoming more common, as seen in a McDonald's television commercial. In their McMasters program, McDonald's offers jobs and training to persons older than fifty-five. The over-sixty-five group will increase to 20 percent of the population in 2020 from 12 percent in 1987 (Rosen and Jerdee 1989). Retirees tend to be loyal, dependable, and service-oriented, but they also tend to need more time off due to illness, work more slowly, and require more training. Most want to work part-time not so much for the money as for the socializing. Because most are receiving Social Security benefits, they do not want to work too many hours and earn too much money; otherwise they would have to pay some money back to Social Security.

According to the Vocational Rehabilitation Administration in Washington, D.C., approximately 18,000 people with disabilities are currently working in foodservice. There are many more who are able and willing to work in foodservice but can't find employment. Although often they take longer to train and their productivity is lower, handicapped employees tend to be dedicated, hardworking, and reliable individuals who stay with their jobs.

Other sources of information for recruiting include government agencies. The U.S. Department of Labor can be contacted about specific employment and training programs. State employment services are involved in recruiting, testing, and training unemployed people so they can return to work; state agencies also maintain a job bank, or list of open jobs, in their local offices so employers can register jobs with them. The Private Industry Council administers many government-funded services and programs on a local level; businesses often contribute money toward worthy projects such as job training. City and county governments also sometimes set up job placement assistance programs.

Private employment agencies, in a contingency search, charge a fee to the employer, which the agency does not collect until they place an applicant. Often, if a newly placed employee leaves the job during a specified period of time, referred to as the guarantee period, the agency must find a suitable replacement or return the fee. Usually the amount of the fee is based on a percentage of the employee's salary, although fees are often negotiable. Private agencies prefer to be used exclusively during a job search; however, if they are not providing good results, it is best to ask another agency for applicants as well. Often a private agency will advertise for the company.

Temporary agencies can provide hospitality employees who will stay for as little as one day, or as long as they are needed. The agencies charge by the hour. Although their hourly rates range from 50 to 150 percent higher than a typical salary for the position, this can be offset by not paying this employee any benefits. The higher rate also covers the agency's overhead and profit. There are a small number of temporary agencies specializing in filling positions for hotels, restaurants, and caterers. Temporary agencies seem most able to fill seasonal and emergency fill-in personnel and entry-level utility workers (Coppess 1988). When evaluating temporary agencies, find out how the agency selects and trains employees, if the employees are bonded and covered by liability insurance and workers' compensation, and if there is a money-back policy if an employee does not work out.

Leasing companies are a new concept being used as a source of employees on a more long-term basis than temporary agencies. Typically these companies hire employees who are trained and leased to the hospitality operator. The leasing company essentially acts as the human resource department for the operator, takes over the function of staffing and payroll, and charges a monthly service fee for the leasing service. One Chicago leasing company reports saving restaurants about two percent of their gross payroll (Slater 1988). Employees generally like to work for leasing companies because they frequently offer better benefits and more variety in work settings.

Another source of employees—not always considered—is the prison system. For instance, a major airline and a hotel chain both use inmates to handle reservations. Other methods, such as setting up industries in prisons and placing offenders in the community with a job, are being used to respond to the rising prison population and the increasing financial burden this causes. Not all convicts are hardened criminals, and many are looking for jobs in order to begin reentering society. Some ex-prisoners have useful work skills, including some learned while in prison, and want to hold onto a job. A poll taken by the Florida Prison Industries Placement Service showed much greater employer receptiveness to the idea of hiring ex-offenders than popular opinion might suggest (Henry and Odiorne 1989). Most problems that might occur due to hiring ex-offenders can be resolved by using good hiring and record-keeping practices and providing proficient and fair supervision.

SELECTION

The *selection* process involves matching the right person to the right job. Two documents crucial to selection are the *job specification* and *job description,* which are discussed in detail in chapter 2. Applicants should be matched with the requirements listed in the job specification, and their knowledge, skills, and abilities matched with the tasks detailed in the job description. Good selection practices increase organizational productivity, decrease turnover and replacement costs, and increase job satisfaction.

Steps in selection typically include getting potential employees to complete an application form, screening applications, interviewing, conducting preemployment testing, and making background checks. Once these steps are performed, a selection decision can be made.

Application and Screening

Figure 1-3 shows an *application* form. Almost all organizations use applications. Basic material obtained on an application form includes personal information such as name and address, previous work experience, education, and references, along with miscellaneous information. At the end of each application is a statement the applicant should sign to show that all information is true and that the applicant accepts the employer's right to terminate employment if any information is later found to be false. Mostly as a result of Equal Employment

Opportunity laws, certain questions can or cannot be asked on an application form or during an interview. Table 1-4 reviews examples of lawful and unlawful questions based on federal laws and guidelines. In addition, some states, through their Fair Employment Practice Office, have detailed guidelines on preemployment questions.

Even if an applicant presents a résumé, an application should be filled out. Résumés give the employer only the information the applicant wants that employer to know; applications ask for information based on the employer's needs.

Once an application is completed, it should be screened to determine if the applicant might go through any additional selection procedures. Following are some things to look for on the application and consider:

- Sloppy, hard-to-read handwriting
- Gaps in work history or overlapping jobs
- Frequent job changes
- Reasons for leaving jobs
- Salary history
- Conviction for a crime (only if job-related)
- Training and educational level
- Blank spaces

If an applicant seems promising, the next step is frequently an *interview*.

Interviewing

Purposes for an interview include reviewing and verifying education and prior work history, asking for additional information of knowledge and skills, observing poise and communication skills, drawing out character traits and motivations, and informing the applicant more fully about the job and the organization. Interviewing is a skill that requires practice.

Before interviewing, preparation is needed. Review the application once again in order to jot down any specific questions for the applicant. Also review the job description, job specification, wages, and benefits. A prepared list of general questions for applicants can be helpful and lends consistency to the process. Select a quiet place that will be private and without distractions or interruptions during the interview. Alert anyone else who will be involved in the interview process.

The interviewer should always start the interview on time, greet the applicant warmly by name, and introduce himself or herself by name and title. Start

Personnel Management
Application For Employment

Date

Month   Day   Year

Equal Opportunity/Affirmative Action Employer

The company will not discriminate against an applicant or employee because of race, sex, age, religious creed, political affiliation, national origin, sexual preference, handicap, or any veteran status.

Last Name   First   Middle Initial   Social Security Number

Present address (Street & Number)   City   State   ZIP Code   Home Phone Number

Address where you may be contacted if different from present address   Alternate Phone Number

Are you 18 years of age or older? _____   U.S. Citizen or Resident Alien? ☐ YES ☐ NO   If no, indicate type of visa

JOB INTEREST

Position you are applying for: Type of position you eventually desire:

Occupational Objective

Applying for ☐ Full Time   Weekends ☐ Yes ☐ No   Part Time Hours Desired:
           ☐ Part Time

When would you be available to begin work?

Have you previously been employed by us?   Previous Position(s) with this Company
☐ Yes ☐ No   If yes, when?

How were you referred to this company?
☐ Advertisement   ☐ Employee Referral   ☐ Employment Agency   ☐ Your Own Initiative   ☐ Other

Other than traffic violations and summary offenses, have you ever been convicted of a crime? If yes, describe in detail.

Physical Record:
Give Details:

Do you possess any physical disabilities which would prevent you from performing the duties required in the position sought?
☐ Yes ☐ No

PERSON TO BE NOTIFIED IN CASE OF EMERGENCY

Name

Address

Phone Number

EDUCATION

School	Name and Address	Dates Attended From Mo. & Yr.	To Mo. & Yr.	Circle Highest Year Completed	Type of Degree	Major Subject
HIGH SCHOOL LAST ATTENDED				1 2 3 4		
COLLEGE, UNIVERSITY OR TECHNICAL SCHOOL				1 2 3 4		
COLLEGE, UNIVERSITY OR TECHNICAL SCHOOL				1 2 3 4		
OTHER (Specify)						

List Friends or Relatives Working for this Company

Name _____ Position _____ Dept. _____

Name _____ Position _____ Dept. _____

Figure 1-3. Employment application.

PREVIOUS EMPLOYMENT—BEGIN WITH PRESENT OR MOST RECENT POSITION

1. Employer   May we contact?   Yes_____   No_____   Employed From   To

Address (include Street, City, State and Zip code)   Telephone Number

Starting Position   Salary

Last Position   Salary

Name and Title of Last Supervisor   Telephone Number

Brief description of duties:

Reason for Leaving:

Disadvantages of Last Position:

2. Employer   May we contact?   Yes_____   No_____   Employed From   To

Address (include Street, City, State and Zip code)   Telephone Number

Starting Position   Salary

Last Position   Salary

Name and Title of Last Supervisor   Telephone Number

Brief description of duties:

Reason for Leaving:

Disadvantages of Last Position:

IF MORE THAN TWO PREVIOUS EMPLOYERS, PLEASE LIST OTHERS HERE

Employment Dates		Company and Address	Position or Type of Work	Salary or Wage	Reason for Leaving
From	**To**				

Please indicate if you were employed under a different name than the one shown on the first page of this application in any of your previous positions.

Employer	Name Used

REFERENCES—OTHER THAN RELATIVES OR FORMER EMPLOYERS

Name		Occupation
Address		Phone Number
Name		Occupation
Address		Phone Number

Employment is dependent upon satisfactorily meeting the medical standards for hire.

Permission is given to investigate previous employment, educational background and references. The facts set forth in my application are true and complete; I understand that false statements on this application shall be considered sufficient cause for rating me ineligible for employment or for dismissal after employment.

Date _____   Signature of Applicant _____

Figure 1-3. (*Continued*)

Table 1-4. Lawful and unlawful questions for job applicants

Subject	Unlawful	Lawful
Name	What is your maiden name?	What is your full name? Have you ever worked or attended school under a different name?
Age	Date of birth? Age? Dates attended school?	Are you 18 or older?
Sex or marital status	Sex? Are you married, divorced, separated, or single? Are you pregnant, or intending to become pregnant? Do you have any children? What is your spouse's name and job?	
Race and national origin, citizenship	Race? Color of skin, hair, eyes? Request for photograph Where were you born? Of what country are you a citizen? Are you a native-born U.S. citizen? Date when acquired citizenship? What is your native language?	Are you a U.S. citizen? Do you have the legal right to live and work in the United States? For how long? If job-related, what foreign languages do you speak fluently?
Religion	Religious preference? Religious holidays observed?	Can you work the days this job requires?
Health	What is your health status? Any physical or mental disabilities? Any recent or past illness or operations? Date of last physical?	Do you have any health concerns that might interfere with your ability to do this job? Are you willing to take a physical if the nature of the job requires one?
Arrests	Ever been arrested?	Ever been convicted of a crime? If so, when, where, and what was the nature of the offense? (If crime is job-related, employer may refuse to hire.)
Notify in emergency	Who should be notified in an emergency, and what is their relationship?	Who should be notified in case of emergency?
Member of groups	Any memberships?	Belong to any job-related groups or organizations?

Table 1-5. Types of interview questions

Type of Question	Examples
Open	What in your background qualifies you for this position? Can you tell me something about the best boss you ever worked for? How did you feel about working with customers?
Closed	Do you like your present job? Did you get to work on time in your last job?
Direct	What are you looking for in terms of wages? How long were you in your last job?
Reflective	Do you mean you left your last job because they did not pay you enough? Am I hearing you tell me that you have good interpersonal relation skills?
Probing	What were some of the reasons for leaving your last job? What is your experience in handling reservations?
Situational	If a customer complained that her meat was too well done, what would you do? If I were your last boss, what kind of reference would I be giving you?
Loaded	Wouldn't you prefer the night shift? We are looking for a motivated person for this position. Are you motivated?

with some small talk on a neutral topic or offer the applicant a cup of coffee as a way to create an informal atmosphere and develop rapport. A seating arrangement that does not put a desk or table between interviewer and applicant is also conducive to developing rapport. At this point, it is a good idea to describe what will occur during the interview, such as discussing the applicant's qualifications, the nature of the job, and the company and answering questions.

To conduct the actual interview, it is important first to understand the types of questions that can be asked. Table 1-5 contains examples of each type discussed here. Open questions require the applicant to discuss something about himself or herself. On the other hand, closed questions can be answered with a yes or no. Direct questions can be answered with a specific piece of information. Reflective questions restate what the applicant said in order to gain more clarification. Probing questions seek more information. Situational questions ask what the applicant has done in certain circumstances in the past or would do in hypothetical situations. Loaded, or leading, questions give the desired answer to the applicant; they should be avoided. Depending on the type of information desired, different types of questions can be appropriate. To learn the most about an applicant, open, reflective, probing, and situational questions should be emphasized. To save time and avoid discrimination, standardize the types of questions asked for a particular job, and be sure to base questions on job duties and requirements.

During the interview, information is gathered about the applicant's background and qualifications, the job is fully explained, and often a tour of the work area takes place. The applicant should be made fully aware of job tasks and responsibilities, work hours, overtime requirements, policies and procedures, wages and benefits, company history and structure, and any probationary period. Both the applicant's suitability and his or her desire to perform the job within all its constraints need to be assessed during the interview.

In closing the interview, there should be time for the applicant to ask any further questions. At the same time, the applicant should be asked for any feelings about the job, and told when a decision will be made and how he or she will be notified.

Tips for interviewing include the following:

1. Be nonjudgmental during the entire interview process. Accept what is said and don't jump to conclusions. A poor interviewer reaches a decision in the first five minutes.

2. Recognize any personal biases and try not to let them be influential. Do not look for clones of oneself, and do not look for the same kind of person for all jobs.

3. Spend most of the time listening.

4. Listen for clues to the applicant's needs, wants, and motivating factors.

5. Make notes openly so that vital information is not forgotten.

6. Repeat or paraphrase the applicant's statements to attain better understanding.

7. Use pauses to allow the applicant to open up.

8. Respond to what the applicant is conveying through words and body language.

9. Paint a realistic picture of the job. Be honest. Make no promises that cannot be kept. Provide information freely.

10. Avoid halo error, which is when the interviewer judges an applicant favorably due to only one strong characteristic. The opposite of this can be called horns error, in which the applicant is rated poorly due to one weak point.

Preemployment Testing

Preemployment testing covers a wide variety of testing devices that are used to help select the best candidate for the job. Psychological, performance, and intelligence tests are some examples. All tests must meet guidelines for non-discrimination according to the EEO Uniform Guidelines on Employee Selection Procedures. Tests must be related to successful performance on the job—in other words, valid—and yield consistent results—in other words, reliable. Tests are available that are either commercially made or custom-made. Each needs to be evaluated in terms of legality, cost, time to administer, and corporate policy.

Most *psychological tests* are paper-and-pencil tests designed to measure aspects of personality that affect performance. They include attitude, honesty, and personality tests. The former measure attitudes, feelings, and beliefs. Honesty tests are the most commonly used psychological tests. They are paper-and-pencil tests used to locate high-risk applicants for positions in which dishonesty would be damaging to the organization, particularly in which dishonesty would be hard to detect. They are relatively inexpensive, not offensive to candidates, and quick to administer. One example is the Reid Honesty Test, which is a four-part paper-and-pencil test requiring forty-five minutes. It asks questions about personal honesty, drug use, and attitudes toward punishment of theft. Personality tests, such as the Minnesota Multiphasic Inventory, are designed to reveal psychological characteristics felt relevant to a particular job. Different tests focus on psychological characteristics such as emotional stability or ability to handle stress.

The London House Corporation has designed a paper-and-pencil test for hourly employees; referred to as the personnel selection inventory, it is available in ten different test forms. It tests for some of the following: honesty, drug avoidance, customer relations attitudes, emotional stability, safety, employability index, and detailed personal and behavioral history. It costs under twenty dollars to administer and can be completed in less than an hour. The test meets the Uniform Guidelines of Employee Selection Procedures regarding the construction and validation of psychological tests.

Performance tests require candidates to perform part of the job for which they have applied. For example, an applicant for a cooking position may be asked to prepare a given recipe; a front-of-the-house employee in a restaurant may be asked to set a table after being shown how it is to be done.

At the end of 1988, the Polygraph Protection Act took effect. The intent of this law was to forbid the use of a *polygraph,* or lie detector, to screen job applicants, a practice some hospitality operators previously used. The lie detector can still be used to investigate theft, if there is reasonable suspicion and advance notice is given.

A last form of testing some employers use involves medical examinations. State or local agencies may require them for food handlers, and many health care institutions require them for all new employees in the foodservice department. Some medical exams include drug testing, usually through urinalysis. Drug testing is probably the most controversial preemployment test. Some states have laws regulating its use, but generally the courts have upheld drug testing.

Background Checks

The most common form of *background investigation* is the reference check. According to the federal Bureau of National Affairs, about 90 percent of employers use a reference check to verify previous employment information, and 50 percent verify educational information (Von der Embse and Wyse 1985). Only the application form and interview are more widely used as selection techniques. Checking references has several purposes: to make sure the information is not misstated, to provide additional information about the applicant, and to reduce the possibility of being sued for negligent hiring, an issue to be discussed in the next section. Before checking references, obtain a signed waiver and release statement from the applicant to obtain references from previous employers and release from liability any organization or person requesting or supplying information.

A major concern regarding reference checks has been whether the reference cited is willing to provide detailed, candid information about an applicant. This problem stems from the Family Educational Rights Privacy Act of 1974 (FERPA), which gives students the right to examine their school files so they would know if the file contained any false or damaging information. FERPA was eventually extended to include employee personnel records. Because employees now can read reference letters, which previously employers were not legally required to reveal, employers are tending to dilute the value of their reference letters after seeing applicants take legal measures if they disagree with information in the letters.

In one survey of human resource managers, 43 percent judged the reference letter to be somewhat valuable, while 38 percent considered it of little value (Von der Embse and Wyse 1985). To increase the usefulness of reference letters, employers can do two things. First, they can have the applicant fill out and sign forms to be used in checking references, and ask applicants if they wish to sign a statement to waive their rights to see the completed reference letters. In addition, employers can be as specific as possible about the information they would like, in order to increase the possibility of getting reliable, thorough responses.

Most managers prefer checking references by telephone, as this method results in more useful, candid information and is relatively inexpensive and fast. Following is a sample list of questions to ask during a telephone reference check:

1. What are the dates of the applicant's employment with your organization?
2. What was the applicant's title when the person started and when he (or she) left?
3. What were his (or her) primary job duties and responsibilities?
4. How would you describe the applicant's performance compared with that of others?
5. How were the applicant's attendance and lateness records?
6. How did the person get along with others? Did he (or she) function as a team member when appropriate?
7. How much supervision was required?
8. How would you rank the quality of the person's work?
9. How motivated and enthusiastic was the worker toward his job?
10. What was the person's salary when he (or she) started and upon leaving?
11. Why did the person leave the job?
12. Would you rehire the applicant? Why or why not?
13. Is there anything else of significance we should know?

When checking references by phone, be confident, persistent, and assertive. Tell the person the information is confidential, and always be sure to speak to the applicant's former supervisor.

When checking educational background, there are companies that offer verification services, such as the National Credential Verification Service in Minneapolis. They can also verify professional memberships and awards.

Another way to check an employee's background is through the use of public records. Employers can look at criminal records, driving records, workers' compensation records, federal court records, and educational records. Information from these sources can be used to disqualify an applicant only if it is job-related and is consistently applied in the selection process.

Criminal records are available through either a state central repository or the county. The county tends to be quicker, less costly, and often more informative over the telephone. The information is usually more complete than the state's, but if many counties have to be contacted, it may be easier just to contact the state.

Driving records are available through a state motor vehicle office. Driving records generally can be obtained inexpensively by mail. An employer can use this information to cross-check whether date of birth and other information are accurate.

Workers' compensation records can reveal if a candidate has a past history of injury on the job and if so, if the person has been cleared to resume full duties. These records are available through the state.

Federal court records can also be obtained. Federal records generally include civil, bankruptcy, and criminal cases. In addition, educational records can always be verified through the individual educational institutions.

Selection Decision

Once information is compiled on various candidates for a job, it must all be evaluated in order to determine whom to hire. Some managers evaluate candidates by examining what is referred to as *can-do* and *will-do factors.* Can-do factors are covered in the job specification or requirement form. Job specifications spell out the knowledge, skills, aptitudes, and work history considered important to successful job performance. Will-do factors include motivation, work interests, and personal characteristics. In the hospitality industry, for example, the latter might include the ability to communicate with guests and work under pressure. In many entry-level hospitality jobs, the candidates can do the job but lack the motivation or interest required so that they will do it very well. Table 1-6 contains survey results showing characteristics that employers look for in potential hourly employees in hotels and restaurants. A written evaluation of each applicant should be written to help ensure that each person was given fair and equal consideration.

If the selection process is neglected and employers make a practice of just hiring "warm bodies," they are leaving themselves open to being sued for *negligent hiring,* in addition to previously mentioned undesirable results such as high turnover rates and poor-quality products and services. In the past ten years, lawsuits for negligent hiring have increased tremendously. The employer has the duty of due care, which means taking reasonable and appropriate precautions to avoid hiring and retaining employees who might harm other workers or the public as in assault and battery. To avoid liability for negligent hiring, the employer can do the following:

1. Conduct a thorough background check of job candidates. Verify employment, education, and residential background. Also require veterans to provide a copy of their DD214 form, which shows an honorable discharge.
2. Check out gaps in employment and short residency periods.
3. Examine state laws on hiring candidates with criminal records. Check for a criminal record if felt to be needed.

Table 1-6. Characteristics employers look for in potential hourly employees in hotels and restaurants

Hotel	Restaurant
Appearance	Dependability
Reliability	Personality
Past experience	Flexibility
Positive attitude	Appearance
Work ethic	Honesty
Personality (outgoing)	High energy
Skills	Past experience (work history)
Attendance	Team orientation
Willingness	Positive attitude
Stability	Good communication skills
Quality	Self-starter
Transferability	Stability
Team worker	Intelligence
Honesty	Service attitude
	Customer awareness
	Pride
	Work ethic (hard worker)
	Demonstrated productivity (organized)
	Smile
	Manners
	Ambition
	Integrity
	Willingness to learn

Source: VanDyke and Strick 1988.

4. When checking out work references, ask about problem behavior such as excessive absenteeism and lateness, lying, violence, inability to get along with others, and drug or alcohol abuse.

Once the candidate is selected, the person must be notified and a *job offer* extended. This is typically the responsibility of the human resource department, which should confirm the job title, working arrangements, wages, and starting date with the selected candidate. The person is also normally asked to make a decision within a certain period of time. If there is no human resource department, it is preferable for the manager supervising the new employee to make the offer. Depending on the position and the organization, the candidate may be asked to sign an offer letter, in which the terms of employment are described.

SUMMARY

Staffing is a major function within human resources management and consists of three basic components: human resource planning, recruiting, and selecting. There are a number of federal laws and executive orders, as well as state and local laws, regarding employment discrimination. The intent of Equal Employment Opportunity laws is the employment of individuals in a fair and nondiscriminatory manner, without regard to race, color, religion, sex, national origin, or pregnancy. Employment includes hiring, compensation, and terms or conditions of employment. EEO laws try to correct problems of protected groups including members of minorities, females, older people, and those with physical disabilities. Affirmative action is a policy that goes beyond EEO by requiring organizations to correct past discriminatory practices through extra efforts to recruit, hire, and promote qualified members of protected groups.

Human resource planning is the process of reviewing the personnel required to ensure that the appropriate number of employees with the required skills and other desired qualities are available when needed. It involves forecasting needs or demands, analyzing the supply of qualified applicants, and balancing supply and demand.

Hospitality operators are having problems getting qualified employees on the payroll; and this will continue. Some of the reasons for this include the declining supply of 16-to-24-year-olds, who are an important component of the hospitality job force, as well as high turnover and relatively low wages. In response to this, operators are using various techniques, such as increasing wages, to recruit and retain employees.

Recruitment refers to the search for individuals from both inside and outside the organization in sufficient numbers and with appropriate qualifications to apply for vacancies. Human resource managers typically help in recruitment. There are many ways to recruit employees, and new sources of employees including women, senior citizens, the handicapped, and ex-offenders are being tapped.

The selection process involves matching the right person to the right job. Two documents crucial to selection are the job specification and job description. Good selection practices increase productivity, decrease turnover and replacement costs, and increase job satisfaction. Steps in selection include obtaining a completed application form, screening applications, interviewing, conducting preemployment testing, and making background checks. Once these steps are performed, a selection decision can be made.

STUDY QUESTIONS

1. Describe the pros and cons of hiring from within the organization, and of going outside.
2. Why is human resource planning a planning technique?
3. What are the key documents used in matching jobs to applicants, and how are they utilized?
4. Describe recruitment methods you have seen hospitality operators use. Can you think of any recruitment methods not listed in this chapter that would bring in applicants?
5. Why are some hospitality operators recruiting the handicapped, senior citizens, and ex-offenders? Do these groups have any special needs? If so, describe them.
6. What is the basic intent of EEO laws? What is the intent of an affirmative action program, and who has these programs?
7. Explain what is meant by adverse impact and the 80 percent selection guideline.
8. Check the Sunday want ads for ones placed by hospitality firms. Do any use discriminatory words such as waitress, barmaid, and so on?
9. Which types of interview questions draw out information?
10. How do you put a job applicant at ease at the start of an interview? Why?
11. On what basis can preemployment tests be used? Describe at least three different ones.
12. Describe the human resource department's role in staffing.
13. What can be done to reduce turnover in the hospitality industry?
14. How would you go about doing a background check on an applicant for a cook's position? Are there any preemployment tests that you might want done?
15. What is an exit interview?

REFERENCES

Arthur, Diane. 1986. Preparing for the interview. *Personnel* 63(2):37–49.

Bargerstock, Andrew S. 1989. Recruitment options that work. *Personnel Administrator* 34(3):52–55.

Berger, Raymond M. 1987. How to evaluate a selection test. *Personnel Journal* 66(2):88–91.

Besnoff, Larry. 1989. Avoiding claims of negligent hiring. *Supervisory Management* 34(8):11–16.

Bove, Robert. 1987. In practice: Hotel industry grapples with high turnover. *Training and Development Journal* 41(4):14.

Broadwell, Martin M., ed. 1985. *Supervisory Handbook.* New York: John Wiley & Sons.

Brown, Darrel R. 1985. Sharpening your job interviewing techniques. *Supervisory Management* 30(8):29–32.

Carlino, Bill. 1988. The labor crisis: Looking for solutions. *Nation's Restaurant News* (May 30):F1, F6, F10.

———. 1989. Operators tap disabled to ease labor shortage. *Nation's Restaurant News* (March 6):1, 66.

Cook, Suzanne H. 1988. Playing it safe: How to avoid liability for negligent hiring. *Personnel* 65(11):32–36.

Coppess, Marcia Hibsch. 1988. Temps: Can they help your labor shortage? *Restaurants USA* 8(1):16–18.

Davidson, Jeffrey P. 1986. Checking references. *Supervisory Management* 31(1):29–31.

Elliott, Travis. 1983a. *Profitable Foodservice Management Through Recruitment and Selection of Employees.* Washington, D.C.: National Restaurant Association.

———. 1983b. *Profitable Foodservice Management Through Reduction of Employee Turnover.* Washington, D.C.: National Restaurant Association.

Equal Employment Opportunity Commission. 1974. *Affirmative Action and Equal Employment:* A Guidebook for Employers. Vol. 1. Washington, D.C.: U.S. Equal Employment Opportunity Commission.

Evans, Deane. 1988. Rules ban polygraph testing. *Nation's Restaurant News* (November 28):47.

Evans, Karen M., and Randall Brown. 1988. Reducing recruitment risk through preemployment testing. *Personnel* 65(9):55–64.

Feuer, Dale. 1987. Coping with the labor shortage. *Training* 24(3):64–75.

Fryar, Carolyn. 1988. Managing fluctuating workloads with temps. *Management Solutions* 33(2):23–27.

Frydman, Ken. 1989. Equipment solutions. *Nation's Restaurant News* (May 22):F20.

Glover, Julie Ashworth, and G. Roger King. 1989. Traps for the unwary employer. *Personnel Administrator* 34(7):52–55.

Granrose, Cherlyn S., and Eileen Appelbaum. 1986. The efficiency of temporary help and part-time employees. *Personnel Administrator* 31(1):71–83.

Henry, J. Patrick, and George S. Odiorne. 1989. Eleven myths about hiring ex-offenders. *Personnel* 66(2):27–30.

Hergenrather, Edmund R. 1988. 32 points no interviewer should miss. *Recruitment Today* 1(1):28–32.

Hiemstra, Stephen J. 1987a. *Analysis and Future Needs of Human Resources Used in the Lodging Industry.* West Lafayette, Ind.: Purdue Research Foundation.

———. 1987b. Factors affecting the supply and demand for employment in the lodging industry. *Hospitality Education and Research Journal* 11(3):135–41.

King, Paul. 1989. Working with alternatives. *Food Management* 24(3):126–35.

Kohl, John P., and David B. Stephens. 1989. Wanted: Recruitment advertising that doesn't discriminate. *Personnel* 66(2):18–26.

LaGreca, Genevieve, and Mona Rosenberg. 1987. *A Primer on How to Recruit, Hire and Retain Employees.* Washington, D.C.: National Restaurant Association.

Long, Richard C. 1988. Public records: What's missing from most background checks. *Recruitment Today* 1(1):40–45.

Madison, Roger, and Barbara Knudson-Fields. 1987. The law and employee-employer relationships: The hiring process. *Management Solutions* 32(2):12–20.

McCool, Audrey C. 1988. Older workers: Understanding, reaching and using this important labor resource effectively in the hospitality industry. *Hospitality Education and Research Journal* 12(2):365–76.

Meyer, Robert, and Gerald C. Meyer. 1988. Older workers: Are they a viable labor force for the hotel community? *Hospitality Education and Research Journal* 12(2):361–64.

Miller, Ernest C. 1980. An EEO examination of employment applications. *Personnel Administrator* 25(3):63–81.

Mondy, R. Wayne, Robert M. Noe, and Robert E. Edwards. 1986. What the staffing function entails. *Personnel* 63(4):55–58.

National Restaurant Association. 1986. *Foodservice and the Labor Shortage.* Washington, D.C.: National Restaurant Association.

———. 1988. *A 1988 Update: Foodservice and the Labor Shortage.* Washington, D.C.: National Restaurant Association.

———. 1989. *Foodservice Employment 2000: Exemplary Industry Program.* Washington, D.C.: National Restaurant Association.

Rosen, Benson, and Thomas H. Jerdee. 1989. Investing in the older worker. *Personnel Administrator* 34(4):70–74.

Ryan, Monnie. 1989. Getting through to them: Behavior-based interviewing. *Restaurants USA* 9(5):18–20.

Scalise, David G., and Daniel J. Smith. 1986. Legal update: When are job requirements discriminatory? *Personnel* 63(3):41–48.

Schuster, Karolyn. 1988. The people puzzle. *Food Management* 23(4):110–34.

Sims, Calvin. 1988. Robots to make fast food chains still faster. *The New York Times* (August 24):D5.

Slater, David. 1988. Hiring dilemma: Where will the workers come from? *Restaurants USA* 8(8):11–17.

Stanton, Erwin S. 1988. Fast-and-easy reference checking by telephone. *Personnel Journal* 67(11):123–30.

VanDyke, Thomas, and Sandra Strick. 1988. New concepts to old topics: Employee recruitment, selection and retention. *Hospitality Education and Research Journal* 12(2):347–60.

Von der Embse, Thomas J., and Rodney E. Wyse. 1985. Those reference letters: How useful are they? *Personnel* 62(1):42–46.

Chapter 2

Analyzing and Designing Jobs

KEY QUESTIONS

1. Why and how is job analysis performed?
2. What are the purposes of job descriptions and specifications?
3. How are job descriptions and specifications written?
4. What are the two major thrusts of job design?
5. What methods can be used to redesign jobs to increase employee satisfaction?

KEY TERMS AND CONCEPTS

Job	Position description
Position	Duties
Occupation	Tasks
Career	Responsibility
Job analysis	Knowledge
Job design	Abilities
Job descriptions	Skills
Job specifications	Aptitude
Job context	Personality
Task inventory	Work simplification
Functional job analysis	Time and motion studies
Job evaluation	Job enlargement
Reliability	Job enrichment
Validity	Job rotation

It is first essential to define the term *job,* as well as other related terms (table 2-1). A job consists of related activities and duties, performed on a regular basis for a set amount of compensation, and is the building block of an organization. Jobs provide the basis for forming work groups or teams, departments, and larger units and for achieving the organization's objectives. Jobs in a food-service company may include servers, cooks, and managers. The number of *positions* in an organization, on the other hand, equals the number of employees. For example, in a restaurant there may be four cook's positions. An occupation is a group of similar jobs found in different organizations. Lastly, a career is a sequence of occupations, jobs, and positions that a person has during his working life.

Table 2-1. Definitions

Term	Definition
Job	A group of identical or similar activities and duties, performed for an organization in exchange for set compensation
Position	A given individual performing one or more jobs; there are as many positions as there are employees
Occupation	A group of similar jobs found in different organizations
Career	A sequence of occupations, jobs, and positions that a person has during his working life
Job description	The detailed definition of a job as a whole, relating the what, how, why, and where of the functions involved
Job specification	The requirements of the person occupying a certain job, including knowledge, skills, abilities, other personal characteristics, and work history
Task	A distinct work activity with a specific function—for example, making change
Duty	A segment of work activity comprising one task or several related tasks with an identifiable output—for example, a housekeeper's cleaning of a room
Responsibility	A description of the results expected or how accountable an employee is for something delegated to him or her

Because organizations experience change, jobs need to be studied periodically to assure an efficient arrangement of work without duplication or gaps. This requires both *job analysis,* which examines the actual requirements of a job, and *job design,* which examines the ideal requirements of a job. *Job descriptions* and *job specifications* are two vital human resource tools associated with job analysis and design.

JOB ANALYSIS

Job analysis involves collecting, analyzing, and synthesizing job information for use in human resource and other managerial functions. In brief, job analysis tries to present a picture of how the world of work looks at a specific moment. The primary purpose of job analysis is to form the basis of the job description, a vital tool that documents in detail what a worker does.

The Job Analysis Process

Job analysis involves a series of steps. First, the problems to be resolved through job analysis must be identified in order to select the right jobs for study and define both the scope of the analysis and uses of the information obtained. Second, the job analysis is designed, selecting appropriate sources of information and methods of collecting it. Sources may include employees, supervisors, and customers. Three principal methods used to collect information include observation of the work being performed, interviews with those employees or their supervisors, and distribution of written material such as questionnaires, logs, or checklists for completion by employees or supervisors. The third step is the job analysis itself, which includes collecting, analyzing, and synthesizing the desired information. Finally, the information is applied as previously determined. For instance, it may be used to develop job descriptions, job specifications, or performance criteria for evaluations.

Job analysts specifically examine a job's input, throughput, and output, as detailed in figure 2-1. For example, a cook uses organizational input, such as cooking equipment and raw foods, as well as his own input—knowledge, skills, and abilities—to cook foods. Cooking is the throughput; in other words, the processing that links input to output. The output—prepared food—represents both a product and a service. Additionally, the analyst considers the *job*

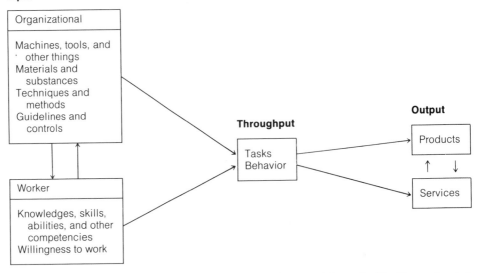

Figure 2-1. Common elements of job situations. (Reprinted from Jai V. Ghorpade, *Job Analysis: A Handbook for the Human Resource Director,* © 1988, p. 26. Reprinted by permission of Prentice Hall, Inc., Englewood Cliffs, NJ.)

context, or the conditions in which the work takes place. Some job context variables include layout and design of the workplace, other physical conditions, work flow, conditions of employment such as pay and benefits, and inter-relationships with other jobs.

There are a number of job analysis methods, which differ in objectives, procedures, and results. Some require the employee or the analyst or both to start from scratch, while others use standardized formats for analyzing jobs, which then allow comparisons with other jobs. Some methods focus directly on the job itself and are called job-oriented. Others focus on the worker, such as the person's abilities and skills, and are referred to as worker-oriented. No one method is best, and one should be chosen based on the particular purposes of the job analysis and the type of data needed.

One method is a *task inventory.* This is a questionnaire listing various tasks, which the analyst uses to define the principal ones that account for an employee's job. The task inventory is usually developed for only one job or a class of related jobs with similar tasks. Although it is an efficient way to collect quantitative data from a large number of employees, task inventories can be expensive and time-consuming to develop.

Another approach is *functional job analysis,* which is based on the assumption that every job requires a worker to function in some degree in relation to data, people, and things. One system of functional job analysis, which the U.S. Department of Labor developed, is shown in table 2-2. The job analyst determines the involvement of the employee for each function listed. Within a restaurant there are commonly nine functional activities: management, supervision, purchases, receiving and storage, production, service, cleanup, maintenance, and records.

Table 2-2. Department of Labor worker functions

Data	People	Things
Synthesizing	Mentoring	Setting up
Coordinating	Negotiating	Precision-working
Analyzing	Instructing	Operating/controlling
Compiling	Supervising	Driving/operating
Computing	Diverting	Manipulating
Copying	Persuading	Tending
Comparing	Speaking, signaling	Feeding
	Serving	Handling
	Taking instructions, helping	

Why Perform Job Analysis?

Job analysis information serves as the primary resource for writing job descriptions, which are mostly written summaries of task requirements, and job specifications, or written summaries of worker requirements. These two documents are crucial to recruitment, selection, and placement of employees, as discussed in chapter 1. The job specification, which identifies knowledge, skills, abilities, and other qualifications required for effective job performance, is used primarily for recruitment and selection. This is also useful in developing criteria and standards for evaluating performance (see chapter 4).

Job analysis is used for other human resource functions, including *job evaluation*—a ranking of jobs based on their worth to the company—and compensation. The primary function of job analysis regarding compensation is in determining compensable factors, job attributes such as knowledge that are used in appraising the worth of jobs.

Job information gleaned from analysis is also useful in determining the orientation, training, and development needs of an organization. Analysts can design and evaluate training that teaches specific knowledge and skills needed for a job. Job analysis also helps differentiate between a training need and a management problem.

Because job analysis clarifies the nature of jobs and the interrelationships among jobs, it can be used to design jobs—for example, to minimize duplication and enhance efficiency within an organization. It may also show the need to change staffing levels or reassign staff, or signal managers and supervisors to modify areas of control. Job analysis data can also be used in human resource planning, which means activities directed at making sure there are human resources available to attain future organizational objectives.

Problems with Job Analysis

A major problem in doing job analysis is that although it is necessary to obtain data from employees, unfortunately they do not always give high-quality information. Employees may not be informed on how to fill out job analysis forms or why it is so important to do this task well. Top-management support of job analysis is crucial for both employees and managers to undertake job analysis seriously. Employees need enough time to complete the analysis and also, where possible, the opportunity to participate in the design of the analysis exercise. Without proper training and guidance, employees may distort the data requested, intentionally or unwittingly. For example, a foodservice supervisor may think his or her position should be upgraded, and therefore purposely add to or misrepresent the position's duties to make it look as if he or she is really doing a higher-level job.

There are many ways to conduct a job analysis, yet often the method chosen is the one with which the human resource manager is most familiar (Wright and Wexley 1985). For instance, the use of questionnaires is very common; although this method is economical and fast, the quality of the data is not as good as using multiple gathering methods. The use of several methods increases the *reliability,* or consistency, of the data. In other words, will employees give the same information when asked about their work duties in several different ways? Using several methods also helps the *validity* of the results. Validity is the degree to which the method actually measures what it is supposed to. If an employee is asked to identify work activities, it is likely some job dimensions will be forgotten. However, if the method focuses on how the person's time is used, more information will be presented, which will increase the validity of the study.

JOB DESCRIPTIONS

The information obtained through job analysis forms the foundation of the job description. The job description relates the what, how, why, and where of a job.

Components of Job Descriptions

There is some disagreement as to what a job description should include, but widespread agreement as to what it should not include. A job description should not refer to the person doing the job, as it is written for a job, not a person. The job description also should not include worker qualifications. This should appear separately in the job specification. In addition, a description of when tasks are accomplished should be put into a more detailed *position description,* not into the job description. Job descriptions need to include identification of the job, a job summary, a list of *duties* (segments of work activities consisting of specified *tasks*), the job context, and any supplementary information (Ghorpade 1988). A sample job description is shown in figure 2-2.

Job identification includes the job title, such as cook, which needs to be descriptive of the work to be done and, when possible, the level within the organization. For example, the title head cook may involve some supervision and be at a higher level in the organization. Job titles should not include the terms *man* or *woman.* This section may also include alternative titles, subtitles, the division or section within the organization, grade level such as cook I or cook II, location of the job, whether it is exempt or nonexempt, and the reporting relationship both above and below the job. An exempt job is exempt from federal minimum wage and overtime pay requirements. Both exempt and nonexempt jobs are discussed in more detail in chapter 6.

Job Identification

Job title: Storekeeper
Reports to: Chef
Department: Kitchen
Exempt or nonexempt: Nonexempt

Job Summary

Storekeeper receives, stores, issues, and inventories food, beverages, and equipment used by the kitchen staff.

Job Duties

1. Receives and checks incoming stock for accuracy of amount, billing price, and quality, using vendor's invoice and department purchase order, which includes written specifications. Follows posted receiving procedures to ensure receipt of appropriate quality and quantity of products.
2. Unpacks supplies, and removes emptied containers to disposal area to decrease pest problems.
3. Dates and stores all stock in proper storage area (including dry, refrigerated, and freezer storage). Rotates stock, using first-in/first-out principal to ensure freshness.
4. Issues stock during posted hours, using stock requisition forms.
5. Cleans and maintains all storage areas according to posted cleaning schedule.
6. Takes physical inventory on a weekly basis, using inventory book to ensure accurate food costing and purchasing.
7. Performs other related duties as requested.
Equipment used: Battery-operated forklift, flatbed trucks, pallet jack, and scales.

Job Context

Contacts: Frequent contact with vendors' drivers and kitchen staff.
Level of supervision: Minimal
Physical conditions and demands: Receiving dock is outdoors and can be hot and humid in summer. Kitchen is air-conditioned but noisy and crowded at peak production times.
Work hazards: Strenuous job requires frequent heavy lifting of up to eighty pounds, pushing, and pulling. Back injuries possible.

Prepared by _____ Date: _____
Approved by _____ Date: _____

Figure 2-2. Job description.

A job summary should be only one to two sentences long and explain concisely the what and why of the job. It need not go into specific tasks or results expected, simply the major duty and purpose as it affects the organization.

The list of duties and tasks includes more detail on the what, how, and why of the job. The what refers to the nature of the specific tasks that make up the overall duties. How refers to the techniques and methods, resources, guidelines, and controls involved in a job. Employees use various resources in performing job duties, such as materials, tools, equipment, and other work aids. These should be mentioned in the description of duties and tasks. Often, when equipment is particularly important in doing a job, it is listed separately on the job description. Guidelines are the established policies and procedures and standard practices followed in the hospitality industry. Controls refer to the amount of supervision from above that the job requires, as well as any it involves over other personnel. By describing the extent of guidelines and controls, the job description reveals how much the employee determines his or her own performance. As for the why of the job, that refers to the purpose or results of the duties. The term *responsibility* refers to results expected, or how accountable an employee is for something delegated to him or her.

The job context answers the following questions:

1. What personal contacts does the job require, both within and outside the organization?
2. What are the physical conditions, such as temperature, humidity, noise, and ventilation?
3. What are the physical demands of the job?
4. What are the work hazards?
5. What are the personal demands, such as stress?

Writing Job Descriptions

The first question to answer is who will write the job description. Typically, a supervisor writes job descriptions for nonexempt employees, particularly when several employees, such as dishwashers, have the same job description. At managerial levels, managers are often asked to write their own job descriptions, which may then be reviewed and revised by their supervisors or, better yet, by experts who check for structure, style, and content. If managers are asked to write their own job descriptions, training is indeed required.

The *Dictionary of Occupational Titles* is a publication of the federal Department of Labor that contains standardized and comprehensive descriptions of over twenty thousand jobs. Hospitality jobs are listed under service occupations. For example, a waiter or waitress is described as someone who

> Serves meals to patrons according to established rules of etiquette, working in formal setting: Presents menu to diner, suggesting dinner courses, appropriate wines, and answering questions regarding food preparation. Writes order on check or memorizes it. Relays order to kitchen and serves courses from kitchen and service bars. Garnishes and decorates dishes preparatory to serving. Serves patrons from chafing dish at table. Observes diners to fulfill any additional request and to perceive when meal has been completed. Totals bill and accepts payment or refers patron to CASHIER (clerical) II. May carve meats, bone fish and fowl, and

prepare flaming dishes and desserts at patron's table. . . . (U.S. Department of Labor 1977)

Designed for use by the U.S. Employment Service, this book can be an excellent source to consult when writing job descriptions.

The most difficult section to write in the job description is the one on duties and tasks. First, job duties and tasks must be identified so as to describe the employee's contacts with data, people, and things. Each job duty and task needs to be explained precisely, using active rather than passive verbs (table 2-3). Job duties and tasks may be described in quantitative terms, such as how often a task is done or how much time is spent on a task, or in evaluative terms describing, for example, the complexity or importance of a certain duty. In any case, employees must be able to understand the language used.

Traditional job descriptions do not tie the duties and tasks to the big picture, that is, their importance to the larger organization and its goals. Another

Table 2-3. Specific active verbs for job descriptions

Functions	*Active Verbs*		
Compare	check	index	revise
	proofread	classify	verify
	edit	affirm	rate
	catalogue		
Contact	call	interview	conduct
	notify	refer	facilitate
	visit	attend	consult
	inform	collaborate	confer
	correspond	participate	request
	discuss	cooperate	requisition
Control	decide	schedule	employ
	determine	select	secure
	direct	assign	obtain
	authorize	act for	contract
	sign	act	require
	approve	order	follow up
	assume	initiate	expedite
	conduct	implement	correct
	execute	release	keep
	delegate	oversee	ensure
	represent	arrange	maintain
	manage	anticipate	cancel
	supervise	coordinate	close
	administer	route	adopt

Table 2-3. *(Continued)*

Functions	Active Verbs		
Count	add	inventory	remit
	total	measure	disburse
	balance	calculate	sell
	bill	reconcile	collect
	invoice	compute	appraise
	figure	compile	evaluate
	extend	pay	
Design	develop	institute	create
	plan	select	originate
	organize	define	formulate
	establish	prepare	
Operate	center	carry	feed
	align	handle	type
	clear	collate	process
	stack	dissemble	batch
	open	assemble	sort
Recommend	advise	submit	promote
	apprise	suggest	contribute
	consult	propose	interpret
	counsel		
Record	register	disseminate	merge
	receive	list	place
	code	issue	file
	note	furnish	transfer
	describe	render	tabulate
	outline	post	chart
	summarize	prepare	lay out
	write	process	amend
	compose	enter	locate
	draft	attach	find
	copy	delete	trace
	circulate	itemize	consolidate
	distribute	arrange	
Study	examine	ascertain	test
	audit	inspect	survey
	investigate	observe	scan
	analyze	sample	screen
	review	estimate	search
Teach	train	instruct	guide

Source: Reprinted by permission of the publisher, from *Building a Fair Pay Program* © 1986 Roger J. Plachy. Published by AMACOM, a division of American Management Association, New York. All rights reserved.

method of writing about job duties does involve explaining not only what needs to be done but also why it is important to the organization in terms of results (Plachy 1987). Writing job descriptions in regard to both duties and their results gives the manager an opportunity to show an employee why job duties are performed, why they are important. Such a results-oriented statement involves three components: an active verb, what the action results in (the why), and the description of the duty (the how). For instance, a traditional duty-oriented statement for a maître d' may note, "Greets customers courteously." This statement could be made results-oriented by noting, "Makes customers feel welcome and comfortable by greeting them courteously within one minute of arrival." An alternative to this format is to state the result first, then list under it the duties and tasks used to achieve it. This format may be desirable when results tend to be related to many duties and tasks.

A final duty included in most job descriptions states something to the effect that the employee "performs other job duties as needed." This statement is put in to allow for emergencies and changing work conditions. Job descriptions also should be revised once a year to allow for changes within an organization.

A last note about writing job descriptions concerns their length. Although it is not desirable to have lengthy job descriptions, length should be dictated by the purposes the job descriptions will serve within the organization.

Uses of Job Descriptions

Job descriptions probably have the potential to be the most powerful management tool of all. There are dozens of ways to use job descriptions, although most organizations use them in only five or six problem areas. One reason they are not used more often is that they are often poorly prepared. One essential function of job descriptions is to make clear to both management and employees exactly who does what. Managers use them to assign and evaluate work. For employees, a job description lets them know what is expected of them and, particularly in the case of one that is results-oriented, explains clearly the importance of the various parts of the job; this may serve to help motivate employees.

Other uses of job descriptions include providing information essential to recruitment, selection, and placement, such as helping to develop application blanks and to explain jobs to potential employees. Job descriptions also are essential to human resource planning and serve as the foundation for performance evaluation. They also permit accurate and defensible assignments of job and pay levels, thereby supporting job evaluation systems. Job descriptions are used to help in training and development, as well as career guidance. Job descriptions also provide the information needed for affirmative action and Equal Employment Opportunity reporting in order to ensure compliance.

In addition, job descriptions can be used in building teams within an organization. Often an employee or manager will give preference to his work unit's goals, rather than to those of the organization. This can be seen, for instance, in the tension felt in some restaurants between the cooks and the servers. Each group has the same goal, serving the customer with high-quality food in a timely fashion, yet that may be hard to believe when a cook is complaining that a server's orders are illegible, and the server is screaming back that the cook takes forever getting orders ready. Job descriptions can be used to make all parties aware of each other's duties in order to bring about increased understanding, appreciation, and support for the roles of co-workers. In this manner, workers can act as a team and help one another instead of criticizing one another.

Job descriptions are also helpful to the new manager who needs to learn who does what. In addition to familiarizing the manager with the various jobs, descriptions can be used to spot areas of work overlap or duplication, or other reasons for work studies in order to design improvements.

Although job descriptions are traditionally used for recruitment, selection, and placement of employees, they are less frequently used for outplacement, or help in finding new jobs for employees who are leaving. Managers can use job descriptions as a guide in giving written and oral references for departing employees; in turn, employees can use job descriptions to help prepare résumés.

Legal Concerns of Job Descriptions

In order to be legally defensible, if necessary, job descriptions first need to be written down. They also must reflect the actual jobs within the company. In other words, generic job descriptions developed without the particular organization in mind, or job descriptions that are too broad, are likely to cause problems in court. Because job descriptions are viewed as the basis for making other personnel decisions, it is essential that job descriptions be relevant and that the tasks described be critical to job performance. From a legal perspective, the job descriptions should at the very least state the tasks involved in the job.

JOB SPECIFICATIONS

In general, a job specification spells out requirements of whatever person would occupy that job. Specifications list various characteristics; tests are used to find out if an applicant possesses those characteristics. Specifications such as "ability to work grill during busy breakfast period" are commonly seen in classified advertising. Job specifications spell out the qualifications and personal characteristics, as well as work history, considered important to successful performance of a job (Ghorpade 1988). Personal characteristics necessary in the hospitality industry, for example, might include the ability to communicate with guests and to work under pressure. A sample job specification appears in figure 2-3.

Components of Job Specifications

The first part of the job specification consists of statements of *knowledge, abilities, aptitude, skills,* and other qualifications needed to perform the job. Knowledge consists of a body of information a worker has that can be applied toward performing a job task. Abilities refer to competence in performing tasks or behavior. Aptitude means the potential to do or learn something. Skills refer to physical abilities and aptitudes, such as the ability to carry a fifty-pound sack of flour. A knowledge, skill, or ability, or any combination of the three, can be called a competency, or qualification fitting a person to a particular requirement.

The next part of the specification deals with *personality* and related characteristics. Whereas the previous part describes what a person is able to do in certain areas, measures of personality and related characteristics help evaluate how a person has achieved his or her current level of expertise and the chances that the person will use such expertise to serve the organization.

Personality is a combination of psychological characteristics or variables describing how people respond to other people, objects, and situations. Some

---

Job title: Storekeeper
Knowledge: Receiving, storing, issuing, and inventorying methods. Quality and grades of foods, beverages, and equipment.
Skills and abilities: Follow oral and written instructions. Perform basic mathematical calculations addition, subtraction, multiplication, and division). Count accurately. Apply policies and procedures for this area. Perform heavy physical work, including lifting up to eighty pounds.
Personality and related characteristics: Must use good judgment for safety in area. Must show initiative, due to minimal supervision and large value of stock. Must work well with others, due to frequent contacts with drivers and department staff.
Work history: One year of experience as storekeeper preferred.
Education: High school graduate preferred. Ability to read and do basic mathematical calculations is required.

Prepared by _____ Date: _____

Approved by _____ Date: _____

Figure 2-3. Job specification.

key personality aspects include reserved or outgoing, serious or happy-go-lucky, tough-minded or sensitive, practical or imaginative, self-assured or apprehensive, and relaxed or tense. Knowledge of an employee's personality is valuable to the extent that it allows the manager to understand and predict that employee's behavior in specific work settings. Researchers in the field of organizational behavior have done studies aimed at, for instance, predicting performance quality and quantity from a knowledge of personality. The field of organizational behavior is still in its infancy, however, with respect to the specific personality characteristics that influence employee behavior and performance at work.

Related characteristics include interests, values, attitudes, and motivation. Interests are inclinations toward particular activities, such as working with the public, and also include hobbies and recreational pursuits. Values are general guides to behavior that give direction to life and show what a person tends to do with his or her time. A foodservice director in a hospital may value, or consider important, helping sick patients get well through good food. Attitudes include feelings with regard to some specific matters such as types of people, social groups, and institutions. Personality and related characteristics must always be job related.

The last components of the job specification are work history and education. Generally, a minimum level of experience and education is required for many positions; additional experience may be cited as preferred or desired.

Writing Job Specifications

When stating knowledge, abilities, aptitude, skills, and other qualifications, it is easier and more accurate to start the sentence with "knowledge of" or "skill in." Next, it is best to show the link between the qualification and the specific task to be performed. For example, "ability to cook for preparation of five-course banquets." When thinking of what is required to do a job, part of the process should include separating those qualifications needed to do the job minimally from those needed to perform it in a superior manner. In other words, minimal "required" qualifications must be separated from additional "desirable" ones. Also, specifications need to be as detailed as possible concerning the type and degree of competence needed.

Uses of Job Specifications

Job specifications are essential for recruitment, selection, and promotion. For example, detailing the knowledge, abilities, skills, and other qualifications provide information needed to formulate application forms and to determine if an applicant is qualified. Job specifications also are used in human resource planning, job classification and evaluation, training and development, and performance evaluation. The information in job specifications also enables companies to meet Equal Employment Opportunity requirements or satisfy the legal exception known as a bona fide occupational qualification, or BFOQ (see chapter 1).

Legal Concerns of Job Specifications

The main legal concern is the potential for discrimination when using a job specification for hiring, promotion, or any other activities that match a job and an employee. Job specifications must be not discriminatory but discriminating, meaning capable of distinguishing between acceptable and unacceptable levels of job performance. Specifications must be determined from the actual duties and needs of the job, not the preferences of the employer. As discussed in chapter 1, such characteristics as race, color, sex, national origin, age, and handicaps are protected under various laws unless an exception can be proved to be a business necessity.

JOB DESIGN

While the job analyst examines existing jobs, the job designer actually creates jobs, giving them their mission, methods, and place in the organizational structure. Although they perform different functions, the job designer may redesign a current job by using information the job analyst has obtained. The purpose of job design is to improve efficiency within an organization and at the same time recognize the needs, both mental and physical, of the employee doing the job.

Industrial engineering emerged from the scientific management school. Frank Gilbreth and Frederick Taylor were the originators of the scientific management movement and contributed much of the theory. The aim of scientific management was to have employees work as much like machines as possible. Industrial engineering evaluates work methods and determines time standards to improve efficiency. This is accomplished by performing *time and motion studies.* Time studies involve establishing the time required to perform a task; motion studies involve finding the best method of performing a task. *Work simplification* is the process of making a job easier. Following are some work simplification principles applicable to foodservice.[1]

---

[1] Ross, Lynne Nannen. 1972. *Work Simplification in Food Service.* Ames, IA: Iowa State University Press. Reprinted by permission.

1. Make rhythmic and smooth-flowing motions.
2. Make both hands productive at the same time.
3. Make hand and body motions few, short, and simple.
4. Maintain comfortable working positions and conditions.
5. Locate materials for efficient sequence of motions.
6. Use the best available equipment for the job.
7. Locate activity in normal work areas when possible.
8. Store materials in an orderly manner.

While improving efficiency is one goal of job design, another is to keep in mind the needs of the employees. *Job enlargement, job enrichment,* and *job rotation* are three techniques used in job redesign to make work more rewarding and the environment less stressful.

Job enlargement, also called horizontal loading, widens the scope of a job by asking an employee to perform a greater number of tasks. The tasks are similar to the current ones but offer more variety. The hope is that adding tasks will decrease boredom. An example of job enlargement in a kitchen would be training the pot washer to wash dishes, too.

In job enrichment, also called vertical loading, the employee is given more freedom, control, and/or responsibility over his work. Vertical loading refers to adding to a job such elements as allowing the employee to become more responsible for a total job cycle, from planning and organizing to evaluating results. For example, an assistant cafeteria manager may be asked to plan and implement special theme days for the operation.

Job rotation refers to employees who do different jobs on a rotating schedule. For example, in some fast-food restaurants, the employees are called "crew members," and each is trained to handle as many positions as possible to allow job rotation. Some benefits of this may include increased scheduling flexibility, leaner staffing, higher quality of output, and greater productivity.

SUMMARY

A job consists of related activities and duties, and is the building block of an organization. Jobs provide the basis for forming work groups or teams, departments, and larger units, and achieving the organization's objectives. Because organizations experience change, jobs need to be studied periodically through job analysis to assure an efficient arrangement of work without duplication or gaps. Job analysis is a technique of examining the actual requirements of a job. There are various ways to do a job analysis, such as a task inventory or a functional job analysis. To collect information for the job analysis, methods may include observing work, interviewing employees and supervisors, and obtaining completed written records such as questionnaires or logs. Job analysis yields two most important human resource documents used in recruitment and selection: job descriptions and job specifications.

Job descriptions need to include identification of the job, a job summary, a list of duties (segments of work activities consisting of specific tasks), the job context, and any supplementary information. Job descriptions are crucial so that both the manager and the employee know what is expected on the job. They also perform other functions. The job specification consists of statements of knowledge, abilities, aptitude, skills, and other qualifications needed to perform the job, as well as work history and education desired.

The job designer creates a job, giving it its mission, methods, and place in the organizational structure. The purpose of job design is to improve efficiency in an organization and at the same time recognize the mental and physical needs of the employee. Using industrial engineering techniques such as time and motion studies, the most efficient way to perform a task can be determined. Job enlargement, job enrichment, and job rotation are three techniques used in job redesign to make work more rewarding and the environment less stressful.

STUDY QUESTIONS

1. What is involved in doing a job analysis, and who within an organization may be involved?

2. Critique a job description and a job specification from a local hotel, motel, or restaurant. Do they include all the information listed in this chapter? Are they specific and job-related?

3. Examine a job description for a current or recent job. Was it accurate, clearly worded, up-to-date, and comprehensive?

4. Describe how you could use job enlargement, enrichment, and rotation at a hotel property or foodservice company.

5. Can you use job enrichment techniques as the solution to problems such as unhappiness with pay or benefits?

REFERENCES

Buford, James A., Bettye B. Burkhalter, and Grover T. Jacobs. 1988. Link job descriptions to performance appraisals. *Personnel Journal* 67(6):132–40.

Elliott, Travis. 1983. *Profitable Foodservice Management through Job Analysis, Descriptions and Specifications.* Washington, D.C.: National Restaurant Association.

Field, Hubert S., and Robert D. Gatewood. 1987. Matching talent with the task. *Personnel Administrator* 32(4):113–26.

Ghorpade, Jaisingh V. 1988. *Job Analysis: A Handbook for the Human Resources Director.* Englewood Cliffs, N.J.: Prentice-Hall.

Grant, Philip C. 1988. What use is a job description? *Personnel Journal* 67(2):44–53.

Kennedy, William R. 1987. Train managers to write winning job descriptions. *Training and Development Journal* 41(4):62–64.

Lo Bosco, Maryellen. 1985. Job analysis, job evaluation, and job classification. *Personnel* 62(5):70–74.

Markowitz, Jerrold. 1987. Managing the job analysis process. *Training and Development Journal* 41(8):64–66.

Musselwhite, W. Christopher. 1988. Knowledge, pay, and performance. *Training and Development Journal* 42(1):62–65.

Plachy, Roger J. 1987. Writing job descriptions that get results. *Personnel* 64(10): 56–63.

Ross, Lynne Nannen. 1972. *Work Simplification in Food Service.* Ames, Iowa: Iowa State University Press.

Scollard, Gene F. 1985. Dynamic descriptions. *Management World* 14(5):34–35.

U.S. Department of Labor. 1977. *Dictionary of Occupational Titles.* Washington, D.C.: U.S. Government Printing Office.

Wright, Patrick M., and Kenneth N. Wexley. 1985. How to choose the kind of job analysis you really need. *Personnel* 62(5):51–55.

Chapter 3

Training

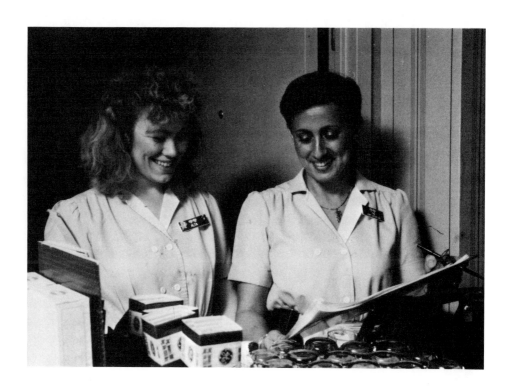

KEY QUESTIONS

1. How do you define training, learning, and coaching?
2. What are the objectives of training, and why is it so important to the hospitality industry?
3. Under what circumstances is learning enhanced?
4. How do you orient new employees?
5. How do you develop a training program?
6. What teaching methods can be used to convey information to employees and managers or supervisors? When is each one appropriate?
7. Why do some training programs fail?
8. What training resources are available to people in the hospitality industry?

KEY TERMS AND CONCEPTS

Training
Learning
Coaching
Adult learning theory
Orientation
Orientation checklist
Orientation packet
Training program
Training lessons
Needs assessment
Job skills training
Learning objectives
Audiovisual hardware and software
On-the-job training (OJT)
Lecture
Demonstrations

Tell, show, do, review
Behavior modeling
Programmed instruction
Structured discussions
Brainstorming
Case discussions
Role playing
Simulations
Games
Evaluation
Follow-up
Coaching
Job rotation
Self-study
Special projects and assignments
Mentors

A National Restaurant Association study of what the foodservice industry will look like in the year 2000 concluded that the industry will have to meet an increased need to train and develop its employees (National Restaurant Association 1988). Factors influencing *training* in the hospitality industry today include stiff competition, demanding and knowledgeable customers, and a labor shortage. These factors by themselves already point to an increased need for training, which is being felt outside of the hospitality industry as well. In a 1988 survey of *Personnel Journal* subscriber organizations, respondents reported a 38 percent increase in training expenditures over a similar period in 1986 (Grossman and Magnus 1989).

In the hospitality industry as a whole, unfortunately, training is a neglected function. Very often training is left to chance, or to another employee who really has little desire or ability to train new employees. Training requires a time commitment, which is tough to find in a business with so much time pressure. So if someone does not find the time for training, what happens? Managers will lose control over some very important aspects of their business, such as work methods, quality control, quality service, and performance standards. In other words, the housekeepers might all clean the rooms differently, the cooks might each provide different-sized portions for the same menu item, and the guests might not be welcomed quickly or treated very well.

Therefore, the need for training, *learning,* and *coaching* is clear. Training means to instruct and guide the development of a trainee toward acquiring knowledge, behavior (skills), and attitudes to meet a specific need. Most training in the hospitality industry is centered around orientation, job skills, and attitude development for both new and current managers, supervisors, and hourly employees. The overall goal of training is to bring about a desired level of work performance. Learning refers to knowledge the trainee gains through observation and study, resulting in a change in behavior or attitude. Coaching reinforces the learning acquired in training and is usually done on the job.

It is important to examine why training is important, how adults learn best, and how to develop a training program, as well as keys to excellent training programs and resources.

OBJECTIVES AND BENEFITS

Training has a variety of objectives:

- Orienting new employees to the organization and their jobs
- Helping employees perform their current jobs well
- Helping employees qualify for future jobs
- Keeping employees informed of changes within an organization
- Providing opportunities for personal development

Once the objectives are stated, it is easy to see the benefits of having training programs. Training increases productivity because employees do their jobs more efficiently. Now management can spend more time planning and organizing and less time putting out fires. With good training programs, there are fewer errors or problems such as accidents, which are counterproductive. Instead, the quality of both products and services is more consistent. Costs also are lower, due to less waste, fewer accidents, less breakage, and so on.

Both employees and guests end up more satisfied due to training. If employees are doing their jobs well, the guests know that, which decreases complaints and also makes them more likely to return. Employees are more confident and proud of what they are doing and make fewer mistakes. They are more likely to feel they belong to the organization—in other words, loyal—which can translate into lower absenteeism and turnover rates and lower recruiting and training costs. In essence, training gives the employee a dual message: "You are important to this organization, and we care about how you do your job."

In summary, training produces confident and competent employees who are more likely to stay at their job. These employees are also more likely to serve the guests in an appropriate manner.

HOW ADULTS LEARN BEST

Many tips and tricks for teaching adults are derived from research and *adult learning theory*. They can be categorized into three areas: the motivation of adult learners, the design of training programs for adults, and classroom work with adults.

Motivation:

Adults can't be forced to learn.

Learning is not its own reward; most adults seek out learning because they have a use for the knowledge or skill being sought.

Adults pursue learning experiences in order to cope with life-changing events such as a promotion, termination, or move to a new city.

Training programs:

Material for learning should be relevant, realistic, and practical. Adults prefer a straightforward, how-to style of teaching.

Adults come to the classroom with much prior experience, so they need to integrate new ideas with what they already know. Information that differs radically from what they already know will be integrated more slowly, as the old information has to be reevaluated.

Adults like to know what the purpose of the training is and how it will benefit them.

Adults learn best when given the big picture first. Next the material should be split up into small doses, going from simple to complex.

Adults generally like to participate in training and to practice new skills.

Adults learn best using different teaching methods and audiovisual or visual aids.

Material should be presented at a speed that permits mastery.

Being very self-conscious of errors, adults tend to take fewer risks in training sessions. They also do not like to compete with one another.

Adults prefer self-directed learning over group learning led by a professional. The self-directed learning is not necessarily isolated and still includes contact with people.

The adult learner should be involved in the development of training programs in order to make the programs more acceptable to them.

Classroom:

The learning environment must be comfortable, informal, quiet and without interruptions, and well lighted; surroundings should be pleasant.

Adults have much life experience, which can be tapped in the classroom to add to the class.

Adults need to be treated as adults in training.

Classes should not be too long—fifteen to thirty minutes is adequate in most cases.

Repetition and feedback such as praise are two valuable tools in the classroom.

Although these tips can't be universally applied to all adults and all training situations, they are true in the majority of cases.

ORIENTATION

Orientation is a specific type of training designed for new employees. Its purposes are to make new employees knowledgeable about their new job and at the same time give them a feeling of belonging to a competent organization where procedures and standards are important. If a new employee starts and is asked to begin working with another employee immediately without any formal orientation, the new employee is likely to feel somewhat confused and bewildered. When a manager takes the time to greet new employees and go through orientation procedures, it gives the employee the message that both he or she and the job are important.

The following topics should be discussed during orientation:

- The history, organization, and objectives or philosophy of the company
- Policies and procedures such as dress code, conduct, work schedule and breaks, tips, and parking
- Performance specifics, including job description, detailed position description, performance standards, and performance evaluation
- Training programs
- Disciplinary procedures
- Pay and benefits
- Immediate training concerns—for example, sanitation and safety

The orientation session itself should be held preferably on the employee's first day of work. Depending on its length, it may be split into two or more sessions. The new employee should not be overloaded with too much information at once. Either the employee's supervisor or another manager can conduct the session. The best way to cover the needed information is to devise and use an *orientation checklist* of all the topics to be covered (fig. 3-1). Another feature of the checklist is that upon completion of orientation, it should be signed by both parties. The checklist then becomes documentation that the employee was oriented to the new job.

Upon completion of part or all of the listed items, the employee should be taken on a tour of the facility and introduced to other employees. It is important for a manager who takes a new employee around to meet others not to express any opinions about anyone. This is unfair to new employees, who need to form their own opinions.

Once the orientation process is completed, the employee should receive an *orientation packet,* which is basically written information about everything covered during orientation. It should include benefit forms and literature, the job description, a listing of performance standards, an evaluation form, a work schedule, information on company holidays, an organization chart, a listing of pertinent policies and procedures, material on sanitation and safety basics, a union contract (if applicable), and a map of the facility and parking lots. Some of this information can be summarized into a booklet format—figure 3-2 shows a partial sample—which is handed to the employee along with the new job and position descriptions, performance evaluation form, and work schedule.

EMPLOYEE NAME _____   JOB TITLE _____   DATE OF HIRE _____

_____ 1. Welcome to the department: give tour of department and introduce other employees. Review map. Get locker information from secretary.

_____ 2. Explain function of the department, its place in the organization and departmental line of authority. (Give organizational chart.)

_____ 3. Outline duties, responsibilities and expectations of job. (Give job description and job duty schedule.)

_____ 4. Discuss performance appraisals. (Give performance evaluation form.)

_____ 5. Discuss dress code and uniform policy. Fill out uniform request form.

_____ 6. Review hours of work and weekends off. Explain holiday coverage. Review overtime and pay differential. Show where schedules are kept. (Give copy of schedules.)

_____ 7. Review work breaks and meal break.

_____ 8. Explain departmental request procedure for time off. Show where to get forms.

_____ 9. Discuss call-in policy and number to use. Discuss need of doctor's note if out sick for three or more days.

_____ 10. Review salary and when and where to pick up paycheck.

_____ 11. Review employee concerns procedure.

_____ 12. Indicate importance of reporting the following to the supervisor: any accident, major or minor (explain incident report procedure); change in address or phone number; any problems that come up at work.

_____ 13. Review importance of caring about others and team approach.

_____ 14. Discuss rules on telephone use and how to answer the telephone.

_____ 15. Review traffic control policy.

_____ 16. Explain Equal Employment Opportunity policy.

_____ 17. Discuss promotional and transfer opportunities.

_____ 18. Show locations of closest fire extinguishers, alarms, and exits. Review fire procedures.

_____ 19. Discuss disaster plan.

_____ 20. Discuss safety, personal hygiene, and sanitation.

_____ 21. Explain importance of training, and show where training schedule is posted.

_____ 22. Discuss right-to-know program.

_____ 23. Demonstrate use of all equipment in employees' work area, and allow employee to show competence using, plugging in, and unplugging all equipment.

EMPLOYEE COMMENTS: _____

_____

_____

_____

_____

EMPLOYEE SIGNATURE: _____ Date: _____

SUPERVISOR SIGNATURE: _____ Date: _____

DEPARTMENT MANAGER SIGNATURE: _____ Date: _____

Figure 3-1. New employee orientation checklist.

> # Traffic Control
>
> Only foodservice and housekeeping employees who are picking up trash are allowed into the department. All others must remain by the main entrance unless they have appointments with someone in the department. If you see someone who does not belong in the kitchen, please don't hesitate to ask, "May I help you?" They are probably looking for someone or need something.
>
> # FIRE!!
>
> The steps to be taken in case of a fire are:
>
> Persons Discovering a Fire:
>
> 1. Report the fire. Every fire must be reported, *regardless* of the type and extent.
>
>   a) Pull the fire alarm box handle
>   b) Dial 88 for the operator—say
>   where the fire is located
>   what is the type and extent, if known
>   who is calling
>
> 2. Reduce the spread of fire and smoke by closing all doors and windows. *Doors and windows are to remain closed until all-clear is given.*
>
> 3. React smoothly and quickly by using the closest *proper* extinguisher as directed on the equipment.
>
> 4. Keep all doors closed and do not use elevators.

Figure 3-2. Part of an employee orientation handbook.

DEVELOPING A TRAINING PROGRAM

Training programs can be developed to train new employees in their new jobs or retrain current employees. Training programs may also aim to upgrade employees' knowledge, behavior, or attitudes. A training program is really a series of *training lessons*. The general steps to be followed in developing a training program are outlined in figure 3-3.

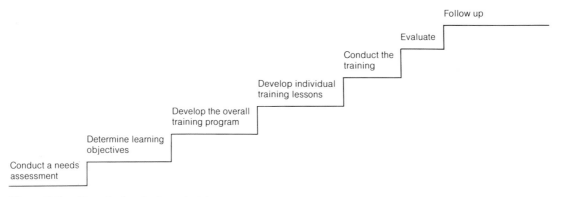

Figure 3-3. Steps in developing a training program.

Conducting a Needs Assessment

The first step in developing a training program is to make a *needs assessment,* or determination of what training is needed. Training programs should be designed both to orient new employees and to train them to perform any job. This second type is referred to as *job skills training,* which can also be used to retrain current employees when it is found, for instance, that the quality of service has decreased.

Evidence that training is needed includes unhappy guests or employees, low productivity, low sales, high costs, poor product quality such as unappetizing food, or a high accident rate. Techniques that are used in needs assessment include observing performance and comparing it to previously established standards, checking key indicators such as the evidence noted above, or surveying employees and managers as to where more training is needed.

Determining Learning Objectives

Now the actual purpose of the program must be defined. Broad, general *learning objectives* should be set for the overall training program. In addition, specific performance-based objectives are set, which will be used to guide the training lessons. Performance-based learning objectives should be realistic, easily understandable, measurable, and achievable. Then both the manager and employee will know clearly what is expected to result from the training. This makes evaluation of the program much easier.

Developing the Overall Training Program

Once the broad objectives for the training program are determined, the following need to be identified: the specific content matter, how much is to be taught at a time, and when, where, and to whom it will be taught. Costs must also be considered during this process.

The first step in a job skills training program is to analyze the job, if this has not already been done (see chapter 2). Each task or distinct work activity needs to be identified, and its procedures and rationale explained. This then becomes the content of the training program, which very often is derived from established policies and procedures within the organization. If developing a training program on sanitation and safety, for instance, the manager may wish to consult several books on these topics, in addition to looking up any relevant policies and procedures.

Determining how much to teach at a time and when to teach it depends on many factors. Employees should not be inundated with too much information in any training situation, either on the job or in the classroom. Classroom training sessions lasting from fifteen to thirty minutes are generally in order, and should be arranged when employees can afford to leave their work location without undue concern about their job not being done. If this is never really possible, training can be done at the beginning or end of a shift or another time; other employees can also be scheduled in advance to cover the positions of employees who need to attend training sessions.

When deciding where to hold the training, consider whether the work location or a classroom environment would be best. It is also necessary to decide which group of employees to target for the training—in other words, for which employees the training will be relevant.

Developing Individual Training Lessons

By this point the objectives and content are detailed for each training lesson. Teaching methods, audiovisual aids, and a trainer are still needed. Part of a sample training lesson appears in figure 3-4.

Audiovisual aids have sound and visual characteristics that make teaching and learning easier. They include films, slides, slide tapes, flip charts, transparencies, boards, simulators, and videotapes. *Audiovisual hardware* is the equipment used in presentations, such as a slide projector. *Audiovisual soft-*

LEARNING OBJECTIVE 2: Identify situations after which hand washing is necessary.

KEY CONCEPTS	TRAINER'S DIRECTIONS
2A. Hand washing: When? After you: smoke eat use the restroom touch money touch raw or cooked foods touch your face, hair, or skin cough, sneeze, or blow your nose comb your hair handle anything dirty	2A. Ask employees first when they think they should wash their hands. Using a visual aid, explain when and why. Why? When you smoke, your fingers come in contact with the saliva in your mouth. Why? When you eat, your fingers come in contact with the saliva in your mouth. Why? Your body, feces, and urine are full of bacteria. Why? Money is very dirty! Why? They may both contain bacteria. Why? Bacteria are all over your body. Why? These actions spread bacteria. Why? Your hair is full of bacteria. Why? Bacteria are likely to be present.
2B. Same as above	2B. Use an audiovisual aid and be sure to fill in any content not covered

Figure 3-4. Part of a training lesson on hand washing.

ware, also referred to as off-the-shelf training programs, run through the hardware. When choosing audiovisual software, consider such factors as cost, availability of the hardware, durability, portability, and ease of use. Also consider that in order to be effective, visual presentations should be simple, concise, uncluttered, relevant, realistic, colorful, easy to read, and accurate; pictures should be used to supplement words.

Whereas content represents what training is meant to convey, teaching methods involve how the content will be conveyed to the employee successfully; in other words, it changes behavior or attitudes or both. Table 3-1 lists teaching methods as related to the level of learner participation. The selection of an appropriate teaching method is crucial to the success of a training program.

Probably the most common teaching method used for employees is what is commonly referred to as *on-the-job training (OJT).* With this method, the new employee works with a peer or a manager or supervisor on the actual job. *OJT* is of little use if the employee is put with someone who either can't or doesn't want to train a new person or if the structure of the training is loose. Although this method has the potential to provide good hands-on experience, it has been badly abused in what has been referred to as the "buddy system." What happens here is that the job takes priority, so that the trainee may not get much explanation of what to do and also may spend too much time doing menial jobs without any significance, such as running for supplies.

OJT can work well when certain conditions are met. First, the trainer must be willing and able to train a new employee. Next, the training should be structured with specific tasks to be accomplished within certain time frames. Procedures, along with their rationale and performance standards, should be taught and the trainee allowed to do parts of the job of the trainer, when ready.

Table 3-1. Teaching methods as related to level of learner participation

Level of Learner Participation	*Method*
Learners listen and watch	Lectures, demonstrations
Learners listen, watch, and read	Programmed instruction
Learners listen, watch, read, move, write, or respond	Structured discussions, behavior modeling
Learners manipulate	Performance tryout
Learners make decisions	Brainstorming, case discussions, role playing, simulations, games

Adapted from: Laird, Dugan, *Approaches to Training and Development,* © 1985, Addison-Wesley Publishing Co., Inc., Reading, MA. Fig. 10.2 on page 132. Reprinted with permission of the publisher.

The trainee should be frequently questioned for understanding and trained off the job as well for the best results.

Other teaching methods are described below. Most are used with groups, but many can also be used in one-on-one training. The methods vary in terms of how much the employees can participate. Participatory techniques are good to use with topics that are open to discussion and analysis, or when teaching new skills that can be demonstrated and practiced. When using any technique in which employees are asked to discuss and analyze chosen topics, the group members must be ready and willing to participate and the trainer must be skilled in group dynamics (see chapter 11).

In the *lecture* method, the trainer does all the talking, making for a relatively passive and unstimulating experience for employees unless the trainer has exceptional presentation skills. While providing much information quickly, it does not encourage retention. Lecturing is a good method to get basic information across to a large number of people. This method is better when combined with teaching aids, questioning of both trainer and employees, and structured discussion.

With *demonstrations,* the trainer shows one or more trainees how to perform a specific skill, such as checking in a hotel guest or starting the dishwasher. It is suitable for learning many procedures and skills. Demonstrations typically are followed by performance tryouts, during which the employees get to practice the skills demonstrated. These methods work best when the skills are presented one step at a time and the employees practice after each step. This method is excellent at getting employee involvement, but requires some time to do properly.

A traditional approach to training developed during World War II uses the three methods discussed up to this point. The combined method has four steps: *tell* (lecture), *show* (demonstration), *do* (performance tryout), and *review.* It is an excellent method to teach new skills. It is also used to learn new behavior, under the name *behavior modeling.* The first step in behavior modeling is to explain the behavior needed to perform a task, such as how to deal with a complaint from a guest. Next, the trainer may demonstrate the desired behavior or use a medium such as video to do so. The employees are then asked to practice the procedure, and they receive feedback on their attempts. Behavior modeling is an excellent method for employees to try out new behavior in a safe environment. This method requires some time investment as well as a skilled trainer to oversee it.

Programmed instruction uses a manual or teaching machine such as a computer, instead of a trainer, to present programmed material, or subject matter with organized, logical sequences that demand continuous responses on the part of the employees. After being given a small chunk of information, the employees must each answer a question, by either writing it down or pushing a button on the machine. If the answer is right, the employee continues to the next segment of information. If the response is wrong, the employee must try until he or she gets the answer right. Programmed instruction is useful because it involves the employee, feedback is instant, and each employee can select his or her own pace.

Structured discussions are conversations between employees aimed toward meeting specific predefined objectives. In a class on kitchen safety, for example, employees may be asked to split up into small groups and develop ideas on how to prevent common kitchen accidents such as burns, falls, and fires. These ideas are usually read back to the trainer, who writes them down for all to see. The trainer must be skilled at keeping the class on track.

Brainstorming is a form of discussion in which employees are asked to generate ideas spontaneously on a given topic without evaluating them. For example, a group of cooks may be asked to brainstorm ideas on how to save energy. Next, the group analyzes the ideas and decides which ones they want to use to develop a plan of action.

Case discussions use case studies, or descriptions of real-life situations, which the employee or group studies, discusses, and answers questions about. For example, with a case study about an outbreak of food-borne illness, employees may be asked to determine what led to it. Case studies allow for analysis and application of information. As in brainstorming, there must be ample time for this method, and the trainer must be skillful in leading discussions.

In *role playing,* employees simulate a specific real or hypothetical situation involving two or more people. In health care, for example, employees may reenact delivering the wrong meal to a sick patient. This technique can be used to examine current behavior or try out new ones to build skill and confidence. The role playing itself is usually followed by discussion and analysis. It also requires much time and a skillful trainer, particularly because adults often do not want to participate.

Simulations duplicate a general real-life job situation. For instance, a simulation of a hotel front desk can be made , at which employees can practice their skills without causing any problems for actual guests. It is an excellent method, if a simulation model is available, to provide realistic job-related learning experiences.

Games may be simulations that are made competitive. Games may also be like those for children—that is, they have a set of rules and a defined objective to meet. They may be designed for one person or for groups. Good games are hard to develop but are generally fun for employees.

A final method to be discussed is really not a separate method, but some hospitality people think it not only is one but also is the be-all and end-all of training: videotapes. Videotapes are an audiovisual aid that can be effective as a medium to help accomplish learning objectives. They are useful in demonstrating behavior and dialogue as well as content that is hard to explain verbally. They are also useful in giving a consistent message within a large organization, such as a hotel chain with many different locations. They are not as useful when the material is very technical or thorough or if it is not appropriate for the employees' educational level and previous experience. Like any audiovisual aid, videotapes must be relevant and accurate in order to succeed. Homemade videotapes are not so well received, because employees will compare their quality to the better quality they see constantly on television.

Conducting the Training

Selecting a trainer and training that person to do a good job may be difficult. Ideally a manager or supervisor is probably the best choice for training. In the case of on-the-job training, if a competent employee can train, it is advisable to compensate that person in some way, because the employee is being asked to take on another significant responsibility. Examples of rewards for trainers include pay increases, a bonus, a new title at a higher level, special privileges, or some mark of distinction, such as a pin.

Being a good trainer requires a variety of characteristics; the person should be

- Knowledgeable
- Enthusiastic and interested
- Funny
- Clear and concise
- Responsive to employees
- Sincerely caring in attitude toward employees
- Patient
- A good role model
- Organized
- Able to put employees at ease
- Good at asking and answering employees
- Good in classroom management skills
- Good in reinforcement skills

All training sessions should be documented as to what was taught, who attended (confirmed with signatures), and date and time. A training record for each employee should also be maintained (fig. 3-5). These records are useful for monitoring an employee's performance and also as backup in employee discharge cases.

Evaluating

Making an *evaluation* is the crucial process of determining if training objectives were accomplished. It can occur both during and after the training. Formative evaluation uses observation, interviews, and surveys to monitor training while it is going on. Summative evaluation measures the results of the training after the program is completed, looking at it in five different ways:

1. *Reaction:* Did the employees like the program?
2. *Knowledge:* Did the employees learn the information taught?
3. *Behavior:* Are the employees using the new skills or behavior on the job?
4. *Attitudes:* Do the employees demonstrate any new attitudes?
5. *Productivity:* Did the training increase productivity, and was it cost-effective?

Various techniques can be used to answer these questions. Evaluation forms (fig. 3-6) can be filled out anonymously by participants, to determine what they liked and did not like about the training. Tests are frequently given at the end of training sessions to determine if the employees know the information or skills covered. For instance, a dishwasher may be asked the correct temperature for the final rinse and then asked to demonstrate how to pick up dishes without contaminating them. Results can also be measured through observation of employee behavior and monitoring of critical indicators such as the number of guest complaints, level of repeat business, and so forth. Questionnaires can be used with both guests and employees to collect information. After collecting information from various sources using different techniques, the person doing the evaluation needs to compare the results to the learning objectives to determine if the training indeed succeeded in bringing about the desired changes.

Following Up

Of all the steps in training, the follow-up is perhaps the most important. Unless there is follow-up to ensure that employees are using what they were taught, the expense and efforts made to train may be lost. Follow-up can be accomplished through *coaching,* which is a two-step process. First, job performance is analyzed. Next, performance is reinforced or corrected face-to-face. Coaching

EMPLOYEE NAME: _____

JOB TITLE: _____ DATE OF HIRE: _____

TRAINING ATTENDED	DATE	DATE	DATE	DATE

Figure 3-5. Sample employee training record.

Name of Class: _____ Name of Trainer: _____

Today's Date: _____

Do not sign this form! This is your opportunity to evaluate anonymously the training you have just received.

Please check the response that most accurately reflects your evaluation.

1. Amount of material
   _____ Adequate   _____ Too Much   _____ Too Little

2. Level of class
   _____ Appropriate   _____ Too Basic   _____ Too Advanced

3. Length of class
   _____ Appropriate   _____ Too Long   _____ Too Short

4. Opportunity to participate in class
   _____ Adequate   _____ Much Opportunity   _____ Too Little

5. Presentation of class
   _____ Interesting   _____ Very Interesting   _____ Boring

6. Helpfulness of Trainer
   _____ Appropriate   _____ Very Helpful   _____ Needed Help

7. Overall rating of class
   _____ Excellent   _____ Good   _____ Adequate   _____ Poor

Any additional comments:

Thank you!

Figure 3-6. Sample class evaluation form.

is a continual process that checks the results of training and also the progress toward goals set in performance evaluation sessions (see chapter 4). Following are some coaching tips:

1. Be a coach, not a drill sergeant. Don't stay constantly on employees' backs, watching or criticizing everything they do. The purpose of coaching is to help employees grow and improve their job performance. Being friendly and using praise does wonders.

2. When analyzing someone's job performance, if there appear to be problems, find out the possible causes. Be sure to discuss the situation with the employee. Does the employee know—and understand clearly—what to do? Does the employee know his or her performance is not satisfactory? Ask

the employee questions, preferably open-ended, in an effort to help, not punish.

3. When job performance is found to be in need of correction, first get an agreement with the employee that a problem exists. Next, discuss together some possible solutions and mutually agree on action to correct the concern. Follow-up is of course necessary. Recognize achievement.

4. Listen to the employee during the coaching session. Be supportive and helpful.

5. Correct errors promptly and in private. Employees are very sensitive about being told in front of their peers that they are doing something wrong. Unless the error could have grave consequences, wait at least to pull the employee aside long enough to tell him or her how to correct it.

6. Recognize when someone has reached his or her potential.

MANAGERIAL AND SUPERVISORY TRAINING

Training for managers and supervisors follows the general guidelines discussed up to this point. Some additional methods of training are used for these people. They include *job rotation, self-study, special projects and assignments,* and *mentors.* Often a hotel or foodservice company will begin a new manager by training the person to work in all areas or departments. This is referred to as job rotation. Self-study might include correspondence courses. Special projects and assignments are non-routine tasks that expose the person to new areas.

A mentor is someone who develops another individual and assists that person in a career within the organization; mentors serve as role models and teach, guide, coach, and counsel their subordinates. In this manner, mentors help an organization by having skilled and knowledgeable subordinates. The mentor also benefits by receiving admiration and seeing his or her managerial methods used. There are no formalized systems for mentors in the industry except for apprenticeships for culinary professionals (Coppess 1989). In a survey sent to two hundred general managers in hotels (Rutherford and Wiegenstein 1985), approximately two-thirds of respondents reported having had a mentor. The study showed that general managers who had mentors progressed faster in their careers than those who didn't. It was reported that mentors helped subordinates feel confident and provided guidance about career moves.

In another survey of foodservices, including those within hotels, it was found that the average length of managerial training was thirteen weeks. The most popular teaching method used was on-the-job training. Management training cost an average of $1,250 per week.

TRAINING: A CASE STUDY

Domino's Pizza operates 3,800 stores within and outside the United States. Franchisees own about 70 percent of all Domino's outlets. Training at Domino's is decentralized in structure and responsibility. There are regional training centers, which are used for its manager-in-training programs; about 85 percent of all training for employees is OJT. Thirteen regional training directors train supervisors, who each oversee six to eight stores. Supervisors then train store managers, which takes about ten months, and the latter then train their employees (Feuer 1987).

There are five distinct employee jobs at each store, and employees are cross-trained to handle all of them—phone answerer, pizza maker, oven tender, router, and driver. Each store has a videocassette recorder, and for a minimal cost any of fourteen video training packages on subjects such as orientation, delivery, and pizza making can be bought. Managers are taught to use the "tell, show, do, review" approach in training employees. Domino's also uses visually appealing posters with work-related tips, posted in appropriate places. Near the oven, for example, is a poster showing the perfect pepperoni pizza, which serves as a useful reminder to the oven tender.

Domino's franchisees can either send their managers to regional training centers or do all the training themselves, but all trainers must be certified by Domino's. In order to teach the manager-in-training program, the trainer must attend a course on how to teach the classes and then actually teach them before receiving certification. After certification, the trainer is continually monitored, and certification will be—and has been—taken away if standards are not being met. Most franchise contracts in the industry require the franchisor to provide a certain level of training before a new franchise opens. This is often supplemented with regional meetings and national conferences once or twice a year.

KEYS TO EXCELLENT TRAINING PROGRAMS

Table 3-2 describes the most common reasons for unsuccessful training, as cited in a survey of training and development executives from many industries conducted in December 1985 and January 1986 by Opinion Research Corpo-

Table 3-2. Why training fails

Reason for Failure	How Often Cited (%)
No on-the-job rewards for actions and skills learned in training	58
Insufficient time to execute training programs	55
Unsupportive work environment for new behavior learned in training	53
Lack of motivation among employees	47
Inaccurate analyses of training needs	40
Insufficient funding of training program	21

Source: Copyright 1986, *Training and Development Journal,* American Society for Training and Development. Reprinted with permission. All rights reserved.

ration for the American Society for Training and Development. What can be done to make training successful? Plenty.

Employees need incentives to learn new skills—or anything else. The incentive could be simple praise or recognition, for example by giving the employee a certificate or pin, or could include a pay increase, job title change, or better benefits.

Training programs need to be planned in advance. This can help in terms of allowing enough time for the program and getting support for it. Trainers need to be carefully selected and taught to train effectively.

Top corporate management must support training programs, which, after all, better enable employees to absorb the mission and guest-service philosophy of the organization. Top management can support programs by helping to find the time, money, and expertise to get them going.

Likewise, managers and supervisors need to reinforce what was learned in training, after employees return to their work stations, and they need to create a motivating work climate (see chapter 9). Managers also need to be good role models, by being enthusiastic, competent, calm, organized, consistent, fair, visible, and respectful of guests, employees, and peers.

HOSPITALITY INDUSTRY TRAINING RESOURCES

Many resources are available to help someone who is setting out to develop a training program. It is a waste of money to develop a training program and related materials from scratch if something already exists that may be adaptable to the person's specific needs. Following is a list of resources—places, people, and materials—that may be helpful (for address and telephone information, see appendix A):

1. Local colleges, universities, and vocational-technical schools that have a foodservice or culinary curriculum; they typically provide credit and non-credit courses in many areas such as business, management, supervising, training, and foodservice topics. Faculty members and graduate students can also help in developing and implementing training programs.

2. Industry associations such as the Educational Institute of the American Hotel and Motel Association (AHMA), the Educational Foundation of the National Restaurant Association (NRA), and the American Management Association, which offer a variety of seminars, correspondence courses, books, and training materials.

3. Professional training societies, such as the Council of Hotel and Restaurant Trainers (CHART) and the American Society for Training and Development (ASTD).

4. The local Red Cross and police and fire departments.

5. State and local health departments, which can be valuable resources for sanitation and safety programs.

6. Sales representatives of food products, supplies, and equipment; they may have training materials available.

7. Training consultants; ask the local branch of the AHMA or NRA for information.

8. Packaged training programs, which are available from a variety of vendors including the AHMA and NRA.

SUMMARY

Training means to instruct and guide the development of a trainee toward acquiring the knowledge, behavior, skills, or attitude to meet a specific need. Most training in the hospitality industry is centered around orientation, job skills, and attitude development for both new and current managerial, supervisory, and hourly employees. The overall goal of training is to bring about a certain desired level of work performance. Unfortunately, the hospitality industry has hardly embraced the idea of training, perhaps due mostly to the time constraints and pressures in this business; but with stiff competition, demanding customers, and a labor shortage, it can be a valuable tool to combat turnover, service, and many other problems.

Many tips and tricks for teaching adults are derived from research and adult learning theory. They can be categorized into three areas: the motivation of adult learners, design of training programs for adults, and work with adults in the classroom.

Orientation is a specific type of training designed for new employees. Its purposes are to make new employees knowledgeable about their new job and at the same time give them a feeling of belonging to a competent organization where procedures and standards are important. Orientation checklists and packets are useful tools with which to conduct orientation.

Programs can be developed to train new employees in their new jobs or to retrain current workers. Training programs may also aim to upgrade employees' knowledge, behavior, or attitudes. A training program is really a series of training lessons. Developing a training program follows these general steps: Do a needs assessment, determine learning objectives, develop the overall training program, develop individual training lessons, conduct the training, evaluate, and follow up through on-the-job coaching. There are numerous resources available for development of training programs.

Common teaching methods used in training include on-the-job training (OJT), lectures, demonstrations, "tell, show, do, review," behavior modeling, programmed instruction, structured discussions, brainstorming, case discussions, role playing, simulations, and games. Additional methods for managerial or supervisory training include job rotation, self-study, special projects and assignments, and mentors. A mentor is someone who develops another individual and assists him in career development.

Keys to excellent training in the hospitality industry include an incentive or reward system, advance planning, management support starting from the top, on-the-job reinforcement of training, managers who are good role models and motivators, and carefully selected and prepared trainers.

STUDY QUESTIONS

1. In a prior or current job, describe the extent of training you received and your response to it.

2. A new employee is likely to be anxious about starting a new job. What are some reasons for this anxiety, and how can they be reduced?

3. If you were asked to train a small group of adults in how to make a bed, what are some training techniques you would use based on adult learning theory?

4. What training methods might you use for teaching knowledge, skills, or behavior for the following:

what to do in case of a fire;

how to handle credit card sales at the front desk of a hotel;

how to handle a customer's complaint;

how to tell the doneness of a steak;

how to know when a food is at the right serving temperature.

5. If you are the first training director for a small chain of fast-food restaurants, what might you accomplish during your first year on the job?

6. Table 3-2 shows why training programs fail. Why do training programs succeed?

REFERENCES

Abella, Kay Tyler. 1986. *Building Successful Training Programs.* Reading, Pa.: Addison-Wesley Publishing Co.

American Society for Training and Development. 1986. Employee training in America. *Training and Development Journal* 40(7):34–37.

Arthur, Diane. 1986. The first day at work. *Management Solutions* 31(10):37–42.

Atkinson, Ann, Cindi Branch, and Greg LaHatte. 1987. Training for excellence. *Cornell H.R.A. Quarterly* 28(1):15–17.

Bell, James D., and Deborah L. Kerr. 1987. Measuring training results: Key to managerial commitment. *Training and Development Journal* 41(1):70–73.

Carlisle, Kenneth A., Sheila Murphy, and Cosimo Tripodi. 1986. *Training and Development Journal* 40(1):65–71.

Carter, Janet Houser. 1987. Participatory training, separating fantasy from reality. *Training* 24(6):46–50.

Coppess, Marcia Hibsch. 1989. Mentoring, learning the ropes from a pro. *Restaurants USA* 9(6):12–14.

Coutts, Cheryl Turi. 1987. Taco Bell combats high manager turnover. *Restaurant Business* 86(2):176–78.

Day, Dave. 1988. A new look at orientation. *Training and Development Journal* 42(1):18–23.

Farber, Bonnie, and Florence Berger. 1985. Closing the loop: Evaluating your training programs. *Cornell H.R.A. Quarterly* 26(2):49–53.

Feuer, Dale. 1987. Training for fast times. *Training* 24(7):25–30.

———. 1988a. Tales of small-time training. *Training* 25(2):29–36.

———. 1988b. The key to cloning your own business. *Training* 25(6):25–33.

Finkel, Coleman. 1986. Pick a place, but not any place. *Training and Development Journal* 40(2):51–53.

Forrest, Lewis C., Jr. 1989. *Training for the Hospitality Industry.* East Lansing, Mich.: Educational Institute of the American Hotel and Motel Association.

Foucar-Szocki, Reginald. 1987. Management training in the food service industry: A state of the art. *Hospitality Education and Research Journal* 11(3):217–22.

Fournies, Ferdinand F. 1987. *Coaching for Improved Work Performance.* Blue Ridge Summit, Pa.: Liberty House.

Gray, Norma J. 1986. Training. *Restaurants USA* 6(7):25–27.

Grossman, Morton E., and Margaret Magnus. 1989. The $5.3 billion tab for training. *Personnel Journal* 68(7):54–55.

Hultman, Kenneth E. 1986. Behavior modeling for results. *Training and Development Journal* 40(12):60–63.

Kopp, Thomas W. 1988. Making trainees want to learn. *Training and Development Journal* 42(6):43–47.

LaGreca, Genevieve. 1988. *Training Foodservice Employees.* New York: Van Nostrand Reinhold.

Laird, Dugan. 1985. *Approaches to Training and Development.* Reading, Pa.: Addison-Wesley Publishing Co.

Lambert, Clark. 1986. *Secrets of a Successful Trainer.* New York: John Wiley & Sons.

Lansing, Rick L. 1989. Training new employees. *Supervisory Management* 34(1):16–20.

Lawrie, John. 1988. Are employees using what they learn? *Personnel Journal* 67(3):95–97.

Marshall, Anthony. 1988. Educated employees can help prevent F&B disasters. *Hotel and Motel Management* 203(1):19–26.

McKenzie, Leon. 1986. The supervisor as instructor: Group discussion. *Health Care Supervisor* 5(1):41–51.

National Restaurant Association. 1988. *Current Issues Report: Foodservice Industry 2000.* Washington, D.C.: National Restaurant Association.

Phillips, Jack J. 1986. Training supervisors outside the classroom. *Training and Development Journal* 40(2):46–49.

Rutherford, Denney G., and Jane Wiegenstein. 1985. The mentoring process in hotel general managers' careers. *Cornell H.R.A. Quarterly* 25(4):16–23.

Salter, Charles A., and John B. Knight. 1985. Videotapes—fulfilling the promise. *Cornell H.R.A. Quarterly* 26(2):54–55.

Shore, Lynn McFarlane, and Arvid J. Bloom. 1986. Developing employees through coaching and career management. *Personnel* 63(8):34–41.

Zaccarelli, Herman E. 1988. *Training Managers to Train.* Los Altos: Crisp Publications, Inc.

Zemke, Ron and Susan. 1988. 30 things we know for sure about adult learning. *Training* 25(7):57–61.

Chapter 4

Evaluating Employees

KEY QUESTIONS

1. What is performance appraisal, and what purposes does it serve?
2. Which formats can be used for a performance appraisal instrument, what are their advantages and disadvantages, and how do you select a formats?
3. How do you evaluate employee performance, and which common errors should you avoid?
4. How do you conduct an effective performance appraisal interview?
5. How is performance management different from performance appraisal?

KEY TERMS AND CONCEPTS

Performance appraisal

Performance management

Pay for performance

Performance appraisal format

Performance appraisal instrument

Validity

Reliability

Graphic rating scale

Performance dimension

Behaviorally anchored rating scale (BARS)

Critical incident method

Behavior summary scale format

Management by objectives (MBO)

Essay

Checklist

Forced choice

Subjective evaluations

Halo effect

Horns effect

Error of central tendency

Leniency error

Severity error

Recency error

First-impression and fixed-impression errors

Rule of finger

Performance appraisal interview

Self-appraisal

Management by wandering around (MBWA)

Performance appraisal, the periodic evaluation of an employee's job performance, is one of the more negatively viewed and poorly performed of managerial tasks. Ron Zemke of *Training* magazine states: "Performance appraisals are about as beloved as IRS audits. . . . Evidence has been popping up to suggest that most performance appraisal systems are more noteworthy for the angst they create than the results they achieve'' (Zemke 1985). Managers and subordinates alike generally dislike performance appraisal programs and interviews. Managers often view the performance appraisal program as time-consuming (which it often is), doubt that positive results will follow, and hesitate telling employees they have areas needing improvement. Similarly, employees feel they do not get the chance to say much (which is usually true), the boss is not prepared, and they are being evaluated unfairly, with an emphasis on the negative rather than the positive.

The term *performance appraisal* itself implies that the boss is scrutinizing the weaknesses of the employee. As far back as 1957, Douglas McGregor suggested in the *Harvard Business Review* an emphasis away from appraisal to analysis, in which employees examine their own strengths and weaknesses and play an active role in the performance evaluation process (McGregor 1987). Participative management practices continue to influence the area of performance evaluation; so do the U.S. courts, which only recently started to examine performance appraisal systems for fairness. As a result, here are some recommendations for a legally defensible management system of performance appraisal:

1. Evaluation of job performance should be based on performance standards derived from a thorough job analysis of the skills, tasks, and knowledge required to perform the job. As much as possible, performance standards should be observable, measurable, and objective.

2. Performance standards must be communicated to and understood by employees in advance. This is frequently done by giving employees up-to-date and realistic job descriptions, performance standards, and an appraisal form.

3. The dimensions of job performance must be clearly defined and behaviorally based; in other words, descriptive of what people do.

4. When using rating scales, avoid abstract terms such as *loyalty* and *dependability*. Keep response categories brief, consistent, and behaviorally based.

5. Employee performance should be documented throughout the evaluation period, not just at the end. Specific performance problems should be documented on the appraisal form.

6. Management should encourage specific activities to improve problem performance areas.

7. Personnel decisions, such as promotions and demotions, should be consistent with the performance appraisals given.

8. Promotion criteria should be clearly understood and communicated, and consistently applied.

9. An appeal process is essential for employees who disagree with their supervisor's appraisal.

10. It is desirable to train those who rate performances, including specific written instructions, or to have an audit mechanism to check on the accuracy of ratings.

In a 1987 survey of organizations belonging to the Personnel and Industrial Relations Association of Southern California, 94 percent had formal performance appraisal programs, though small organizations were twice as likely not to have a formal program. Some organizations, such as small independent restaurants, have not set up any evaluation system (Locher and Teel 1988). Where formal programs do exist, there may be problems related to implementation, evaluation, or support. The policy and procedures set up for the program may be poorly understood, simply not followed, or not examined on a regular basis for improvement; management might not provide the support or commitment needed to operate the program successfully.

Evaluation of employees means much more than an annual assignment from the human resource department. It is a managerial function and responsibility that is critical to motivating employees and improving their performance and productivity. People are the major asset of all organizations, particularly service organizations. Performance evaluation is the key to utilizing and developing employees, and companies that realize this have replaced simple performance appraisal programs with a year-round cycle of continual *performance management* (fig. 4-1). In addition to reviewing performance formally at specific intervals (customarily once a year), a performance management program involves ongoing observation, assessment, documentation, and coaching of employees. In this manner, the yearly performance appraisal is less likely to create anxiety, because performance is monitored more closely.

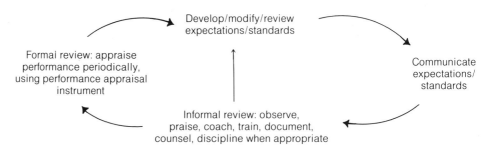

Figure 4-1. The performance management cycle.

The performance appraisal process warrants a more detailed examination of its roles or uses, the design of an evaluation form or instrument, ways of rating employees' performance, and communication of the rating during the appraisal interview. It is also desirable to examine a performance management program in greater detail.

ROLES OF PERFORMANCE APPRAISALS

Performance appraisals have various roles or uses in hospitality organizations. The 1987 survey mentioned previously indicates that appraisals are used most widely for compensation decisions, performance improvement, and feedback to employees (table 4-1). When exploring the roles of performance appraisal, it is possible to view them from the perspectives of the employee, the supervisor, and the organization.

A performance appraisal lets each employee get an answer to the question "How well am I doing?" This is an opportunity for employees not only to get feedback on how well they are meeting standards, but also to communicate and discuss their performance and what is expected of them. If problem areas of work performance are identified, an employee may be advised to undergo

Table 4-1. Primary use of appraisals

Purpose	Organizations (%)
Compensation	75
Performance improvement	48
Feedback	40
Documentation	30
Promotion	25
Training	7
Transfer	7
Discharge	6
Layoff	2
Personnel research	2
Manpower planning	2

Source: Lochner, A. H., and K. S. Teel. 1988. "Appraisal Trends," copyright September 1988. Reprinted with permission of *Personnel Journal,* Costa Mesa, CA; all rights reserved.

training. Very often, the performance appraisal acts as the basis for an employee's salary increase (referred to as *pay for performance*) or promotion. Opportunities for career and personal development also can be discussed at this time. Performance appraisals can contribute toward an employee's satisfaction and motivation, particularly when done in an appropriate manner.

For the manager, evaluating employee performance has various roles. By forcing the manager to observe and be involved in the employees' work, it improves productivity as poor performance is identified, coached, and improved. It also increases communication between manager and employees, allows the manager to get to know the employees better, and consequently strengthens the manager-employee relationship.

For the organization, performance appraisals are used to improve communication and manager-employee relationships, remind employees of the company's goals and missions, determine training needs, and thereby improve performance. This may then lead to increased morale and decreased turnover. Performance appraisals are also often used to support wage and salary decisions or justify job actions such as promotions, demotions, termination, transfer, and layoffs. Two additional roles of performance appraisals include helping to define staffing needs and to diagnose organizational problems.

PERFORMANCE APPRAISAL FORMATS

A variety of written *performance appraisal formats* or methods exist to document employee performance. Which format is selected depends to a large extent on the purpose of the performance appraisal; the need to collect different types of information in turn requires different methods. The *performance appraisal instrument* refers to the actual form used by the evaluator.

A manager can generally judge how well employees are performing in any of three ways: what they achieve (results or outcomes), what they do (behavior or actions), and what they are (knowledge, skill, abilities). For example, the housekeeping staff in a hotel can be evaluated on results, such as the number of rooms cleaned, and on the process itself, such as how well the rooms are cleaned as compared to predetermined performance standards. Performance standards or criteria translate work requirements, found in the job analysis, into levels of acceptable or unacceptable performance. Performance standards can be either quantitative, such as the number of covers or tables a waiter serves, or qualitative, such as the courtesy of a front desk employee in dealing with customers. As much as possible, performance standards should be objective, quantifiable, measurable, observable, achievable, job-based, documented, and agreed upon in advance. Avoid vague words such as *approximately, appropriate, reasonable,* and *adequate.* Figure 4-2 depicts possible appraisal formats, depending on what is going to be evaluated.

To be used successfully, and therefore fulfill their roles within an organization, performance appraisal instruments—the evaluation forms—need to be both practical and acceptable to raters and employees alike. In order to be practical, the instrument must be *easy* to understand and use. In order for it to be acceptable, raters and employees need to feel the instrument is not just practical, but also valid and reliable.

Validity is the degree to which the instrument measures what it is supposed to. For instance, are the items being rated representative of the important requirements of the job? In order to be valid, instruments need to describe observable, relevant, and quantifiable job behavior. There are times when this is not possible; however, these times should be minimized. *Reliability* refers to consistency of judgment among raters. For example, if three different people evaluate an employee and they are equally qualified to do so, are the ratings consistent? This is particularly important to employees who are often aware of and sensitive to inconsistencies. By involving employees to some extent in the development of the instrument, there is generally greater employee acceptance and satisfaction with performance appraisals.

Graphic Rating Scale

The most popular format used to appraise performance is the *graphic rating scale.* Figure 4-3 depicts one that, though still in use, has some serious handicaps. This scale delineates rating factors for a certain job, then formulates rating or response categories, from unsatisfactory to outstanding. The rating factors are known as *performance dimensions:* the categories of duties and responsibilities that constitute a job. Many different graphic rating scales exist, with most

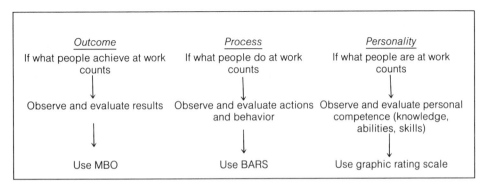

Figure 4-2. Selection of performance appraisal formats.

Factors	Unsatisfactory	Conditional	Average	Above Average	Outstanding
Quality of work					
Quantity of work					
Job knowledge					
Cooperation					
Dependability					
Attendance					
Appearance					
Get along with others					

Figure 4-3. Sample graphic rating scale.

differing in how the various performance dimensions and response categories are defined.

Performance dimensions are often based on personality traits considered important to good job performance, such as dependability, communication, and cooperation. The use of such traits in job evaluations should be avoided unless they can be defined in terms of observable, job-related behavior. For instance, dependability can be rephrased as "comes to work on time."

Graphic rating scales can be used to examine areas of an employee's competence, such as knowledge, abilities, and skills, and motivation, as related to job performance. Competence in hotel or restaurant managers might include knowledge of the customer base, ability to be a team player, and decision-making skills. Competence must be behaviorally based in order to be rated accurately and objectively.

Rating or response categories are on a scale, or continuum. The scale may be marked by numbers or by vague adjectives such as *satisfactory* or *poor,* which defy valid measurement. Response categories should be behaviorally based, unambiguous, and relevant to the dimensions being rated and the job. In general, five to nine response categories produce the most consistent ratings. For example, response categories for the performance dimension "ability to adjust and use recipes" may range from "employee can always be counted on to accurately adjust recipes and follow instructions to the letter as evidenced by consistent and high-quality products" to "employee frequently makes errors adjusting and following recipes as evidenced by products of inconsistent quality."

One advantage of this method is that it singles out both poor and high performers; however, it does not distinguish well among relatively average employees. Midrange ratings tend to be inconsistent. Although the method is less time-consuming to develop and use, special care must be taken to ensure properly defined performance dimensions and response categories. Because the scales are generally standardized for a job, they can be used to compare one employee to another. The scales also force the rater to consider several dimensions of performance. Unfortunately, this method alone gives the employee little idea of how to improve.

Behaviorally Anchored Rating Scale (BARS)

The *behaviorally anchored rating scale (BARS) is a fairly new method that* combines the graphic rating scale with what is called the *critical incident method*—a process of examining and documenting observed on-the-job *behavior that is judged to be directly related to job performance, in order to* draw a fairly clear picture for evaluation. Actual descriptions of types of significant job behavior (critical incidents) for different job dimensions are anchored on a numerical scale (fig. 4-4). A rater uses the critical incidents, or anchors, which the raters actually develop, to compare employees' actual performance. Each employee is not rated on specific critical incidents; rather, the anchors are used as a basis for observations about job-related behavior.

Developing an evaluation tool using the BARS format requires a series of steps:

1. *Critical incidents:* People who are either employees, managers, or supervisors are asked to give specific examples of effective and ineffective performance.

2. *Performance dimensions:* The developers of the performance appraisal instrument then normally categorize the critical incidents into five to ten performance dimensions.

3. *Recategorization:* This time, a new group of job participants is asked to assign a list of critical incidents to specific job dimensions.

4. *Scaling of critical incidents:* The group from the previous step is usually asked to rate behavior as to how effectively, or ineffectively, it represents performance in the given dimension. Vertical rating scales with seven to nine points are common.

5. *Final instrument:* Using various statistical methods on the data gathered from the two previous steps, a final performance appraisal instrument is completed.

The BARS format has many advantages, but some disadvantages as well. BARS is relatively easy to use, gives a clear idea of what the standards are, measures more objectively and accurately, and increases the consistency of

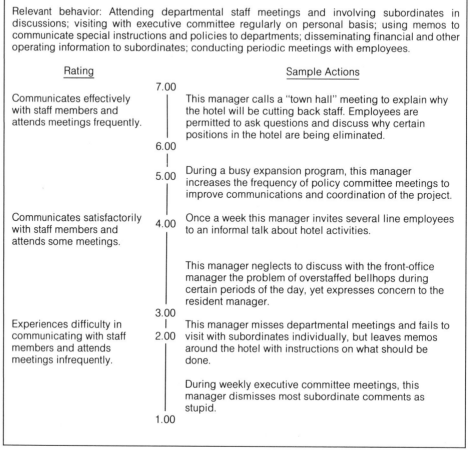

Relevant behavior: Attending departmental staff meetings and involving subordinates in discussions; visiting with executive committee regularly on personal basis; using memos to communicate special instructions and policies to departments; disseminating financial and other operating information to subordinates; conducting periodic meetings with employees.

Rating		Sample Actions
	7.00	
Communicates effectively with staff members and attends meetings frequently.		This manager calls a "town hall" meeting to explain why the hotel will be cutting back staff. Employees are permitted to ask questions and discuss why certain positions in the hotel are being eliminated.
	6.00	
	5.00	During a busy expansion program, this manager increases the frequency of policy committee meetings to improve communications and coordination of the project.
Communicates satisfactorily with staff members and attends some meetings.	4.00	Once a week this manager invites several line employees to an informal talk about hotel activities.
		This manager neglects to discuss with the front-office manager the problem of overstaffed bellhops during certain periods of the day, yet expresses concern to the resident manager.
	3.00	
Experiences difficulty in communicating with staff members and attends meetings infrequently.	2.00	This manager misses departmental meetings and fails to visit with subordinates individually, but leaves memos around the hotel with instructions on what should be done.
		During weekly executive committee meetings, this manager dismisses most subordinate comments as stupid.
	1.00	

Figure 4-4. Sample BARS scale for rating hotel manager's communication skills. (From Umbreit, Eder, and McConnell 1986. Reprinted by permission of *The Cornell H.R.A. Quarterly.*)

ratings by various raters. BARS also provides more useful information on employee strengths and weaknesses and is likely to stimulate discussion of performance. Two major disadvantages of BARS are that it requires much time and money to develop and it measures activities, not results. Another problem occurs when the rater cannot find an anchor to match to an employee's performance. BARS also would be difficult to maintain in cases where job duties change frequently.

The *behavior summary scale format* method was developed due to possible problems with the BARS format of finding similarities between employees' performance and the behavioral anchors. Instead of specific behavioral anchors, this format uses more generalized ones.

Management by Objectives

Management by objectives (MBO) is a concept that was formalized in Peter Drucker's 1954 book, *The Practice of Management.* Drucker did not originate this idea; several influential management theorists previously championed the managerial use of objectives. Although there are many varieties of MBO, in general an employee is told the objectives of the company and asked how he or she can contribute to these objectives. The employee then pursues the objectives, to some degree independent of the boss. This contrasts with management by control, in which an employee is told exactly what to do, and how and when to do it.

Management by objectives is not a system or procedure in that, for example, organizations have developed MBO goal-setting and evaluation forms. Rather, MBO is a concept, a philosophy, a behavioral orientation. MBO represents managerial behavior characterized by looking into the future, setting useful and attainable objectives, then communicating and guiding employees toward these objectives. It also acknowledges that employees need to play a major role in setting their own objectives.

How useful is MBO as an evaluation format? MBO is not meant to be used solely for evaluating employees, for many reasons. MBO only shows results, but tells little about performance or what a person did to get those results. The person may have done very little to achieve a certain outcome. The achievement of most objectives depends to some extent on factors that the employee does not control. MBO also focuses too much on numbers, such as sales figures in a foodservice company or the average annual room rate in a hotel, and not so much on how to change or improve the numbers. In addition, if employees are allowed to set their own objectives, they will tend to choose short-term ones that are achievable to the detriment of long-term or more difficult goals. It can also be hard for an employee to set reasonable goals six to twelve months ahead. If an objective needs to be revised during the year, the employee may hesitate telling the supervisor because that could require a lot of convincing. Therefore, it is unlikely that objectives will change with a changing environment. Further, a manager cannot compare results of MBO evaluations among several employees, because each has a unique set of goals with different degrees of difficulty.

MBO does, however, have some distinct advantages as an evaluation and planning tool. It allows employees to be involved in setting their own goals, which generally improves performance. The goal-setting process itself is motivating, because an employee who is directly involved is much more likely to become committed to achieving the objectives than if they are imposed. MBO also may enhance the quality of the supervisor-employee relationship. In addition, this method focuses on quantifiable and objective measures of accomplishment, so there is little subjectivity.

Other Performance Appraisal Methods

Other methods include the *essay,* the *checklist,* and *forced choice.* In the essay format, the rater may be asked to describe overall performance or write about specific performance dimensions. It is a popular method used for management personnel. There are usually open-ended questions, such as "What are this employee's strengths in planning and organizing," regarding an employee's strengths and weaknesses, potential, and suggestions for improvement. It is a very time-consuming method, however, and difficult for managers with poor writing skills. Checklists involve checking off from a list of behavioral statements those that describe an employee's performance, such as "Employee maintains good attendance record." With this method, the manager describes more than evaluates job performance. A more sophisticated form of the checklist is the forced choice format. The rater must choose between statements that seem equally favorable or unfavorable but are actually designed to distinguish between successful and unsuccessful performance. The overall rating is obtained by applying a scoring key to the rater's selections. The rater does not know the scoring behind the statements, to ensure objectivity and accuracy. Besides being hard and costly to develop, however, this method may encounter resistance because the rater does not know the scoring weights for each statement.

Which Format Is Best?

No one format clearly wins out over all the others. Each has good and bad points. The format or formats chosen will no doubt be influenced by available time and money as well as whether results, behavior or actions, or personal traits are to be evaluated. For example, an evaluation form that uses MBO for measuring results and BARS for measuring actions and relevant personal traits may be appropriate for certain people in management and for hourly employees.

EVALUATING EMPLOYEE PERFORMANCE

The rater, or evaluator, has the responsibility of rating an employee's performance and communicating this to the employee. By far the majority of employees in an organization—about 88 percent—are considered average; about 5 percent are outstanding, and 7 percent are rated poor (Girard 1988). But a number of factors exist that can result in common rating errors.

A major error related to rating employee performance results from *subjective evaluations*. It is difficult to evaluate objectively when only job performance is being examined, as each evaluator brings to the rating process personal attitudes, values, perceptions, prejudices, stereotypes, and emotions. Personal values and prejudices, such as racial bias, can replace an organization's standards of performance. Objective evaluation involves appraising an employee's performance, not the employee.

The *halo effect* refers to letting the rating of one factor in which an employee does very well, such as being cooperative, positively influence the rating of other factors. For example, a cook who does very well in the area of good sanitation practices and always has a neat, clean appearance may also be rated well on the ability to produce high-quality food, which may not be the case. The opposite of the halo effect is the *horns effect,* in which a poor rating in one aspect of the evaluation negatively influences the rating of other factors.

The *error of central tendency* states that evaluators tend to rate everyone about the same, due to an inclination to avoid extremes when rating anything. Typically, employees are ranked as average or just above average.

Leniency error occurs when the evaluator is too generous with the ratings due to a tendency to want to be everyone's friend, and to avoid the unpleasant tasks of confronting and discussing performance problems and dealing with employee defensiveness. Evaluators inflate ratings for other reasons as well: to avoid confronting hard-to-manage employees with their poor performance, to help someone whose performance is declining due to personal problems, to make their department look good, to make sure the employees get a decent raise, or to encourage an employee whose performance is poor overall but who has made much progress prior to the appraisal. One problem with being lenient, however, is that if an employee's performance slips and the person gets fired, he or she could win a case in court when the many good ratings are brought to light. Another problem with leniency is that because employees are never told of their deficiencies, their performance and productivity do not improve, and they are less likely to be promoted. The opposite of leniency error is *severity error,* in which everyone is rated poorly. This may occur because the rater is a perfectionist, so that few measure up to his or her tough interpretation of the performance standards.

Recency error occurs when the employee is rated only on his or her most recent performance. Performance review should not begin a month before the yearly review session; it actually starts a full *year* before. Recency error occurs frequently, because the rater has insufficient or erroneous documentation of employee performance so that only vague, general statements based on recent observations are written. This can upset the employee, especially if earlier incidents of outstanding performance are forgotten.

First-impression and fixed-impression errors both refer to a rater who has limited insight into an employee's performance. In first-impression error, the evaluator rates an employee solely on the rater's first impression of the employee, not on subsequent performance. In fixed-impression error, the evaluator typically bases an employee's performance on only a few observations, which form the basis for evaluation.

In addition to these rating errors, length of service and previous reviews can affect ratings significantly. It is often difficult for raters to give an employee a less than satisfactory evaluation after many years of satisfactory service or previous good evaluations.

When evaluating an employee's performance, remember: rate the performance, not the employee. Also get input from others who have some working relationship with the employee. Where there is substandard performance, be specific with examples and ask "Why?" These are some of the reasons employees may not be performing up to standards:

- Poor communication of job duties and performance standards
- Insufficient training, lack of skills
- Over- or underqualification for the job
- Inconsistency or lack of enforcement of policies, procedures, and performance standards
- Lack of support to meet employee's needs for equipment, materials, advice, praise, and so on
- Poor communication within the organization
- Boredom, lack of growth
- Poor working conditions
- Work overload
- Personal problems
- Physical limitations

Managers should use the so-called *rule of finger,* which means looking closely in the mirror before pointing a finger of blame at an employee. Perhaps the employee was not given enough support, for example. It is also necessary to put on the evaluation form examples of what constitutes examples of the employee's behavior, to back up the ratings. And it is important to keep fairness in mind when evaluating performance; a manager should ask himself or herself, "If this were my review, how would I react?"

THE PERFORMANCE
APPRAISAL INTERVIEW

The *performance appraisal interview* is a time to give encouragement and work on improving performance and building commitment to the organization. If it is done only once a year, it is probably too late to give praise or to remedy most problems that occurred during the past twelve months. This is a time to help, not reward or punish. Unfortunately, many performance appraisals have salary review as a major purpose and function. Whether happy or unhappy with the increase, the employee tends not to focus on the evaluation as much as on the increase. It is best to conduct two performance appraisals per year, six months apart, with one to review performance and one for salary administration.

The performance appraisal interview refers to the preparation as well as the interview itself. Here are some guidelines to follow for these two steps:

Preparation

1. In advance, explain the performance appraisal instrument and interview process thoroughly to the employee.

2. If applicable, ask the employee to fill out a self-evaluation form. Explain that his or her feedback is important in this process, and ask the employee to fill out the form as completely and honestly as possible.

3. Set an appropriate time for the interview that is convenient for the employee. Pick a place to hold the interview that is quiet and informal, and where there will be no interruptions; some employees find the boss's office can be threatening or intimidating, so consider choosing a neutral place. Tell the employee about the time and place.

4. Review the entire file and fill out the performance appraisal form, using the employee's self-evaluation if available.

5. Consider giving the employee a copy of the completed performance appraisal about a day before the interview. This allows the employee adequate time to read and think about the evaluation as well as develop responses.

Interview:

1. Establish and maintain a friendly, relaxed, trusting atmosphere by
   - Sitting side by side
   - Maintaining good eye contact
   - Explaining that honesty and feedback are important and that the discussion will be on performance, not personality
   - Starting with a statement of purpose and agenda

- Watching for any nonverbal language—such as gestures or facial expressions—indicating employee tension, anxiety, or misunderstanding
- Using positive, constructive language instead of negative language, such as substituting *concern* for *problem,* or *potential growth area* for *shortcoming*
- Listening
- Being a counselor or coach instead of a judge
- Being specific, with examples, and avoiding generalities

2. Using the performance appraisal form, start with a discussion of the employee's strengths and offer praise. Next, identify and ask for feedback on areas that need improvement, first citing specific examples of poor performance.

3. Get an open discussion going by
- Avoiding reading the evaluation form
- Asking the employee for an assessment of his or her own performance before discussing the evaluation
- Avoiding too many questions with yes or no answers; use some open-ended questions such as "What help could you use to improve?"
- Being constructive with any criticism

4. Don't allow the conversation to drift to unrelated areas or to another employee's performance. If personal problems come up, be careful about getting involved; don't play therapist. Instead, suggest sources of help.

5. If the employee disagrees with the assessment of problem areas, listen and be open-minded; the employee may describe previously unnoticed situations.

6. Strive to reach consensus on what areas need improvement and on a plan of action, or growth plan, to build on both the employee's strengths and weaknesses. Make sure this plan has deadlines and is specific, realistic, behavioral, measurable, consistent with the organization, and clear to the employee.

7. Ask the employee for feedback on one's own managerial performance or comments on working conditions and supervisory relations.

8. Summarize and conclude on a positive note by, for example, telling the employee how important his or her contribution to the organization is.

As part of some performance management systems, employees are asked to fill out a *self-appraisal* form, which is given to the manager either prior to or during the performance appraisal interview. Self-appraisal can be surprisingly accurate, though many employees tend to underrate themselves, particularly the better ones, while less effective employees may overrate themselves. If the employee is given the chance to participate, and the manager really reads and takes the self-appraisal seriously, the worker gets a message that his or her opinion matters, resulting in less defensiveness and a more constructive interview. It also can improve motivation and job performance. Self-appraisal is particularly justified for employees who are on their own most of the time.

A PERFORMANCE MANAGEMENT PROGRAM

The crucial step in performance management (see fig. 4-1) that distinguishes it from simple annual performance evaluations is the informal review. This step includes observing employee performance, praising, coaching, and training (see chapter 3), as well as documenting, counseling, and disciplining (see chapter 14). Informal reviews should occur frequently during the year, which can do much to reduce undue anxiety about the yearly performance appraisal. These informal reviews involve what is called *management by wandering around (MBWA),* which refers to being with employees on their own turf, making observations, asking questions, offering comments, and so forth. Management visibility to employees, as well as to customers, has always been an important practice for managers in the hospitality field.

The performance management system has requirements similar to those for the performance appraisal instrument. It needs to be practical, acceptable to both raters and employees, relevant, valid, reliable, free from bias, supported by management, participative, and able to distinguish between various levels of performance.

A component of performance management that is absolutely vital is the training of raters. Although spending time and money on training those who do the rating will not solve everything, it will probably help the system work better. Elements of rater training might include the purposes of the system, ways to coach and appraise performance, typical rating errors, ways to record specific examples of behavior and use the appraisal forms, and ways to conduct performance appraisal interviews and develop improvement plans. Knowing alone will not necessarily change a rater's behavior; change can be stimulated by having raters actually practice and then receive feedback on how they use forms, document performance, and conduct performance appraisal interviews. Methods of doing this might include role playing, videotapes, or behavioral modeling. Practice in making ratings generally improves skill and increases reliability or consistency. By discussing the subjective errors made in the rating process, it is hoped they will not occur as frequently.

SUMMARY

Performance appraisal, the periodic evaluation of an employee's job performance, is one of the more negatively viewed and poorly performed of managerial tasks. Performance appraisals have various roles or uses in hospitality organizations. These might include providing information for salary review, performance improvement, and feedback to employees.

The performance appraisal format selected depends to a large extent on the purpose of the performance appraisal, which requires different information to be collected and in turn requires different methods. Formats include the graphic rating scale, behaviorally anchored rating scale (BARS), behavior summary scale format, management by objectives (MBO), essay, checklist, and forced choice. No one format clearly wins out over all the others. The format chosen will no doubt be influenced by time and money available, as well as whether results, behavior or actions, or personal traits are to be evaluated.

A manager generally can judge how well employees are performing in any of three ways: what they achieve (results or outcomes), what they do (behavior or actions), and what they are (personal competencies). Some errors that raters typically make in evaluating employee performance include subjective evaluation, the halo effect, the error of central tendency, leniency error, recency error, first-impression error, and fixed-impression error. When rating an employee's performance, be sure to evaluate the performance, not the employee. Also, be fair, consistent, and use the so-called rule of finger before blaming an employee for poor performance. The performance appraisal interview consists of both preparation and the interview itself, and there are guidelines for handling both successfully.

Performance evaluation is the key to utilizing and developing employees, and companies that realize this have replaced simple yearly performance appraisal programs with year-round performance management programs. The crucial step in performance management that distinguishes it from annual performance evaluations is the continuing information review. This step includes a degree of observing employee performance, praising, coaching, training, documenting, counseling, and disciplining during the year, between performance appraisals.

The performance management system has requirements similar to those of the performance appraisal instrument. It needs to be practical, acceptable to both raters and those rated, relevant, valid, reliable, unbiased, supported by management, participative, and able to distinguish between various levels of performance.

STUDY QUESTIONS

1. What are the purposes of performance appraisal?
2. Describe the characteristics of an ideal appraiser.
3. Can discussions of job performance be kept separate from salary review? How or how not?
4. What performance standards can be developed for evaluating the following jobs:
   server in a white-tablecloth restaurant;
   concierge in an upscale hotel;
   cook in a cafeteria operation;
   front desk clerk in a medium-sized property.
5. Discuss how you would ascertain if someone was performing poorly, and factors you would consider.
6. How can you minimize defensiveness in a performance appraisal interview?
7. What can you do to involve employees in the performance management process?
8. How do you recognize an effective performance management system?
9. For a housekeeper in a hotel, which format or formats might you choose for a performance appraisal?
10. What can you do to avoid errors in evaluating employees?

REFERENCES

Bernardin, H. John, and M. Ronald Buckley. 1981. Strategies in rater training. *Academy of Management Review* 6(2):205–12.

Borman, Walter C. 1979. Format and training effects on rating accuracy and rater errors. *Journal of Applied Psychology* 64(4):410–21.

Cascio, Wayne F. 1982. Scientific, legal, and operational imperatives of workable performance appraisal systems. *Public Personnel Management Journal* 11(4): 367–75.

Cascio, Wayne F., and H. John Bernardin. 1981. Implications of performance appraisal litigation for personnel decisions. *Personnel Psychology* 34(2):211–26.

Editors of the Alexander Hamilton Institute. 1986. Will your next performance appraisal land you in court? *Management Solutions* 31(7):4–9.

Ferris, Gerald R., and David C. Gilmore. 1985. Appraisals everyone can agree on. *Management World* 14(8):12–15.

Fowler, Aubrey R., and Stephen C. Bushardt. 1986. T.O.P.E.S.: Developing a task oriented performance evaluation system. *SAM Advanced Management Journal* 51(4):4–8.

Geber, Beverly. 1988. The hidden agenda of performance appraisals. *Training* 25(6):42–47.

Girard, Richard. 1988. Is there a need for performance appraisals? *Personnel Journal* 67(8):89–90.

Grant, Philip C. 1987. A better approach to performance reviews. *Management Solutions* 32(3):11–16.

Greenwood, Ronald G. 1981. Management by objectives: As developed by Peter Drucker, assisted by Harold Smiddy. *Academy of Management Review* 6(2): 225–30.

Harper, Stephen C. 1986. Adding purpose to performance reviews. *Training and Development Journal* 40(9):53–55.

Jacobs, Rick, Ditsa Kafry, and Sheldon Zedeck. 1980. Expectations of behaviorally anchored rating scales. *Personnel Psychology* 33(3):595–640.

Kane, Jeffrey S., and Kimberly A. Freeman. 1986. MBO and performance appraisal: A mixture that's not a solution. Part 1. *Personnel* 63(12):26–36.

———. 1987. MBO and performance appraisal: A mixture that's not a solution. Part 2. *Personnel* 64(2):26–32.

Kirkpatrick, Donald L. 1986. Performance appraisal: Your questions answered. *Training and Development Journal* 40(5):68–71.

Krantz, Shelley. 1983. Five steps to making performance appraisal writing easier. *Supervisory Management* 28(12):7–10.

Levine, Hermine Zagat. 1986. Performance appraisals at work. *Personnel* 63(6): 63–71.

Locher, Alan H., and Kenneth S. Teel. 1988. Appraisal trends. *Personnel Journal* 67(9):139–45.

Malinauskas, Barbara K., and Ronald W. Clement. 1987. Performance appraisal interviewing for tangible results. *Training and Development Journal* 41(2):74–79.

Mallinger, Mark A., and Tom G. Cummings. 1986. Improving the value of performance appraisals. *SAM Advanced Management Journal* 51(2):19–21.

Martin, David C., and Kathryn M. Bartol. 1986. Training the raters: A key to effective performance appraisal. *Public Personnel Management* 15(2):101–9.

McConnell, Charles R. 1987. An integrated view of performance appraisal. *Health Care Supervisor* 5(4):61–78.

McEvoy, Glenn M. 1988. Evaluating the boss. *Personnel Administrator* 33(9): 115–20.

McGregor, Douglas. 1987. An uneasy look at performance appraisal. *Training and Development Journal* 41(6):66–69.

McKinnon, D. Kim. 1987. Three steps to increasing supervisory success. *Management Solutions* 32(1):12–14.

Metz, Edmund J. 1988. Designing legally defensible performance appraisal systems. *Training and Development Journal* 42(7):47–51.

Phillips, Kenneth R. 1987. Red flags in performance appraisal. *Training and Development Journal* 41(3):80–82.

Plachy, Roger J. 1983. Appraisal scales that measure performance outcomes and job results. *Personnel* 60(3):57–65.

Rarick, Charles A., and Gerald Baxter. 1986. Behaviorally anchored rating scales (BARS): An effective performance appraisal approach. *SAM Advanced Management Journal* 51(1):36–39.

Regel, Roy W., and Robert W. Hollmann. 1987. Gauging performance objectively. *Personnel Administrator* 32(6):74–78.

Rice, Berkeley. 1985. Performance review: The job nobody likes. *Psychology Today* 19(9):30–36.

Romberg, Robert V. 1986. Performance appraisal, 1: Risks and rewards. *Personnel* 63(8):20–26.

Schneier, Craig Eric, Richard W. Beatty, and Lloyd S. Baird. 1986a. How to construct a successful performance appraisal system. *Training and Development Journal* 40(4):38–42.

———. 1986b. Creating a performance management system. *Training and Development Journal* 40(5):74–79.

Schneier, Craig Eric, Arthur Geis, and Joseph A. Wert. 1987. Performance appraisals: No appointment needed. *Personnel Journal* 66(11):80–87.

Schwab, Donald P., and Herbert G. Heneman. 1975. Behaviorally anchored rating scales: A review of the literature. *Personnel Psychology* 28(4):549–62.

Smith, David E. 1986. Training programs for performance appraisal: A review. *Academy of Management Review* 11(1):22–40.

Smith, Michael. 1987. Putting their performance in writing. *Management Solutions* 32(3):4–10.

Umbreit, W. Terry. 1987. Achieving content validity in a performance appraisal instrument. *Hospitality Education and Research Journal* 11(3):19–29.

Umbreit, W. Terry, Robert W. Eder, and Jon P. McConnell. 1986. Performance appraisals: Making them fair and making them work. *Cornell H.R.A. Quarterly* 26(4):58–69.

Wehrenberg, Stephen B. 1988. Train supervisors to measure and evaluate performance. *Personnel Journal* 67(2):77–79.

Weiss, Donald H. 1988. The legal side of performance appraisals. *Management Solutions* 33(5):27–29.

Weitzel, William. 1987. How to improve performance through successful appraisals. *Personnel* 64(10):18–23.

Zemke, Ron. 1985. Is performance appraisal a paper tiger? *Training* 22(12):24–32.

Chapter 5

Working Successfully with Unions

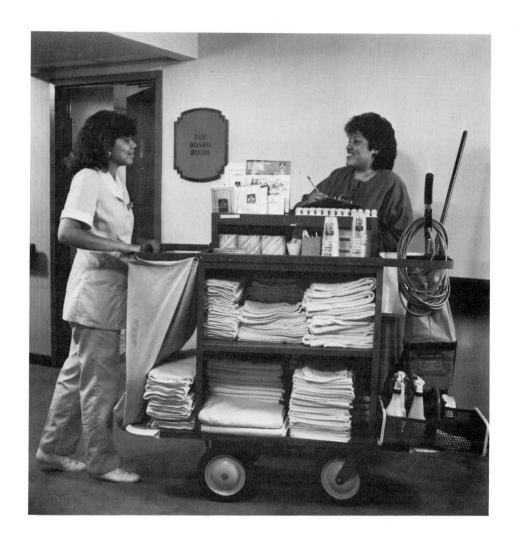

KEY QUESTIONS

1. What types of unions are there?
2. What are the implications of major labor legislation?
3. Why do employees join unions?
4. How do unions become organized within hospitality operations?
5. What are some guidelines for collective bargaining?
6. What is typically covered in a labor contract?
7. How can a hospitality operation avert unionization?

KEY TERMS AND CONCEPTS

Labor contract

Labor relations process

Federations

Industrial unions

Craft unions

Professional unions

Collective bargaining

Bargaining unit

Union steward

Norris-LaGuardia Act of 1932

Wagner Act of 1935 (National Labor Relations Act)

National Labor Relations Board (NLRB)

Taft-Hartley Act of 1947 (Labor-Management Relations Act)

Mediation

Arbitration

Right-to-work laws

Union shop

Closed shop

Agency shop

Open shop

Landrum-Griffin Act of 1959 (Labor-Management Reporting and Disclosure Act)

Union organizing

No-solicitation rule

Authorization cards

Representation election

Election campaign

Decertification

Strike

Picket

Boycott

Management-rights clause

Grievance procedures

Preventive labor relations

Unions are organizations that employees designate to represent them collectively in bargaining with the employer for wages and other conditions of employment. The objectives of a union include obtaining improved wages and other employment conditions in the *labor contract,* increasing membership, and administering the contract. The labor contract is a written agreement negotiated between management and the union that governs the conditions of employment. The various reasons for and methods of unionization, and union-related objectives and activities, are referred to as the *labor relations process.*

In the hospitality industry, unions have been most successful at organizing larger properties in such metropolitan areas as New York, Chicago, Minneapolis, San Francisco, Las Vegas, and Atlantic City. Unions obviously have more to gain economically from organizing larger numbers of employees. There has been a significant decline in union membership nationwide since 1970, partly because white-collar ranks have increased and the number of manufacturing jobs is decreasing. Blue-collar workers traditionally have been more likely than white-collar workers to join a union, although many white-collar employees have become unionized. Union membership has also declined because the success rate of union organizers has declined while the rate of voting out an incumbent union has increased.

Today less than 20 percent of the total work force are union members. About eight percent of hotel and restaurant workers belong to a union, and hotel workers are much more likely to be unionized than restaurant workers (Bertagnoli 1989). Unions often find it hard to organize a restaurant because of the high turnover rate of employees. With the current shift from manufacturing to service jobs in the U.S., the hospitality industry could be a likely target for unions.

Before examining the labor relations process, and actions that companies take to avoid unionization, it is important to look at some basic information about the nature and history of unions, highlighting significant legislation.

TYPES OF UNIONS

There are three types of unions: international, national, and local. National labor unions have membership solely within the United States. When its membership is from both within and outside the United States, it is referred to as an international union. Local unions represent employees in a limited geographic area, and they constitute the greatest number of unions in the United States. Most local unions are affiliated and operate under the constitution of a national or international union. The local union is run by elected officials who carry out the daily union operations.

Some unions are grouped into *federations,* such as the AFL-CIO (American Federation of Labor and Congress of Industrial Organizations), which are not in and of themselves unions. AFL member unions mostly represent skilled craft workers, while CIO members represent both skilled and unskilled workers in a specific industry. In 1955 the AFL and the CIO merged. Federations function in part to resolve disputes between unions and to obtain favorable laws.

Most unions can be designated as industrial, craft, or professional. *Industrial unions,* such as the Hotel and Restaurant Employees International Union, represent all the employees in a given industry. *Craft unions* represent employees in a single occupation, such as maintenance engineers. *Professional unions* include professionals such as nurses, teachers, and supervisors.

A few more terms related to unions that need to be defined are *collective bargaining,* the *bargaining unit,* and the *union steward.* Collective bargaining is the process by which the labor contract between the union and management is negotiated and enforced. The bargaining unit is a group of two or more employees who share common employment interests and conditions and can be reasonably grouped together for collective bargaining purposes. Union contracts define the bargaining unit—in other words, who can join and be represented by the union. Within a hotel or restaurant, the bargaining unit may include all nonsupervisory personnel or it may be smaller, such as a kitchen unit or bar unit. The union steward, or shop steward, is an employee designated by the union to check on contract compliance and advise employees of their rights and what the union is doing for them. They are trained to identify and negotiate grievances.

SIGNIFICANT LABOR LEGISLATION

The first overt union activity in the United States was in Philadelphia in 1794, when shoemakers tried to get wage increases after their employer cut their pay. The court ruled with the employer. Until 1842 workers were legally discouraged from forming unions; then, in *Commonwealth of Massachusetts* v. *Hunt,* the courts ruled that unions in and of themselves were not criminal, though their conduct might be. Craft unions formed in the second half of the 1800s, and a group of national craft unions called the American Federation of Labor was organized in 1886. During World War I unions grew significantly, but growth slowed during the start of the Great Depression. Before the 1930s, unions were prosecuted in the courts on the basis that they interfered with the employer's right to do business. Injunctions or restraining orders were widely used to control union activities such as work stoppages.

In 1926 came the first significant pro-labor legislation: the Railway Labor Act, which covered nonmanagerial rail employees, and later was extended to include airlines workers. This legislation allowed employees to be represented by a union and to engage in union activities. It also established the National Mediation Board to conduct union elections and legitimized collective bargaining for railway employees.

The *Norris-LaGuardia Act of 1932* covered private-sector employers and labor organizations. It affirmed the right of unions to organize workers and bargain collectively with the employer, and limited employers' use of injunctions to cases in which danger to life or property was possible. It omitted two important points, which were corrected in the next piece of legislation: it did not require management to bargain collectively with unions or stop management from discriminating against employees involved in union activities.

The *Wagner Act of 1935,* also called the *National Labor Relations Act,* was the most significant piece of labor legislation in terms of impact. It covered all private-sector employers and nonmanagerial employees not covered by the Railway Labor Act. The Wagner Act affirmed the employee's right to organize and engage in union activities and to bargain collectively through representation of their choice, without interference from management. It outlawed unfair labor practices by employers such as interfering with an employee's rights to organize and bargain collectively, refusing to bargain collectively with the union, and firing or not hiring pro-union individuals. The National Labor Relations Act created the *National Labor Relations Board (NLRB),* whose job to this day remains to supervise both unfair labor practices and representation elections, in which a union may be selected as the collective bargaining agent for a bargaining unit.

Between 1932 and 1947 most laws were pro-union. The unions underwent a period of rapid growth and became more militant, as evidenced by frequent strikes. Some unions also received much publicity due to charges of corruption and racketeering.

Then the *Taft-Hartley Act of 1947,* or *Labor-Management Relations Act,* which covers most private-sector employers and nonmanagerial employees except those covered by the Railway Labor Act, put certain restraints on unions. Unfair labor practices by both unions and management were defined. The former include, for example, coercing employees in the selection of a bargaining agent, refusing to bargain collectively with the employer, and charging excessive initiation fees. The National Labor Relations Board was expanded from three to five members and asked to determine appropriate bargaining units and to prevent and deal with unfair labor practices. In addition, the president was given the right to impose an eighty-day cooling-off period to delay a strike if national safety or health is threatened.

The Taft-Hartley Act also established the Federal Mediation and Conciliation Services, which have two major functions. They are notified of contract expirations and offer to help work on new contracts in order to avoid work stoppages. They also keep lists of available arbitrators. *Mediation* refers to the process by which an impartial third party meets with both sides separately and then suggests compromises or actions that will lead to an agreement. A mediator has no authority to force either party to accept anything. In *arbitration,* a third party conducts hearings to help form the basis of his or her decision, which both parties agree in advance will be binding—in other words, both sides must accept the arbitrator's decision.

An important part of the Taft-Hartley Act allows states to pass *right-to-work laws,* which prohibit mandatory union membership. About 40 percent of the states now have these laws. In right-to-work states union shops are illegal. Union shops are companies at which an employee must join the union after a probationary period, which is often 30 days. A closed shop means applicants must be union members in order to be considered for employment, and is forbidden by federal law. In an agency shop, employees don't have to join a union but still must pay a charge. An open shop, on the other hand, means that the employees may elect to join or not join the union. Whether or not they join, the union represents all the employees in the bargaining unit.

Even after the Taft-Hartley Act there were complaints of union corruption and racketeering, so the *Landrum-Griffin Act of 1959,* also referred to as the *Labor-Management Reporting and Disclosure Act,* was passed. It covered private-sector employers and labor organizations. A cornerstone of the Landrum-Griffin Act is the Bill of Rights of Union Members. These include that every union member must be given the right to nominate candidates for union office, vote in union elections, and attend and participate in union meetings. Also included is that union members can sue their union or officers and that a majority vote in a secret-ballot election is required before dues can be increased.

WHY EMPLOYEES JOIN UNIONS

Employees join unions for a variety of reasons, which generally boil down to one of the following:

- Unhappiness with management
- Unhappiness with employment conditions (such as wages)
- Social or peer pressure
- Requirement to join the union

Employees who are unhappy with management often claim unfair job-related policies, such as work schedules or promotions that receive biased enforcement; they commonly cite favoritism by supervisors. Employees may feel that a union will give them more bargaining strength with management than they currently have and will yield positive rather than negative outcomes. Employees who unionize are also likely to be unhappy with employment conditions such as wages, benefits, job security, physical working conditions, and feelings of appreciation. Interestingly enough, the desire to join a union comes more from problems with working conditions than from the nature of the work itself.

There are, of course, circumstances in which employees join the union simply because everyone else is, so they go along with the crowd. In states without right-to-work laws, however, they may be required to join the union.

WHY MANAGERS RESIST UNIONS

Managers frequently voice complaints about unions and use techniques to avoid unionization. Why? They are concerned that unionization will create conflict between employees who support the union and those who reject it. They are also concerned that it may cause lowered employee commitment and productivity, loss of direct communication between employees and management, and increased payroll costs. Additionally, managers may feel some of their rights, such as giving promotions and rewards, will be subject to union rules and/or endorsement.

ORGANIZING A UNION

The first step in *union organizing* of employees is to make contact with them and find out about their complaints and needs. This may be in response to unhappy employees who have contacted the union. In this way the union starts to build a case for itself as their representative in dealing with the employer. The union also tries to determine how vulnerable the employer is. An employer that allows on-premises solicitation by any outside groups or charities, must also let union organizers solicit employees, although this is permitted only in noncustomer, nonwork areas during break periods. If organizers cannot get on the premises to talk to employees because of a *no-solicitation rule,* they will commonly talk to employees in or close to parking lots and at workers' homes and hangouts.

After initial contact is made, the organizers set up a meeting with employees to open channels of communication and to tell them about the advantages of membership. The union establishes an organizing committee of employees who are natural leaders and will hand out union materials and ask other workers to sign *authorization cards* (fig. 5-1); this indicates that those employees want the labor union to represent them in collective bargaining with the employer.

The union organizers' goal is to get at least 30 percent of the employees to sign authorization cards, because then the union can file a petition with the National Labor Relations Board (NLRB) asking for a secret-ballot *representation election*. If 50 percent of the employees sign cards, the union can ask management directly for the right to represent the employees. Management has the right to say no at this point and normally does so, in which case the union must go to the NLRB and there is usually a representation election. If management negotiates or even talks to the union at this point, it may be interpreted by the NLRB as recognition of the union.

Before the NLRB holds the election, it conducts a hearing to determine the makeup of the bargaining unit and to answer other questions. The NLRB determines if the petitioning union really is a labor organization and if there is any reason an election should not be held or should be delayed. If these questions can be resolved, and management and the union agree on what constitutes the bargaining unit and who can vote in the election, a representation election takes place. If they do not agree on the bargaining unit or there are

---

XYZ UNION

Authorization for Representation

I hereby authorize XYZ Union to represent me for the purpose of collective bargaining.

Print name	Date

Sign name

Employer's name and address

Home address and telephone

Department	Job title	Full-time or part-time

Figure 5-1. Authorization card.

other concerns, it causes a delay, which management sometimes uses to its advantage. The disputed groups in determining a bargaining unit are frequently supervisors, part-timers, employees cross-trained in various departments, trainees, and clerical workers.

Once a date is set, the *election campaign* starts. The NLRB monitors campaign tactics for unfair labor practices by both the union and management. There are numerous rules as to what, for example, the employer is and is not allowed to do during a unionization campaign:

An employer may

1. Prohibit union organizers from coming on the premises to solicit, if all solicitation is forbidden and the policy is consistently enforced.

2. Interfere with union organizing activities during the employees' working hours, excluding unpaid breaks.

3. Tell employees that a union can't guarantee job security or pay increases—it can only ask.

4. Provide employees with information about union dues and other expenses, such as initiation fees, which are all used to pay the salaries of the union officials and organizers; with any facts about the union or its officers, even of a critical nature; with reprints of articles about the union if they are based on facts that have been established and are a matter of record; and with any known sections of the union's constitution and bylaws that spell out how the union can fine or assess workers.

5. Tell employees about the loss of income during work stoppages, the possibility of being required to serve on a picket line, and the fact that they can be replaced during a strike as long as it was not motivated by employer unfair labor practices.

6. Inform employees that they do not have to talk with union organizers, that the federal government will take action against any union that tries to restrain or coerce employees from their right not to join a union, that they do not have to sign any union authorization cards passed out or mailed to their homes, and that signing an authorization card does not mean an employee has to vote for the union in an election.

7. Explain to employees that anyone considering joining the union will get no special treatment or favors.

8. Discuss with employees the positive aspects of the current situation, such as competitive wages and benefits and good working conditions, and explain how they compare to those of other employers, whether unionized or not.

9. Inform employees it is management's personal opinion, if asked, that a union is not needed and will not work to anyone's advantage, and that the employer prefers to deal with them directly and individually rather than through an outside third party.

10. Tell the employees about any untrue or misleading statements union organizers have made and explain management's position on issues the union has brought up.

11. Explain to employees that the employer can continue to discipline and discharge them for good cause, as long as such action follows usual personnel policy and practice and is not done based on an employee's interest in the union.

12. Pass out or mail printed antiunion material to employees and to their homes.

An employer may not

1. Promise employees a pay increase, promotion, better working conditions, additional employee benefits, or special favors if they vote against the union or if the union loses the election.

2. Threaten employees with loss of job, reduction of wages, or use threatening or intimidating language that may be designed to influence employees in the exercise of their rights to belong or refrain from belonging to a union, or discriminate in any way against any employee because of support for the union.

3. Threaten to close or drastically reduce operations if the union is voted in.

4. Attend union organizing meetings, spy on union activities, ask employees questions about union activities or the signing of authorization cards, urge loyal employees to try to persuade others to vote against the union, or visit the homes of employees to urge them to campaign against the union.

5. Interfere with solicitation of employees to sign authorization cards during nonpaid hours in noncustomer areas (unless there is a no-solicitation rule).

6. Fire or refuse to hire union sympathizers, without just cause.

7. Ask prospective employees when or after they are hired whether they belong to a union, carry a union card, or have ever signed a union authorization card.

An employer's most effective antiunion campaign stresses the positive points of current working conditions and that the employees can't know for sure what working conditions will be like under the union. The employer should tend to business as usual and not get involved in any action, such as an unscheduled wage increase, which would be considered an unfair labor practice.

The NLRB supplies written notices of the election, which the employer must post in conspicuous places at least three working days prior to the vote. Generally, regular full-time and part-time employees who have been on the payroll at least three weeks are allowed to vote. The secret-ballot election is generally conducted at the workplace, and each side is allowed an equal number of observers in the polling area. Either side may object to how the election is conducted; if any charges are found to be true, this may force another vote.

If a majority of ballots cast in the election are for the union, it becomes the representative of that bargaining unit. The winning party is based on the number of employees who vote in the election, not the total number in the bargaining unit. Whatever the outcome of the election, there can't be another one of any kind in this bargaining unit for another year; then the entire organizing process can begin again (fig. 5-2).

Just as a union can be voted in, so too can the bargaining unit employees vote to drop a union as their representative, in a process called *decertification*. It occurs most often the first year or so after a representation election, which is one reason most unions want three-year contracts. To decertify a union, at least 30 percent—preferably 50 percent—of the members must sign a petition, which is filed sixty to ninety days before their current labor contract expires or between labor contracts. The NLRB then decides whether to hold another representation election. If the employer has in any way encouraged, formulated, or implemented the petition, the NLRB dismisses it. If the election is held, and a simple majority of votes cast are for decertifying the union as the exclusive bargaining agent, the union is in effect voted out.

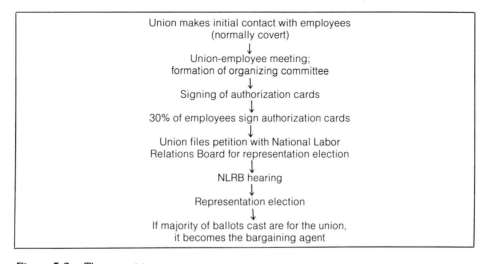

Union makes initial contact with employees
(normally covert)
↓
Union-employee meeting;
formation of organizing committee
↓
Signing of authorization cards
↓
30% of employees sign authorization cards
↓
Union files petition with National Labor
Relations Board for representation election
↓
NLRB hearing
↓
Representation election
↓
If majority of ballots cast are for the union,
it becomes the bargaining agent

Figure 5-2. The organizing process.

The employer is permitted to initiate decertification if there is reasonable doubt that the union represents a majority of the employees. More than one action such as the following is needed to establish reasonable doubt to the NLRB: a majority of employees didn't support a strike, a minority of employees pay union dues, or there has been much turnover since the union was voted in. It is difficult for the employer to prove any of these or other such actions to the satisfaction of the NLRB so that it will call for an election.

COLLECTIVE BARGAINING AND THE LABOR CONTRACT

Collective bargaining refers primarily to the negotiations between the employer and the union to develop a labor contract, as well as the enforcement of the contract. It may also include the use of economic pressure by either side. The union may use work stoppages or ask employees not to buy company products; while management may replace those who walk out, or might even close down the business. Collective bargaining is probably the most complicated area of labor-management relations.

Management has a responsibility to negotiate in good faith with the union's representatives. This includes meeting at a reasonable time and place, making rational and realistic proposals, and, if those proposals are not acceptable, suggesting others. Neither party, however, is required to agree to or give in on any issue. Both sides must bargain in good faith on what the National Labor Relations Board calls mandatory subjects of bargaining. These include wages, benefits, work hours, and other conditions of employment. Nonmandatory subjects of bargaining include those that are not related to wages, benefits, work hours, or other conditions of employment; neither management nor the union can force the other to bargain on these topics.

In order to negotiate a labor contract successfully, the employer must prepare adequately. Preparation includes researching all issues, becoming knowledgeable about the union negotiators, and deciding in advance what areas can or can't be conceded, as well as areas of compromise. Following are other tips for successful collective bargaining with unions:

1. In the first preparatory meeting with the union, set ground rules that may strengthen the employer's position, such as limiting hours to those of the normal workday—long negotiating sessions generally do not help management.

2. One person should keep detailed notes on what occurs at each meeting. All proposals and counterproposals need to be documented, along with when

meetings started and ended and who attended. These notes need to be taken during and right after sessions to ensure accuracy of detail.

3. Get to know the union negotiators, and accept them as equals during negotiations. If management treats a union representative condescendingly, it will not help the employer's position. Also, never underestimate the representatives' abilities at the negotiating table.

4. Communicate regularly with managers and supervisors. Ultimately the managers and supervisors will administer the labor contract, so they need to know what is going on, and they should offer opinions on the issues, since they know best what they can and can't live with.

5. If there is a deadlock, consider federal mediation. Bringing in a mediator shows good faith on the part of management.

A deadlock in collective bargaining may cause the union to *strike, picket,* or *boycott.* A strike is when any number of employees refuse to perform their jobs. If one is called due to bargaining demands, it is called an economic strike. A sympathy strike occurs when union members from one bargaining unit refuse to cross the picket line of another. Unprotected strikes include all other work stoppages, such as unofficial wildcat strikes and job slowdowns, and are generally not permitted by the NLRB. Employers can obtain injunctions or court orders to stop these actions. Because a strike can be risky for the union, it often seeks approval from the membership before calling one, and often this authorization is used in bargaining to get concessions. Before striking, a union will also look at the ability and willingness of its members to weather the hardships of a strike and also determine how well the employer can function during a strike. In order for a strike to be successful from the union's point of view, its members need to remain steadfast in their refusal to work, and the employer's operations need to be crippled.

Strikes are typically accompanied by pickets, or employees who position themselves outside entrances to the property. Pickets carry placards describing their dispute and stating opinions that also serve to discourage other employees from entering the property. Legally, pickets can't block entrances and exits or keep other people from using them; pickets also can talk to, but can't intimidate or threaten, other employees.

Boycotts occur when employees refuse to buy the products of an employer with whom the union has a labor dispute. A boycott obviously must be on a large scale in order to cause damage to an employer. In most cases, boycotts of this nature are legal.

Once it is agreed to, a labor contract typically covers a wide variety of topics, including the following:

- Recognition of the employees' representative
- Wages and fringe benefits
- Working hours and overtime
- Holidays and vacations
- Sick days, personal days, and leaves
- Working conditions and safety rules
- Determination of seniority
- Training
- Job postings, evaluation, promotions, and transfers
- Local union representatives and stewards
- Discipline
- Discrimination
- Grievances
- Strikes and lockouts
- Arbitration
- Reduction or increase in work force
- Representation fee
- Application of provisions
- Duration of agreement
- Modification and termination of agreement
- Notices

Although management may be given the right to administer discipline, for example, it normally must be administered within the guideline of reasonable, clear, publicized, and consistently applied rules; a progressive discipline system may be put in place in which the employee is given many chances to correct a performance problem before losing the job.

The *management-rights clause* in a contract expressly reserves to management certain rights. This clause is of utmost importance to management, because a union will try to become involved in decisions that management previously made exclusively, leaving the latter less freedom to act.

Grievance procedures are also outlined in the labor contract. A grievance is an employee complaint about a section of the collective bargaining contract that the worker feels has been violated. How grievances are handled is crucial to the contract. An effective grievance procedure should progress in a timely fashion and function to get both sides closer together rather than further apart. Grievance procedures differ as to the number of steps, who is involved in each one, the number of days allowed for each to be completed, and the grievance form itself (fig. 5-3). A typical grievance procedure follows these steps:

1. The employee is usually asked to discuss the concern first with the immediate supervisor in the hope of resolving the issue. An employee who is uncomfortable with this may ask the union steward to accompany him or her. Many grievances can be and are resolved at this step. Grievances are often due to misunderstandings that, if the supervisor handles the situation appropriately, can be easily settled.

Employee Name: _____

Department: _____ Job Title: _____

Supervisor: _____

The following is a statement of my grievance, which I am asking my Supervisor to review within five working days of today's date.

_____

_____

_____

_____

_____

_____

| _____ | _____ | _____ |
| Employee Signature | Union Steward's Signature | Date |

Resolution:

_____

_____

_____

_____

| _____ | _____ | _____ |
| Employee's Signature | Supervisor's Signature | Date |

If the grievance is not resolved to the satisfaction of the employee, the Supervisor is asked to proceed to the next step, as outlined in the Personnel Policy and Procedure Manual.

Figure 5-3. A typical grievance form.

2. If the first step did not produce satisfaction, the employee must fill out a grievance form, which helps in two ways: it forces the employee to think through the grievance, which, if it is petty or irrational, may make the employee forget about it; on the other hand, if the grievance is worthwhile, all parties involved will now have a clear and similar idea as to its nature.

3. Next, there is a meeting to resolve the grievance, which the employee, the immediate and a higher-level supervisor, the union steward and chief union steward, and someone from the human resource department all attend.

4. If the employee still is not satisfied, the next step involves another meeting, this time also including top management and high-level union officials.

5. The final step includes mediation or arbitration or both. Both parties will enter the last stage only if each feels it has a strong case. One side might pull out before this if it feels it might lose.

HOW TO AVOID UNIONIZATION

The main objective of *preventive labor relations* is to deter a union from coming in, rather than responding to it once it is in and organizing. The key is early use of preventive strategies, such as keeping wages competitive, especially as many take months to implement. If an employer waits until it is learned that the union is organizing—which of course the union organizers begin to do quietly—a campaign by the employer then will generally do very little to sway employees' opinions. Such a campaign also usually forces several costs on the employer: legal services, loss of employee and management time, and reduced productivity for that period of time. A 1975 study of 146 elections showed a cost per employee of between $100 and $125 (Kilgour 1978), which today would be considerably higher.

Management can use many techniques to avert unionization. Many of them revolve around the notion of having and maintaining a positive, motivating work environment. They all ultimately have to do with creating and maintaining employee satisfaction; employers wishing to remain nonunion should be concerned with this. Employee attitude surveys can help measure satisfaction (see chapter 9). Following are various methods that can help prevent unionization:

Provide competitive wages and benefits.

Have a no-solicitation rule for both employees and others 365 days a year.

Be fair and consistent in managing and disciplining.

Have an effective grievance procedure in place; two-thirds of nonunion organizations have established grievance procedures.

Treat employees as the valuable assets they are.

Offer interpersonal skills training to managers and supervisors to improve their dealings with employees.

Ensure that there is no favoritism for certain employees.

Ask for, and listen and respond to, employees' questions and complaints. Use attitude surveys to identify issues of concern to employees (see chapter 9).

Maintain open and frequent communication with employees.

Don't make promises that can't be kept.

Train managers, supervisors, and hourly employees.

Promote from within.

Sponsor social events for the employees, such as sports and picnics.

Make sure established policies and procedures are communicated to the employees, and consistently and fairly administered.

Make sure the employees know what is expected of them and how they will be evaluated.

Use seniority to some extent in determining wages, promotions, and so forth.

Post open positions on company property.

Document all employee disciplinary decisions.

Maintain a pleasant and safe working environment.

In addition, it is important to talk periodically with local hospitality operators to check on union organizing efforts in the area. Find out who the union organizers are and what they look like, so the management team can be alert to their appearing in the parking lot or even inside the operation. Initial efforts to organize employees are typically done quietly so that management will not know and mount its own campaign. Managers and supervisors also need to listen for signs of union organizing by monitoring employees' behavior. Signs of union interest and solicitation might include increased employee complaints and the more frequent use of terms such as *grievance, representation,* and *seniority.* Other signs are groups of employees having private conversations that stop when a supervisor walks by, employees using a representative to air their complaints, or friendly employees withdrawing from talking with managers or supervisors. As soon as management knows there is an organizing campaign, a labor attorney should be contacted.

WORKING WITH A UNION

If you are working with a union, it is essential to become familiar with the union contract and to oversee its appropriate administration. It is also important to get to know the shop steward, as this person will be handling employee grievances. Although it is very easy to let the relationship between management and the union become adversarial, management should work toward a relationship characterized by trust and common goals.

SUMMARY

Unions are organizations that employees designate to represent them in bargaining collectively with the employer for wages and other conditions of employment. The objectives of a union include obtaining improved wages and other employment conditions in the labor contract, increasing membership, and administering the labor contract. This contract is a written agreement negotiated between management and the union that governs the conditions of employment.

In the hospitality industry, unions have been most successful at organizing larger properties in metropolitan areas. Most unions are local ones that are affiliated with a national or international union. Within each unionized operation, there are defined bargaining units and union stewards. Unions have a long and sometimes stormy history, starting in 1794 with the first overt union activity, in Philadelphia. Unions were initially illegal in most respects but over the years were eventually given various rights and power—so much at one point that laws were formulated to restrain some of their power.

Employees might join unions due to unhappiness with management and employment conditions, social or peer pressure, or a requirement to join. When a union initially tries to organize employees, it does so quietly. The process involves the union setting up an organizing committee, which includes employees and tries to get 30 percent of all the workers to sign authorization cards so that the union can then file a petition with the National Labor Relations Board for a representation election. If 50 percent of the people voting support the union, it will become the sole collective bargaining agent for all the employees who qualify as a bargaining unit. During the campaign and election, there are certain actions the employer may or may not legally take to influence the vote. Decertification is the process by which the bargaining unit employees vote the union out.

Collective bargaining refers primarily to the negotiations between the employer and the union to develop a labor contract, as well as the enforcement of the contract. It may also include the use of economic pressure by either side. The union may use strikes and boycotts, for example, while management may replace strikers or close down the business. Collective bargaining is probably the most complicated area of labor-management relations.

The main objective of preventive labor relations is to deter the union from coming in, rather than responding once it is already organizing. Management can use many techniques to avert unionization, such as maintaining competitive wages and benefits.

STUDY QUESTIONS

1. Why have unions lost membership over the past twenty years?
2. What is an authorization card? What does it mean if you sign one?
3. What rights and responsibilities do unions have? What rights and responsibilities does management have in regard to a union?
4. In a past or current job, why would you or anyone else want a union? Have you or anyone else been dissatisfied enough to want to belong to a union?
5. What is a right-to-work law, and what are its implications?
6. Describe the steps in certifying and decertifying a union.
7. Can an employer do much about keeping a union out once it is organizing in the establishment? Will it have an effect?
8. If you were to go into a collective bargaining session tomorrow, what would you want to know before you went in?
9. What happened to the federal air traffic controllers when they went out on strike? Can that happen to other unions? Under what conditions?
10. Describe ten preventive labor relations techniques.

REFERENCES

Bertagnoli, Lisa. 1989. State of the union varies in industry. **Restaurants and Institutions** 99(8):26.

Bethke, Art, R. Wayne Mondy, and Shane R. Premeaux. 1986. Decertification: The role of the first-line supervisor. **Supervisory Management** 31(2):21–23.

Brett, Jeanne M. 1980. Why employees want unions. **Organizational Dynamics** 8(4):47–59.

Bucalo, John P. 1986. Responding to the causes of unionization with a comprehensive employee relations system. **Personnel Administrator** 31(4):63–84.

Dickens, William T., and Jonathan S. Leonard. 1985. Accounting for the decline in union membership, 1950–1980. *Industrial and Labor Relations Review* 38(3):323–34.

Fulmer, William E. 1981. Step by step through a union campaign. *Harvard Business Review* 59(4):94–102.

Gilberg, Kenneth, and Nancy Abrams. 1987. Countering unions' new organizing techniques. *Personnel* 64(6):12–16.

Hartland, Robert W. 1984. *Responding to Unionization Efforts.* Washington, D.C.: National Restaurant Association.

Henry, Karen Hawley. 1985. Health care union organizing: Guidelines for supervisory conduct. *Health Care Supervisor* 4(1):14–26.

Hopkins, James H., and Robert D. Binderup. 1980. Union elections are seldom won or lost during the campaign. *Personnel Administrator* 25(3):57–61.

Kilgour, John G. 1978. Before the union knocks. *Personnel Journal* 57(4):186–213.

———. 1983. Union organizing activity among white-collar employees. *Personnel* 60(2):18–27.

Kohl, John P., and David B. Stephens. 1985. On strike: legal developments in labor-management relations. *Cornell H.R.A. Quarterly* 25(4):71–75.

PA talks with veteran negotiator Fritz Ihrig. 1986. *Personnel Administrator* 31(4): 55–60.

Pickworth, James R. 1987. An experiential approach to collective bargaining. *Cornell H.R.A. Quarterly* 28(2):60–66.

Swann, James P. 1983. The decertification of a union. *Personnel Administrator* 28(1):47–51.

Wentz, Charles Alvin. 1987. Preserving a union-free workplace, *Personnel* 64(10): 68–72.

Chapter 6

Employee Compensation

KEY QUESTIONS

1. What are the objectives of a compensation program?
2. What is job evaluation, and how is it done?
3. How is a salary structure developed and administered?
4. How do pay surveys fit into the job evaluation process?
5. What are the major provisions of federal laws governing compensation?
6. What are the requirements of a sound employee benefits program?
7. What are the most recent trends in employee benefit plans?
8. What are the major categories of employee benefits?
9. How is a flexible benefit schedule put together?

KEY TERMS AND CONCEPTS

Compensation

Wages

Salary

Incentives

Benefits

Nonexempt employees

Exempt employees

Cost-of-living adjustments (COLA)

Consumer price index (CPI)

Job evaluation

Job-ranking method

Factor comparison method

Compensable factors

Job grade method

Wage classes or grades

Job class

Point method

Point manual

Wage and salary survey

Wage curve

Bonuses

Merit raises

Gain-sharing plans

Lump sum payment

Profit sharing

Fair Labor Standards Act (FLSA)

Comparable worth

Social Security

Workers' compensation

Unemployment compensation

Health maintenance organization (HMO)

Preferred provider organization (PPO)

Defined benefit pension plans

Defined contribution pension plans

Independent Retirement Accounts (IRA)

Flexible benefit programs, or cafeteria programs

Reimbursement or flexible spending account

Employee *compensation* for work performed includes either *wages* or *salary, incentives,* and *benefits.* Wages refer to pay based on an hourly rate, while salary is based on a specific period of time such as weekly or annually. Most nonmanagerial employees in the hospitality field are paid by the hour and are referred to as hourly or *nonexempt employees.* Most managerial employees are salaried and receive the same amount of pay regardless of how much they work. According to federal law, they are *exempt employees* and are therefore not covered by the law's overtime provision (time and a half for all hours over a forty-hour work week). On the average in the hospitality industry, employee compensation makes up about one-third of total sales.

Incentives include onetime payments and other motivational tools used to encourage special work effort. Benefits include legally required ones such as Social Security, health and life insurance, pensions, payment for time not worked, employee services, free meals, and others.

The goals of compensation policies include rewarding employees' performance, being competitive in the labor market, attracting new employees, maintaining equity among employees, and increasing job satisfaction and possibly the motivational level of employees. A goal in nonunion organizations is also to have a compensation package attractive enough to keep out a union.

WAGES AND SALARIES

Many factors affect how wages and salaries are set. These factors include what is currently being paid in the area, the labor market, the minimum wage and other governmental regulations, the worth of the job, the cost of living, the employer's ability to pay, and the presence of a collective bargaining agreement. Pay rates are often adjusted upward to help employees cope with inflation. *Cost-of-living adjustments (COLA)* are seen in union contracts and also in the policies of many nonunion organizations. Usually COLA are based on the *consumer price index (CPI),* a governmental measure of the average change in prices over a certain period of time for goods and services that people buy for day-to-day living.

A good wage system has several requirements, starting with an evaluation of the job, followed by a determination of a wage and salary structure. This process needs to be as accurate as possible to ensure pay equity, or equal pay for equal work, and also to ensure that pay rates are competitive for the area. Clearly written wage policies and procedures are also needed. Wage policies and procedures can include how pay rates and raises are made, how jobs are put into pay grades, and personnel responsibility for the various components of the program. Next, pertinent policies and procedures are communicated to the employees so they understand how the system works. Last, at least once a year the process of job evaluation and determination of wages and salaries needs to be reviewed.

JOB EVALUATION

Job evaluation is the systematic process of determining the relative worth of jobs in an organization, then determining which jobs should pay more than others. Job evaluation also helps to establish which jobs have the same worth to the organization. Because job evaluation is used to set up a salary structure, it is crucial to job satisfaction and productivity.

Job evaluation is fairly simple for foodservices, compared to other industries, because there are rarely more than twenty-five to thirty distinct job classifications. There are more classifications at hotels and motels, but still not nearly the number as in many other industries. One factor that does complicate job evaluation and wages in the hospitality industry is tips. Tips must be considered remuneration and therefore part of wages when setting wage rates. It is not possible to evaluate hotel and motel or foodservice jobs on a standardized basis, because each operation is unique to some extent.

There are several methods of doing a job evaluation: through job ranking, factor comparison, job grades, and points. Both job descriptions and job specifications are useful in this process (see chapter 2).

In the job-ranking method of job evaluation, which is the simplest and oldest one, a job's worth is determined by comparing the entire job with other whole jobs in the organization. Job ranking can be done by a manager who is not a professionally trained wage analyst, with the help of a committee of at least four or five people. This method tends to be subjective and should be used only in smaller operations. Table 6-1 shows a possible job ranking for a small hotel's food and beverage department.

The *factor comparison method* also compares jobs to others, but it is the component parts or factors—referred to as *compensable factors*—making up a given job that are compared, rather than the jobs as a whole. Compensable factors are job elements such as knowledge, skills, efforts (mental and physical), responsibilities, such as supervision, and working conditions, such as stress or hazards. These factors are compared to those of key jobs in the organization, resulting in a factor comparison scale. Table 6-2 shows the ranking of three key jobs as an example, but normally between twelve and twenty key jobs make up the factor comparison scale.

Other methods of job evaluation compare a given job with a scale of worth. The *job grade method* groups jobs into broader, predetermined *wage classes or*

Table 6-1.   Possible job ranking for a small hotel's food and beverage department

Position	Ranking
Manager, food and beverage	Highest
Chef	
Restaurant manager	
Dining room manager	
Cook	
Bartender	
Server	
Storeroom clerk	
Kitchen helper	
Pot/Dishwasher	Lowest

grades that require increasing levels of knowledge, skill, efforts, and responsibility. For example, one such class may include dishwashers, potwashers, and housekeepers. Each *job class* includes a description, against which specifications for the various jobs are compared. In this method, the job is evaluated as a whole.

In the *point method,* which is more objective and popular, the relative value of a job depends on how many points it "scores" when evaluated on the basis of compensable factors (Table 6-3). This method is more refined than either the ranking or grade methods and produces more valid results. Although it is difficult to establish, it is simple to use.

Because management jobs have a broader scope and more complex tasks than others in an organization, they are evaluated using a detailed factor comparison or point method, or some combination of the two.

Table 6-2.   Ranking key jobs by compensable factors

Job	Knowledge	Skills	Efforts	Responsibilities	Working Conditions
Cook	1	1	1	2	2
Server	2	2	2	1	3
Dishwasher	3	3	3	3	1

Table 6-3. Sample listing of points for selected compensable factors

Factors	Points per Job by Degree of Difficulty		
	1st	*2nd*	*3rd*
Job	10	25	40
Knowledge	Use of reading and writing	Use of reading and writing	Use of reading and writing
	Use of mechanical equipment	Use of basic mathematics	Use of basic mathematics
	Reading and use of fixed gauges	Knowledge of at least one part of foodservice operations such as cooking or serving	Use of computer
			Knowledge of all facets of foodservice operation: menu planning, purchasing, receiving, storage, food preparation, service, sanitation, marketing, human resource management, financial reporting

SALARY STRUCTURE

In order to determine a certain salary or salary range for a given job, that job must be placed in the context of a salary structure, or companywide range of pay rates. The salary structure, in turn, results from conducting a survey of wages and salaries, establishing pay grades with rate ranges, and putting job titles into pay grades.

A *wage and salary survey* covers the wages paid to workers for various employers in an organization's relevant labor market, the area from which employers obtain their workers. By obtaining wage and salary information from other organizations that compete for the same personnel, a company is able to offer its employees salaries that are equivalent to—or better than—those paid at the other establishments. It should be done every one to two years.

To conduct a wage and salary survey, the organization identifies key jobs for comparison with the same or similar positions elsewhere. Key jobs, also called benchmark jobs, are recognizable by other hospitality organizations and vary little from operation to operation. Then ten to fifteen other organizations are selected that are not exactly like the surveying one, but rather are representative of the various types of employers—large and small, new and established, and so on—against which the surveying organization could be said to compete.

The survey should be specific about the type of data (wages, benefits, compensation policy) and the degree of detail (hourly, daily, weekly, or monthly), and of experience (new employees, those in midcareer, or more senior ones) necessary. Once the responses are collected and tabulated, the next step in constructing the salary structure can begin.

Once the survey responses are examined, pay grades need to be established (table 6-4). Each pay grade has a minimum or starting rate and a maximum rate. Setting wage ranges within these wage classes enables the salary structure to provide a greater incentive for employees to accept a promotion to a job in a higher class. Two other refinements are advisable: divide the ranges into steps that allow attainment of the top-of-the-range salary within each class based on merit, seniority, or both; and overlap the ranges of adjoining wage classes, so that an employee with experience may be enabled to earn as much as or more than someone with less experience in the next-highest job classification.

To complete the salary structure, each job is placed in its appropriate pay grade on the basis of its evaluated job worth. When examining each job, remember that it is crucial not to look at the performance of the person in the job, but only at the nature of the job itself.

In addition to the pay grades, an organization may need to establish rates of pay for special circumstances, such as night shift or the temporary addition of responsibilities. In these situations, an employee is often paid an additional hourly amount over his or her normal hourly rate.

Table 6-4.   Pay grades and rates

	Hourly pay rate		
Pay Grade	Minimum	Midpoint	Maximum
1	$3.50	$4.25	$5.00
2	4.50	5.25	6.00
3	5.50	6.25	7.00
4	6.50	7.25	8.00
5	7.50	8.25	9.00

INCENTIVES

Incentives include *bonuses, merit raises,* and *gain-sharing plans,* motivational tools used to encourage special work effort. Many employee benefits to be covered in a moment may act as incentives. Bonuses are onetime or periodic payments given in addition to the basic wage to reward employees for extra work done; they may be given for individual or group effort (see chapter 10).

Merit raises are given to an employee based upon level of performance. They are usually given at the time of the performance appraisal interview. In some organizations, raises are not directly tied to performance, but rather are automatic. This method is giving way to merit raises, which are the most popular pay-for-performance method. Employees who believe that their efforts will be rewarded become productive and stay productive. Studies of both executives and employees show that when pay is tied to performance, employees' satisfaction, motivation, and productivity increase. For some people, increased pay uplifts their self-esteem, pride, and prestige.

The use of merit raises will fail to serve its motivational purpose under certain conditions:

- If the performance evaluation system is not functioning effectively
- If employees don't trust the managers who make the decisions that will affect their merit raise
- If managers make their decisions based on favoritism, seniority, or pity
- If employees can successfully pressure their supervisor to give them a higher increase

Table 6-5 shows an example of merit guidelines. Depending on the rating given the employee and his or her position in the wage range within a particular class, wages will increase by a certain percentage. In some cases, the raise is given in a single amount, called a *lump sum payment;* this is often used for employees who are red-circled, which means that their wage rate is at the maximum for their grade.

Gain-sharing plans are programs designed to improve productivity through sharing the financial gains of the organization with employees. The most popular such plan is called *profit sharing.* This involves any method that distributes a portion of the company's profits among the employees. It is common for employees to become eligible after reaching twenty-one years of age and having worked 1,000 hours. In a cash plan, the profits are distributed annually. In a deferred plan, which is more common, there is no significant payment until termination, retirement, disability, or death. Some plans com-

Table 6-5. Sample merit increase guidelines

Performance Rating	Amount of Raise (%), Based on Employee's Position in the Wage Range*			
	Below 25%	*Below 50%*	*Below 75%*	*Below 90%*
Outstanding	15	12	9	6
Good	13	10	7	4
Meets standards	10	7	4	2
Below standards	No raise until performance is brought up to at least "Meets			
Unsatisfactory	standards."			

* If the current wage is between 90 and 99 percent of the wage range, the increase will be to the maximum of the range. For employees who are already at the top of the wage range, a lump sum will be paid.

bine both cash and deferred concepts. According to a 1985 study for the National Restaurant Association (Boyle 1987), 17 percent of restaurants had a form of profit sharing, a figure lower than was found in manufacturing (25 percent) and retail and wholesale (33 percent).

Its advantage is that it can provide an incentive for employee recruitment and retention as well as high levels of performance and productivity; its motivational value may not be so great, however, because it rewards all workers equally, although their performance and efforts are certainly not close to being equal. Additionally, during years when there are no profits to share, it can be demoralizing. In order for profit sharing to be successful, employees must feel they can actively participate in making their organization successful.

GOVERNMENTAL REGULATION OF COMPENSATION

The major federal law regarding wages is the *Fair Labor Standards Act (FLSA),* commonly called the Wage and Hour Act or the federal minimum wage law. The major parts of the act are concerned with the minimum wage, overtime payments, definitions of exempt and nonexempt employees, child labor protection, and equal rights as stated in the Equal Pay Act of 1963 and the Age Discrimination in Employment Act of 1967 (see chapter 1 and table 1-1). For the major requirements of the FLSA as related to the hospitality industry, *see* Appendix D.

The Equal Pay Act of 1963 requires that men and women be paid at the same rate for work that is substantially equal in skills, effort, responsibility, and working conditions. Related to this issue is the more complex one of comparable worth, which concerns certain occupations in which women predominate, such as secretarial work, that have lower pay rates than predominantly male occupations, such as construction, that are different but require similar skills and abilities.

As of January 1, 1990, both private and public employers in Ontario, Canada with more than ten workers are required by law to evaluate jobs in which 60 percent of the employees are women. Jobs must be evaluated on the basis of skill, effort, responsibility, and working conditions. Employers are given a certain period of time in which to start eliminating any pay inequities between women and men. In the United States, twenty-two states have similar legislation that applies only to public agencies (Freudenheim 1989).

Under the Consolidated Omnibus Reconciliation Act (COBRA) of 1986, employers with twenty or more employees must offer them the option to continue health care insurance under the employer's plan if coverage should terminate, such as on resignation. The employee must pay for this coverage, plus a handling fee, and must be able to continue coverage of spouse and dependents as well.

Other legislation affecting benefits includes the Tax Equity and Fiscal Responsibility Act of 1982 (TEFRA), the Deficit Reduction Act of 1984 (DEFRA), the Tax Reform Act of 1986, and Section 89 of the IRS Code. These laws are very complex, making benefit administration more involved and expensive and also making it necessary for some businesses to hire benefit consultants.

EMPLOYEE BENEFITS

Benefits were originally referred to as fringe benefits because they were quite meager and given in addition to the paycheck. Their scope and costs have expanded widely. Employee benefit costs have greatly affected business expenses and profits since enactment of the first state compensation law around 1900 and passage of the Social Security Act of 1935. According to U.S. Chamber of Commerce surveys, costs of benefits have risen from 3 percent of total payroll expenses in 1929 to 36.6 percent in 1984. Of that 36.6 percent, approximately 10 percent goes to paying for legally required benefits, 11 percent for time not worked, and 8 percent to cover health and life insurance; the remaining 7.6 percent pays for other benefits and services. Passage of the Employee Retirement Income Security Act of 1974 (ERISA) and increased Social Security taxes, as well as other legislation and worker demands, have all greatly increased the cost of employee benefits.

A benefits program should meet objectives the organization sets, which are likely to include improving morale, meeting health and security needs, and attracting and motivating employees. An organization's objectives for a benefits program will of course vary by its size, sales volume and profitability, location, and local industry patterns.

A good benefits program allows for employee input through committees, surveys, or other methods, and is communicated clearly to all employees. Under ERISA, employers are required to inform their workers about pensions and certain other benefits in such a way that the average employee truly understands them. Employers should also periodically review the benefits program to be sure that it is meeting employees' needs. The traditional benefit program was designed for a man who was the sole support of his family, with a statistical average of 2.5 children. This situation is no longer true for the majority of working individuals.

Table 6-6 contains a listing of many of the employee benefits that may be available. These include ones that are legally required, health and life insurance, pensions, payment for time not worked, and employee services and other benefits.

Legally Required Benefits

Legally required benefits include *Social Security, workers' compensation,* and *unemployment compensation.* Congress passed the first phase of the Social Security program in 1935. The program is divided into four major parts: old-age benefits, disability benefits, survivors' benefits, and Medicare. The employee pays a fixed percentage of his or her income (in 1990, 7.65 percent of the first $57,000 earned) to the federal government, and the employer pays a similar amount.

Old-age benefits start at age sixty-five, but this is being raised gradually to sixty-seven years of age. In order to receive old-age benefits, an individual must have worked for at least ten years. Persons under seventy who are collecting Social Security payments and are also gainfully employed can earn only so much income before having to pay back some of it to Social Security.

Employees who have been disabled for at least six months, will be disabled for at least twelve more months, and have worked and paid into Social Security for at least five years are also eligible to receive Social Security payments. It is computed similarly to retirement benefits.

Dependents of retired, disabled, or deceased workers are entitled to receive Social Security payments if under eighteen years of age and not married. Other survivors may qualify for payments as well. Medicare is an amendment to the

Social Security Act and is usually treated as a totally separate program from Social Security. Medicare's primary purpose is to help people sixty-five and older pay for health care costs.

The intent of workers' compensation laws is to provide the cost of medical expenses and income to individuals who become hurt on the job (see chapter 7). The payment of workers' compensation insurance is compulsory in most states. Depending on state laws, employers may insure with private companies, join a state insurance system, or become self-insured. The premiums, which the employer usually pays, depend to a large extent on the company's safety record.

Unemployment compensation refers to benefits paid to employees who are laid off from a job for up to twenty-six weeks. These employees must register to receive the compensation and be willing to accept any suitable employment offered. The employee's most recent wage and period of employment deter-

Table 6-6. Categories of benefits

Categories	Benefits
Legally required benefits	Social Security
	Workers' compensation
	Unemployment insurance
Health and life insurance	Group health insurance
	Health maintenance organizations
	Preferred provider organizations
	Dental care
	Vision care
	Prescription care
	Group term life insurance
	Accidental death and disability insurance
	Long-term disability
	Short-term disability
Pensions	Defined benefit
	Defined contribution
	401(k) plan
	Profit sharing
	Independent Retirement Account
	Independent Retirement Account
Payment for time not worked	Sick leave
	Vacation time
	Holidays
	Bereavement
	Breaks
	Jury duty

Table 6-6. *Continued*

Employee services and other benefits	Educational assistance
	Credit unions
	Meals/meal allowances
	Rooms/room allowances
	Uniforms/uniform allowance
	Parking/parking cost assistance
	Employee assistance program
	Wellness program
	Social and recreational programs
	Payroll deductions for additional insurance
	Legal services
	Discount purchases
	Financial planning services
	Preretirement planning and counseling
	Relocation (moving) expenses
	Child care availability/child care assistance
	Awards such as length of service
	Membership in professional and trade associations
	Attendance at industry seminars
	Trade journals and periodicals
	Scholarships for dependent children
	Matched donations to universities and colleges

mines the amount of the benefit. Both the federal and the state governments collect an amount based on percentages of each employee's wages, up to an established maximum; most of the federal money is returned to the states to operate the program.

Health and Life Insurance

Health insurance is the most common benefit in the U.S. In 1983, the most expensive benefit for employers to pay was Social Security pay for retirement. In 1988, health insurance became the most expensive benefit, largely because health care costs have been increasing dramatically since 1965. One result of this has been that more organizations are shifting part of the cost of health insurance onto the employees. By far a majority of employers in the United States offer health insurance to their employees. The National Restaurant Association's Survey of Health Insurance Coverage in the Restaurant Industry

(1987) found that small companies are less likely to provide health insurance coverage. The most common features of the health plans include ninety-day waiting periods, maximum coverage of $1 million, coverage of dependents, thirty to forty hours per week of work required to qualify, and payment by the plan of 80 percent of the benefits after the employee pays the deductible.

More and more employers are offering a *health maintenance organization (HMO)* or *preferred provider organization (PPO)* option. An HMO is an organization of physicians and other health care professionals who provide all services to employees enrolled voluntarily under a prepaid plan. Some HMOs may require a minimal copayment of, for example, two dollars when an enrollee uses services. Plan members must use HMO-approved physicians and hospitals. Often the HMO has its own building in which its health services are provided. HMOs emphasize preventive care, in part to provide care early and keep costs down. PPOs came about, as did HMOs, due to the spiraling costs of health care; both have helped contain costs. PPOs may be either a hospital or a group of physicians offering a plan to provide all medical services for employees using those facilities. Employers usually encourage employees to use the PPO by covering much more of their expenses if they do.

As a general rule, the larger the employer, the greater the number of supplemental health benefits available. From most to least popular, these benefits include dental plans, prescription drug plans, and vision care plans.

The most prevalent life insurance plan is group term life insurance. The most popular benefits in case of death or disability are accidental death and disability (AD&D) and long-term disability (LTD) insurance.

Pensions

Most employers offer some type of retirement or pension plan. Most plans are noncontributory; in other words, only the employer contributes, not the employee. Most are categorized as either *defined benefit* or *defined contribution pension plans.* In defined benefit plans, the amount of the pension upon retirement and the conditions for its payment are known ahead of time. In defined contribution plans, what is preset is how the employer and possibly the employee will contribute to the pension fund, which may be through profit sharing, *Independent Retirement Accounts (IRA),* or other ways. An IRA is a tax shelter available under certain circumstances to individuals who normally use it as a source of retirement income. However, the amount of the actual pension is not determined until retirement, when the value of the funds invested is determined.

Among defined contribution plans, salary reduction or 401(k) plans, named after section 401(k) of the Internal Revenue Code, are the most popular. Employees, particularly in small businesses, can save for retirement through payroll deductions of one to six percent of their paychecks, with the employer possibly matching their savings. All money contributed into the plan is tax-deferred. In most 401(k) plans, full vesting occurs immediately or within five years; this means that an employee who leaves the company has a right to the pension.

FLEXIBLE BENEFIT PROGRAMS

Flexible benefit programs, also called *cafeteria programs* or employee choice plans, offer participants options in terms of which benefits they want and what type of coverage. Reasons for implementing flexible plans include to control the spiraling costs of benefits, better meet the different needs of employees, improve employee satisfaction and morale, and educate employees about actual benefit costs. Although flexible benefit programs have been around since the early 1970s, they are not yet widely used; but their numbers are growing.

Most flexible benefit programs fit into one of three approaches: the core method, the participation option method, and the additional allowance method (Baker 1988). Using the core method, a core plan is devised, with a minimal level of coverage of certain benefits. All employees must keep this core plan and cannot trade it away for other benefits. An employee can then use the dollar difference between a traditional plan and the core plan to purchase more coverage. In the participation option method, employees can choose among several option plans. An employee who wants to purchase more coverage can do so through payroll deduction. By picking a program with less value and less coverage than he or she is currently getting, the employee can take the difference as taxable income. With the additional allowance approach, the employer maintains the existing benefit program but offers an allowance of credits that can be used to purchase more or new coverage; these credits are usually based on the employee's salary and years of service. In almost all programs, employees can make changes periodically, such as yearly.

The three most common flexible benefits are health insurance, life insurance, and dental care. The Internal Revenue Service limits the choice of tradable benefits to medical care, group term life insurance, short- and long-term disability, group legal services, cash or deferred plans under section 401(k), and vacation days.

Flexible benefit plans also often have a feature called a *reimbursement or flexible spending account.* An employee can set aside pretax dollars to pay for goods or services the benefit plan does not cover. These might include contact lenses or dental work that is not part of a dental plan.

Flexible benefit programs are not suitable to every organization. They require much time and effort to get started, and because the idea is new and somewhat strange to many employees, much time and money must be spent to communicate the program to them and help them make their choices.

SUMMARY

Employee compensation includes wages or salary, incentives, and benefits. Wages and salaries are affected by many factors both within and outside the workplace. Job evaluation is used to determine the relative worth of jobs in order to determine how jobs should be paid—in other words, how the job is to be placed in the wage and salary structure. There are four methods by which to evaluate jobs.

Incentives include bonuses, merit raises, and other motivational tools used to encourage special work effort.

Benefits include legally required ones such as Social Security, health and life insurance, pensions, payment for time not worked, and employee services and other benefits such as free meals. The cost of benefits has recently increased tremendously, particularly in the area of health care insurance. In response to this, many employers are asking employees to share in premium costs and pay higher deductibles. Some employers are also instituting flexible benefit programs to get more value for their benefit dollars.

STUDY QUESTIONS

1. What are the components and objectives of a compensation program? Do you feel the compensation program in a current or previous job meets the objectives?
2. Compare and contrast the four methods of job evaluation. Include one advantage and disadvantage of each.
3. What is a wage curve, and what are the two ways to construct it?
4. List two jobs in a restaurant that would be in the same job class, and why.
5. What is the most popular pay for performance method?
6. What are three major trends in employee benefit plans?
7. Ask someone who has a full benefits package to go over each component with you. List and categorize them.
8. What are some benefits of a cafeteria plan?

9. In a past or current job, what benefits have you received?

10. What are the FLSA regulations concerning tips?

REFERENCES

Baker, Carolyn A. 1988. Flex your benefits. *Personnel Journal* 67(5):54–61.

Boyle, Kathy. 1987. Giving employees a share of the business. *Restaurants USA* 7(2):16–19.

Dee, Dorothy. 1987. Fringe benefits. *Restaurants USA* 7(10):29–31.

Elliott, Travis. 1983. *Profitable Foodservice Management Through Job Evaluation.* Washington, D.C.: National Restaurant Association.

Freudenheim, Milt. 1989. A new Ontario law matches women's wages with men's. *New York Times* July 27:1.

Friedberg, Bonnie R., and John H. Callahan. 1987. Employee benefits attract the best. *Restaurants USA* 7(2):10–12.

Grossman, Morton E., and Margaret Magnus. 1988. The boom in benefits. *Personnel Journal* 67(11):51–55.

Hanna, John B. 1986. *Managing Employee Benefits.* Fort Worth: U.S. Small Business Administration.

Mills, Susan. 1988. A review of industry health insurance plans. *Restaurants USA* 8(8):42–44.

Papa, Anne. 1987. Foodservice operators customize benefits. *Restaurants USA* 7(2):13–15.

Sherman, Arthur W., George W. Bohlander, and Herbert J. Chruden. 1988. *Managing Human Resources.* 8th ed. Cincinnati: South-Western Publishing Co.

Stefanick, Gerald J. 1981. What you should know about the wage-hour law. *Cornell H.R.A. Quarterly* 22(1):6–11.

Walker, C. Terrence. 1987. The use of job evaluation plans in salary administration. *Personnel* 64(3):28–31.

Chapter 7

Health and Safety

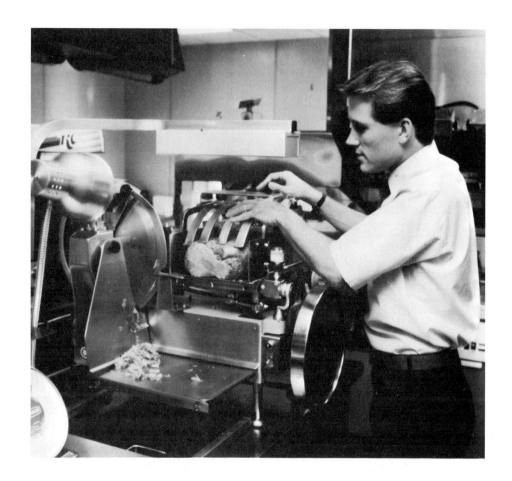

KEY QUESTIONS

1. What health and safety concerns are there within a hospitality organization?
2. What is an employer legally required to do to ensure a healthful and safe workplace?
3. What else can be done to create a healthful and safe working environment?
4. How is stress defined, and how does it affect the body?
5. What is a Type A and a Type B personality, and which one is more prone to stress?
6. What are the major causes of stress?
7. How can you cope with stress?
8. How can you better manage your time?

KEY TERMS AND CONCEPTS

Occupational Safety and Health Administration (OSHA)

Right-to-know laws

Material safety data sheets (MSDS)

Workers' compensation

Employee assistance programs (EAP)

Wellness programs

Safety programs

Safety committees

Stress

Fight-or-flight syndrome

Job burnout

Type A behavior

Type B behavior

Physically induced stress

Emotionally induced stress

Time management

"To do" list

Prioritize

Within any hospitality operation, there are health and safety concerns such as dealing with an alcoholic employee or preventing accidents involving employees and guests. Due to various pieces of legislation, hospitality operators have a legal obligation to perform certain health- and safety-related functions. Besides legal requirements, there are many other health and safety concerns in a hospitality organization, including stress and effective time management.

LEGAL REQUIREMENTS

Occupational Safety and Health Act

In 1971 the Occupational Safety and Health Act became law. Its purpose is to "assure so far as possible every working man and woman in the Nation safe and healthful working conditions and to preserve our human resources." The act created the *Occupational Safety and Health Administration (OSHA)* to establish and enforce necessary safety and health standards, the Occupational Safety and Health Review Commission to judge OSHA's enforcement actions when they are appealed, and the National Institute for Occupational Safety and Health to do research in this area, recommend new standards, and develop educational programs. The act applies to any business, regardless of size, that affects interstate commerce, so almost all businesses are included.

OSHA has the responsibility to set mandatory job safety and health standards, encourage both employers and employees to decrease hazards in the workplace and establish each party's responsibility in such actions, conduct compliance inspections, and ask for record keeping of injuries, illnesses, and fatalities. OSHA states that the employer "shall furnish to each of his employees, employment and a place of employment which are free from recognized hazards that are causing or likely to cause death or serious physical harm to his employees." Although OSHA is a federally run program, the act encourages the states to develop and enforce their own programs, which should be at least as effective as the federal one.

OSHA inspections are made by compliance safety health officers, who generally do not give advance notice. During an inspection they may do any of the following:

1. Check that the OSHA poster explaining the job safety and health protection provided under the act is posted in a prominent place in the establishment.
2. Observe employees' activities and ask them questions.
3. Examine and evaluate the safety and health program, including the training component.
4. Inspect the establishment for safety hazards.
5. Check for availability of appropriate medical first aid services.
6. Examine overall housekeeping.
7. Check emergency procedures.

After the inspection, the officer will review with the managers what was seen, including any violations. Penalties may not be imposed during an inspection, nor can the operation be closed down. The officer returns to the office and prepares a report for the area director, who then determines if any penalties or citations for violations will be imposed. Citations must be posted in the physical area of the violation, and the area director must be notified when the situation is remedied, for which there is a deadline. Employers can appeal through OSHA about citations or proposed penalties and/or any corrections they must make.

In addition to enforcement, which focuses on hazardous industries and workplaces with problems or complaints, OSHA will consult with any employers who wish help in recognizing and correcting safety and health hazards. It is a free, on-site service, which is penalty-free and completely separate from the OSHA inspection effort. The only requirement for the employer is to commit to correcting any safety hazards found.

The foodservice industry was exempted from the record-keeping requirements of OSHA in 1983, with one notable exception: if there is an accident that results in a fatality or hospitalization of five or more employees, the foodservice operator must report it to the nearest area director within forty-eight hours. Hotel and motel operators need to record occupational injuries and illnesses on OSHA Form No. 200 within two working days of notification of such. Only injuries and illnesses deemed recordable by OSHA are put on this form. Every operator also must maintain a log of all workplace injuries and illnesses.

Right-to-Know Laws

By 1988 most American businesses, including hospitality operations, were required to comply with the Hazardous Materials Communication Standard, which OSHA developed. Related legislation has come to be called *right-to-know laws,* because the purpose of the OSHA standard is to give employees the right to know what chemicals they are working with, what the risks or hazards of these chemicals are, and what they can do to limit their risks. Examples of materials that contain hazardous chemicals and are found in hospitality operations include laundry detergent, oven cleaner, all-purpose cleaner, canned fuel for cooking and warming equipment, and pesticides.

Chemicals present physical or health hazards, or both. Physical hazards include being explosive, chemically reactive, or flammable. Health hazards include being irritating, corrosive, poisonous, carcinogenic, or a potential cause of birth defects.

Under the standard, employers must do the following:

1. Post a list of hazardous substances found in the industry.
2. Inventory these products.
3. Post *material safety data sheets (MSDS)*—one for each hazardous product —which explains basically what the substance is, the risks in using it, safe handling practices, and emergency and first aid procedures.
4. Explain to employees how to use the MSDS and product labels. Make sure all hazardous chemicals are labeled.
5. Train employees how to use chemicals properly and handle emergencies.
6. Develop a written hazard communication program describing how the above are accomplished and who is responsible.

Training employees must be done when they are first assigned to a position involving hazardous chemicals and whenever a new hazard is to be used in the area. Training should include how to read and use information on the MSDS and labels; what steps to take, such as the use of protective equipment, to protect employees from hazards; and what to do in an emergency.

Workers' Compensation

By 1920 most states had *workers' compensation* laws; the last state to adopt this type of statute did so by 1929. The intent of workers' compensation laws is to provide medical expenses and income to individuals who become hurt on the job. About 88 percent of the nation's employees are covered. Common features of state laws are as follows:

1. They provide for payment of medical expenses (usually fully covered) and some replacement of lost income (usually one-half to two-thirds), vocational rehabilitation if necessary, and death benefits to survivors.
2. They have basically set up the equivalent of an insurance program, in which the employer pays premiums based on the company's accident rate.
3. It's a no-fault system in that job-related injuries and illnesses are covered regardless of who is responsible.
4. An employee gets the benefits if the injury resulted from an accident that occurred during the course of the worker's employment.

Prior to workers' compensation laws, workers had to sue their employer when work-related injuries or illnesses occurred. This caused expensive lawsuits for the employer, and the employee, if he or she won, received payment only after a lengthy period of time. With workers' compensation laws, employees get prompt and certain payment and employers are protected from costly lawsuits.

HEALTH CONCERNS

An organization's health concerns center around physical and emotional health, and substance abuse. Organizational approaches to other health concerns include employee assistance, wellness, and substance abuse programs.

Physical Health

Of much concern to hotel, restaurant, and institution operators today is the health issue of AIDS. AIDS, which stands for Acquired Immunodeficiency Syndrome, is caused by a virus that makes the body unable to fight disease. There is no cure, and up to 90 percent of individuals with the virus may die from AIDS-related complications. Approximately 20 to 50 percent of AIDS victims have AIDS but do not show any symptoms, and many do not even know they have the disease. AIDS is transmitted by sexual contact, reusing contaminated drug needles and syringes, and receiving blood infected with the virus. AIDS is not transmitted through casual contact, eating food prepared by an AIDS-infected individual, insect bites, saliva, sweat, tears, kisses, the air, using a bathroom, or swimming in a pool.

Most American businesses have failed to develop any AIDS-related policies and procedures or programs (Redeker and Segal 1989). In addition, many employees do not understand how AIDS is (and is not) transmitted. An employee who has AIDS can create much fear and prejudice in employees and guests (if they find out), who may leave and not come back. Hospitality operators need to develop and implement the following steps before this type of incident occurs, in order to minimize their liability. This should be done in consultation with an attorney.

1. *Nondiscrimination policy.* In many states and jurisdictions, AIDS-infected individuals are considered to be handicapped and are therefore protected against any adverse employment decisions, such as being terminated, unless they are job-related. Probably the only job-related condition that may justify termination is poor job performance due to the crippling effects of the disease. AIDS-infected employees should be covered by a nondiscrimination policy that protects their right to obtain and keep their jobs in an

environment free from discrimination as long as they are capable of performing their jobs.

2. *Confidentiality policy.* AIDS-infected employees have a right to ask management to keep any AIDS-related information confidential, regardless of how the employer found out about the information.

3. *Education.* Employees need to be educated about what AIDS is and especially how it is and is not transmitted. This type of education should be mandatory for all employees at all organizational levels. Once employees understand that AIDS cannot be transmitted by working with someone, they will more likely be rational and tolerant if they learn at some future point that a co-worker has AIDS.

4. *Plan for damage control.* Even after implementing the recommendations above, there may be a high level of publicity surrounding a hospitality operation. Plans should be made ahead of time for dealing with this type of problem. The advice of legal counsel and public relations people may be helpful.

Also of concern is the issue of smoking in the workplace. The dangers and costs of smoking are well documented. Smokers cost their employers between $400 to $1,000 more per year than nonsmokers (Voluck 1987). This is due in part to increased costs resulting from higher health and fire insurance and higher rates of absenteeism. The Surgeon General's office has elaborated on the dangers of passive smoking, the inhaling of cigarette smoke by nonsmokers.

More and more businesses, as well as eating establishments, are starting to restrict smoking, increasingly in response to state and local legislation. Employee requests or a desire to enhance the health and satisfaction of nonsmokers have also contributed to this trend. Commonly, an employer sets up smoking areas where nonsmokers will not be exposed. Whereas a nonunion employer may limit or forbid smoking in the workplace, this may be against provisions of the labor contract in a unionized environment. Even if the contract says nothing on this issue, smoking may be seen as an issue affecting employment.

As with AIDS, the legal aspects of smoking in the workplace are evolving and vary from state to state. An employer not providing a smoke-free environment may be found liable in some states for compensatory and punitive damages for employee health problems caused by the effects of smoke. Employers can therefore minimize their risk of going to court by adopting policies that limit smoking to certain areas and involving employees in the implementation of the policy.

Emotional Health

Emotional health is a concern in hospitality operations. Symptoms of strained mental health include typical behavior that becomes exaggerated, behavior that changes radically, and displays of distress symptoms, which can include agitation, depression, difficulty in concentrating, fatigue due to inability to sleep, and weight loss. Approximately 3 percent of employees have problems serious enough to require professional help (Bureau of National Affairs 1978).

Substance Abuse

The two major substances abused in the workplace are alcohol and drugs. Alcoholism, or problem drinking, is viewed as a medical disease with distinguishable causes and treatment. The disease starts with a mild psychological dependence, which turns into a physiological dependence, and then an addictive state. The process takes about ten to twenty years to develop.

Approximately one out of every twenty employees has a problem with alcohol (Nelson 1985). Among the costs resulting from alcoholism, according to the National Council on Alcoholism, are that such employees

- Are absent two times more often than other employees
- Have two to three times more accidents
- Collect three times more sickness and accident benefits (Appelbaum and Shapiro 1989)

In addition to these costs are inefficient work and slowdowns, employee turnover and effect on morale.

Early signs of alcoholism include more frequent latenesses and absences (especially after days off), declining quality and quantity of work, increased arguing with peers and supervisors, and poorly thought-out work decisions. Physical and behavioral signs of alcohol intoxication include bloodshot eyes, flushed face, alcohol smell on the breath, nervousness, impaired judgment, frequent arguing, sudden mood changes, and fluctuating or poor work quality and output. The employee may also take longer breaks, leave work early, and avoid the supervisor.

Drug abuse is less prevalent than alcoholism but poses a different type of problem. Drug abuse can be more difficult to contain, as the drug abuser gets other employees onto drugs and the selling of drugs may start to occur on the work premises. Drugs are not restricted to any one type of employee; they are found at all levels of an organization. Common drugs include cocaine, stimulants, and marijuana, among many others.

The typical so-called recreational drug user, when compared to fellow employees, is late three times more often, asks to leave early over twice as frequently, has twice as many absences of eight days or more, uses three times the sick benefits, is five times as likely to file a workers' compensation claim, is involved in accidents over three times more often, and is 33 percent less productive (Cascio 1986). Additional signs of drug abuse include moodiness, trembling hands, and an unsteady gait.

Hospitality organizations must have a clear policy for on-the-job substance abuse for its employees. Typically, the policy states that working under the influence of any substance will not be tolerated and employees will be sent home. To avoid liability problems, the employer must make sure the employee gets home safely. The substance may be alcohol, illegal drugs, prescription or nonprescription drugs that cause behavior, such as slowed motion, that creates unsafe working conditions. Disciplinary guidelines need to be set for this infraction of work rules, so employees know the consequences of their actions. Many of the legal issues regarding drugs and alcohol in the workplace are not clearly defined, so legal counsel may be necessary.

Drug testing programs are used only by a minority of businesses, often those with compelling safety or national security concerns. The most common response to substance abuse is the employee assistance program.

Employee Assistance Programs

Counseling programs, called employee assistance programs (EAP), are an expansion of traditional occupational alcoholism programs, which began appearing 40 years ago. About one-third of the U.S. work force has access to EAPs. Larger organizations, of over 500 employees, are more likely to have EAPs than smaller companies. Companies such as Marriott Corporation offer counseling and referral services to some of their employees.

EAPs function to help troubled employees in personal crises, as well as those with emotional, alcohol, or drug abuse problems (Liddle 1989). In a time when the hospitality industry needs to retain employees, EAPs can help to get employees back on their feet and back to work.

An organization may hire its own counselors to administer the program or may use outside counseling companies. Outside companies estimate that EAPs cost the employer from 75 cents to three dollars per employee per month. The price varies according to the number of services provided (Liddle 1989). The EAP counselor's office may be within the organization's facility, or purposely located elsewhere to help ensure confidentiality.

When starting an EAP, a company should have a policy statement written to explain its objectives for the program. This statement should include the fact that the EAP is strictly confidential. This information, including how to use the program, should be explained clearly to employees. In addition, managers and supervisors need to be trained how and when to make referrals; if an employee is having problems doing the job, the EAP program should be suggested as a source of help. Referrals are also appropriate if an employee appears quite angry, confused, depressed, or withdrawn.

Effective EAP programs share the following characteristics:

1. The program is accessible twenty-four hours a day, seven days a week.
2. The employees are given the phone number of the EAP office.
3. The program is carried out by qualified professionals who are understanding of personal problems.
4. Involvement of the family is encouraged in situations where it is relevant to treatment.
5. The program should be advertised, and available, to the entire family.
6. Confidentiality must be maintained.
7. The employee should not receive any special favors or exemptions from on-the-job rules during treatment. Disciplinary actions must continue as necessary.

EAP programs most help those people with alcohol, drug, or behavioral problems. It is important that a manager who has an employee with any of these problems can mention and deal with only the resulting poor work performance—in other words, these problems are the manager's business only to the extent that work performance is impaired. The manager should not be passing judgment on an employee who has a drinking problem or moralizing, lecturing, or demanding promises from the employee to stop drinking. The manager can do only two things: recommend the use of the EAP program, and counsel and discipline specific instances of poor work performance.

In the case of the alcoholic, there is one special consideration: alcoholism is considered a disease, so that if an employee is about to be terminated for poor performance, the worker must be given a chance to enter some type of alcohol rehabilitation program. Only if the employee will not agree to go into a program can the manager then fire the person.

Wellness Programs

Promoting good health in the workplace, with what are commonly called *wellness programs,* has been growing in popularity. The overall goals of these programs are disease prevention, detection, and treatment. Major components of health promotion and disease prevention programs include physical fitness, detection and reduction of the risks of hypertension and heart disease, general nutrition, weight control, elimination of smoking, and stress management. They are provided by the employer, usually at minimal or no cost.

A wellness program potentially can result in lower health care costs, increased productivity, reduced absenteeism, lowered turnover, improved employee morale, and increased knowledge of health risks, as well as encouragement and stimulation of positive health attitudes and healthier life-styles. The trend toward wellness programs continues.

An example of a wellness program is one run by General Mills Corporation. General Mills's health education program promotes a healthful employee life-style through education, emphasizing employee awareness and participation. The program, which has been named Framework, incorporates a multidisciplinary approach that includes physical fitness, nutrition, mental health, chemical dependency counseling, first aid training in cardiopulmonary resuscitation (CPR), safety, and recreation. Information about these subjects is presented in seminars, displays, and publications. This material is reinforced by employee participation and one-on-one consultation as the employee desires. The Framework program encourages employees to take responsibility for a positive life-style, both at work and at home.

Substance Abuse Training Programs

In a 1988 survey of businesses with training professionals on staff, about 25 percent of the businesses provided substance abuse training (Schreier 1988). These programs typically focus on facts, policies, and procedures, and are presented to employees, families, supervisors, and managers. Supervisors and managers may also receive information on legal issues involved, as well as on how to identify, confront, and counsel users.

Wellness programs and substance abuse training are much more common in organizations with more than five thousand employees. In a 1988 survey by *Personnel Journal,* approximately half of responding organizations had EAPs and about one-third had health education, promotion, or wellness programs, under whatever name. Their prevalence in the hospitality industry, although not formally researched, is thought likely to be limited primarily to larger hotel and restaurant chains.

SAFETY CONCERNS

Safety hazards in hospitality operations range from built-up grease in the kitchen to slippery guest stairways without handrails. Typical hospitality-related accidents include fires, falls, cuts, and electric shock. They occur because employees are fooling around, rushing, being careless, working under the influence of alcohol or illegal drugs, not paying attention, or overdoing it. Accidents also sometimes occur because employees are ignorant of proper procedures or just feel that accidents are inevitable anyway.

In restaurants alone, there are approximately 500,000 accidents per year in the United States, costing $3.5 billion according to the Federal Bureau of Labor Statistics. The injury rate in the restaurant industry, 8.2 injuries per 100 workers, is higher than the national average. Additionally, almost 50 percent of these accidents involve serious injuries resulting in thirty-five lost work days each (Estrin 1989).

All accidents have one thing in common: a person who may incur pain and suffering and financial expenses. Financial expenses might include lost work time of injured and uninjured workers, management time spent dealing with the problem, overtime, medical expenses, retraining costs, higher workers' compensation insurance rates, and the cost of repair or replacement of anything damaged in the accident. Accidents can also lower morale and damage the reputation of the organization. Whenever guests or employees are hurt, an operator also runs the risk of being sued, which can be quite costly, even if the employer eventually wins the court case. Human error causes the majority of accidents, but unsafe working conditions, such as poor lighting, also encourage accidents. Appendix B, "An Accident Prevention Guide," lists ways to prevent most hospitality-related accidents.

The most serious safety issue operators face is serving unsafe or contaminated food. The Food and Drug Administration reports that between two and four million people become sick annually from food eaten in a restaurant or elsewhere. An outbreak of foodborne illness can close down an operation temporarily or even permanently.

Safety programs are common in hospitality operations as a method to prevent accidents and foodborne illness. They may include some or all of the following components:

- Safety policies and procedures, including sanitation policies and procedures
- Employee training
- Supervision
- A committee on safety
- Inspections for unsafe working conditions and employee practices
- Accident reporting and investigation

The more components are utilized, the more effective is the safety program.

Safety policies and procedures should be written to cover any situation in which there is the potential for an accident. For example, figure 7-1 shows a procedure for proper lifting of objects. The policies and procedures form the basis for an employee training program.

Safety training should start with orientation, and this information should be put into the employee handbook. The accident rate for employees is higher during their first month of employment than any subsequent month. Safety training should be repeated once a year for all employees. Topics for safety training can include safe food handling techniques, personal hygiene, the causes and prevention of different types of accidents, what to do in case of an emergency including first aid and the Heimlich maneuver (to stop choking), how to handle hazardous chemicals safely, and how to use and clean equipment properly. Employees also need to know that accidents don't just happen, that they can be eliminated or at least minimized. As part of their training, employees need to be evaluated on what they know (fig. 7-2) and rewarded or recognized for working safely.

1. *Plan it!*   Do you need help?
   Do you need a cart?
   Where is it going?

2. *Get ready!*

   Squat down with your back straight. Do not bend over from the waist!

   Put one foot alongside the object and one beside it for more stability.

   Grip the object with both hands, one at the bottom corner with palm up, and the other on the opposite top corner.

   Keep arms and elbows close to the body.

   Tuck in your chin.

3. *Lift it!*

   Straighten your knees slowly to stand up, and don't twist your back.

4. *Move it!*

   Keep the object close to you.

   Don't twist your back. If you need to change position, move your feet and entire body.

   Look where you are going.

   Call out "Coming through!" as needed.

5. *Set it down!*

   Do the reverse of Step 3.

   Slide the load into place, watching your fingers and toes.

Figure 7-1.   Procedure for proper lifting.

QUIZ ON PREVENTING FALLS AND STRAINS

Directions: Circle the correct answer.

1. To move two cases of #10 cans from the storeroom to the food preparation area, you should:

    A. Open the boxes, load your arms with as many cans as possible, and take them to the work area.

    B. Properly lift and carry one case at a time to the work area.

    C. Bring a cart with you, and use it.

    D. None of the above.

2. When lifting a load, you should mainly use your:

    A. Arm muscles.

    B. Leg muscles.

    C. Back muscles.

3. You need to lift and move a heavy pot of soup that you are not sure you can handle; you should:

    A. Flex your muscles and do it yourself.

    B. Ask for someone to help you lift and move it.

    C. Split the soup into two pots and then lift and carry it.

    D. Any of the above.

4. When getting ready to lift a heavy object, you should:

    A. Put one foot on each side of the object.

    B. Put one foot alongside and one beside the object.

    C. Put both feet in front of the object.

    D. Don't worry about your feet.

Figure 7-2. Safety quiz for employees.

Managers and supervisors themselves can do much to prevent accidents and foodborne illness. Besides being responsible for carrying out the various components of the safety program, they oversee the day-to-day monitoring and enforcement of safety standards, have to report and correct unsafe conditions, and act as role models. They are vital to creating an environment where safety is practiced and respected.

Businesses often form *safety committees,* which meet periodically to discuss safety matters. A safety committee may include managers, supervisors, and employees from various departments, as well as a human resource manager. The safety committee has many functions, such as developing and

5. When getting ready to lift a heavy object, you should:

   A. Lean over from the waist.

   B. Squat down to the level of the object.

   C. Squat down as low as you can.

6. When getting ready to lift a heavy object, you should:

   A. Keep your arms, elbows, and the object close to you.

   B. Keep your arms, elbows, and the object away from the body.

   C. Do whichever is comfortable.

7. When getting ready to lift a heavy object, you should:

   A. Grab it from the bottom.

   B. Grab it by the sides.

   C. Grab it by the bottom corner and the opposite top corner.

8. The best material for a shoe's heel and sole so you do not fall on wet floors is:

   A. Leather.

   B. Plastic.

   C. Rubber.

   D. None of the above.

9. Describe what to do if a spill occurs.

10. Describe three ways to prevent falls and slips.

11. Describe three precautions in using stepladders.

Figure 7-2. *Continued*

changing safety policies and procedures, reviewing data on number and types of accidents to date, inspecting the facility, and developing, implementing, and monitoring training.

Inspections of the facility should be done periodically to correct any safety-related problems. Appendix C contains a typical safety inspection form for a foodservice company. In addition to managers and supervisors, employees should take part in the inspection process, to encourage them to take a more active role in preventing accidents. Additionally, inspections stressing sanitation should be conducted.

Any accident, no matter how small, should be reported as soon as possible. This is typically accomplished by filling out a standard reporting form. The cause of the accident should be determined in order to take appropriate corrective action. These accident report forms contain much information that can be used for safety training.

STRESS

In the past decade, a lot of attention has focused on the negative health effects of *stress*. Unfortunately, hospitality jobs are highly stressful compared to those in other industries. In a commercial or institutional foodservice, meals must go out on time regardless of how many employees call in sick. Likewise, managers and employees must try to meet the different needs of hundreds of guests every day. Stress management is crucial to the success of hospitality managers, as stress can cause turnover and absenteeism and affect their health and their contributions to the effectiveness of the organization. Stress-related problems cost hospitals, for example, an average of $1,003 per employee annually (Cerne 1988). Several techniques exist, however, for dealing effectively with stress.

Stress Defined

Stress can be defined as the body's response to any demand made upon it. Stress is not merely anxiety or nervous tension. The stressor, or force that elicits the stress reaction, can be either generally pleasant, such as getting married, or unpleasant, such as losing a friend. It comes from two basic forces: the stress of physical activity and that of mental activity. In general, stress from emotional frustration is more likely to produce disease than stress from physical exercise. In fact, physical exercise is relaxing and helps a person deal with mental stress. Even when fully relaxed, people are under some stress: the heart continues to beat, the stomach is digesting recently eaten food, and so forth. A person who had no stress at all would be dead!

Stress, therefore, cannot and should not be entirely avoided. Moderate stress helps most people perform well, but too much stress causes poor performance and inactivity. In addition, a daily grind of chronic stress is worse than a single stressful event. Excessive stress can cause a variety of physical, emotional, and behavioral symptoms, as shown in table 7-1. Each person differs in the amount and type of stress he or she can endure.

Regardless of the source of stress, the body has a three-stage reaction to it, referred to as the *fight-or-flight syndrome:* alarm, resistance, and exhaustion. Anyone may remember going through these stages in a stressful situation such as speaking in front of a large group. In the alarm stage, the body identifies the stressor and prepares for fight or flight. This is accomplished by a release of hormones from the endocrine glands, which among many changes causes an

Table 7-1. Stress symptoms

Type of Effect	Symptoms
Physical	Dizziness, fatigue, sweating, insomnia, headache
Psychological/Emotional	Tension, mental tiredness, inattentiveness, moodiness, agitation, boredom, depression, anxiety, helplessness
Behavioral	Aggressiveness, hostility, apathy, cynicism, withdrawal, inability to concentrate and make decisions, absence from work

increase in heartbeat and respiration, dilated pupils, sweaty palms, and slowed digestion. The person will then choose whether to use this burst of energy to fight or get away from the cause of stress. In the resistance stage, if the stressor continues, the body exerts much energy to resist it. If the stressor does not cease, the body must remain alert and goes into the third stage—exhaustion. Continued exposure to stress at this stage can cause the body to run out of energy. The intensity of the reaction will depend on the person's perception of how severe the situation is.

The fight-or-flight syndrome is a coordinated bodily reaction to meet the requirements of life-and-death struggle or of a quick retreat. Whereas this was essential in the days of our Stone Age ancestors, now when we mobilize our bodies involuntarily for fight or flight, we rarely carry either out, causing health and psychological concerns for the chronically stressed person. The human body is actually capable of destroying itself when forced to maintain a high-stress state of alarm for long periods without relief.

Stress can lead to *job burnout,* which is characterized by fatigue, irritability, a negative attitude, inflexibility, and indecision. Burnout moves through four phases, from emotional exhaustion to cynicism and defensiveness to isolation and finally to a feeling of giving up. At this point, a job change may be necessary.

The Stress-Prone Personality

Researchers have identified two basic types of behavior characterizing people in our society. They are referred to as *Type A and Type B behavior.* Type A behavior is distinguished by impatience, competitiveness, and a heightened orientation toward time and achievement. The Type A person tends to try to do too much work in too little time and is often found doing two things at once. Not surprisingly, the person is frequently a workaholic; but despite working long hours, he or she is not necessarily more productive. The Type A person can't relax without feeling guilty and finds it hard to say no to another project or commitment. Type B people tend to be calmer, less worried, and more realistic in terms of how much work they can accomplish. They are less concerned about time, are patient and mild-mannered, and can relax without guilt.

Studies show that 60 percent of managers and supervisors are Type A (Suojanen and Hudson 1980) people—who are more prone to both stress and heart disease. It is quite likely that the negative health effects of stress include partial blame for heart disease.

Causes of Stress

The primary causes of stress include major life events, social and job-related pressures, and a person's psychological makeup. Physical causes such as bad health result in *physically induced stress;* anxiety from, for example, social or job pressures results in *emotionally induced stress.* Table 7-2 rates the impact of various major life events on a scale from 1 to 100, starting with the most serious causes of stress. At the top of the scale, not unexpectedly, is the death of a spouse.

Table 7-2. Stress from major life events

Life Event	Mean Value (100 = worst)
Death of spouse	100
Divorce	73
Marital separation	65
Jail term	63
Death of close family member	63
Personal injury or illness	53
Marriage	50
Termination from a job	47
Marital reconciliation	45
Retirement	45
Change in health of family member	44

Table 7-2. *Continued*

Life Event	Mean Value (100 = worst)
Pregnancy	40
Sex difficulties	39
Gain of new family member	39
Business readjustment	39
Change in financial state	38
Death of close friend	37
Change to different line of work	36
Change in number of arguments with spouse	35
Mortgage over $10,000	31
Foreclosure of mortgage or loan	30
Change in responsibilities at work	29
Departure of son or daughter from home	29
Trouble with in-laws	29
Outstanding personal achievement	28
Beginning or end of work by spouse	26
Beginning or end of school	26
Change in living conditions	25
Revision of personal habits	24
Trouble with boss	23
Change in work hours or conditions	20
Change of residence	20
Change of school	20
Change in recreation	19
Change in church activities	19
Change in social activities	18
Mortgage or loan of less than $10,000	17
Change in sleeping habits	16
Change in number of family get-togethers	15
Change in eating habits	15
Vacation	13
Christmas or other important holiday	12
Minor violation of the law	11

Source: Reprinted with permission from *Journal of Psychiatric Research*, vol. 11. Thomas H. Holmes and R. H. Rahe. The social readjustment rating scale. Copyright 1967, Pergamon Press PLC.

Social pressures are numerous in American society: to own a house, buy an expensive car, have a job with status and a great salary, and so forth. We tend to identify who we are by what we work as and what we own. Work, therefore, has tremendous significance.

Causes of job stress in the hospitality industry are seemingly innumerable: the guest who wants to change rooms—for the tenth time, or the diner who insists the perfectly cooked steak is overdone, or the employee who isn't sure how to do something but can't find anyone to help. There are eight key factors in a job that affect satisfaction, and any is a potential source of stress: work load, physical conditions, job status, accountability and degree of control, task variety, human contact, and physical and mental challenges.

A person's psychological makeup, including overall outlook on life and level of self-esteem, tremendously influences reaction to stress. Different people perceive stressors in different ways. In addition, emotionally induced stress is caused by a person's own thought processes and is usually due to anxiety about time, a future event, a potentially threatening situation, or dealings with other people. Emotionally induced stress, therefore, is largely self-induced and can, through training, be managed more appropriately than stress from physical causes.

STRESS MANAGEMENT

Strategies to cope with stress include good physical and mental health habits. A balanced life of work and play is important to avoid the ill effects of stress. In addition to helping a person cope with his or her own stress, techniques are available by which managers and supervisors can help their employees cope.

Physical Health

Exercise and good nutrition are important to assure good physical health. Vigorous aerobic exercise two or three times a week is recommended. Walking can also be excellent exercise, if done regularly. For good nutrition, a varied, balanced diet that stresses moderation is important. Table 7-3 lists other recommendations. Related to good nutrition is the importance of not overeating—especially tempting when working in a foodservice business! Here are some tips on how to avoid this problem:

Set regular times to sit down and eat a balanced meal.

When taste-testing food, just taste it!

Table 7-3. Nutrition recommendations

Problem	Recommendations
Fats and cholesterol	Reduce consumption of fat (especially saturated fat) and cholesterol
	Eat vegetables, fruits, whole grain foods, fish, poultry, lean meats, and low-fat dairy products
	Use food preparation methods that add little or no fat
Energy and weight control	Achieve and maintain a desirable body weight
	Balance energy (caloric) intake with energy expenditure
	Limit consumption of foods relatively high in calories, fats, and sugars
	Minimize alcohol consumption
	Expend energy through regular, sustained physical activity
Complex carbohydrates and fiber	Eat more whole grain foods and cereal products
	Eat more vegetables (including dried beans and peas) and fruits
Sodium	Reduce intake by choosing foods relatively low in sodium
	Limit the amount of salt added in food preparation and at the table
Alcohol	Use only in moderation (no more than two drinks a day), if at all
	Avoid drinking alcohol if pregnant

Source: U.S. Department of Health and Human Services 1988.

Do not eat dinner so late that there is no time to work it off.

Do not sit and eat with customers.

Plan to eat healthful snacks, such as fresh fruit, between meals.

Do not eat while walking through the kitchen.

There are other worthwhile habits for good physical health. Six to eight hours of sleep each night is vital for functioning well during the day. Arrange periodic vacations: everyone needs a break from time to time, to get away from everything. Do not smoke cigarettes; use alcohol only moderately, if at all; and avoid other drugs. Finally, schedule regular physical and dental checkups, to make sure there are no hidden physical health problems.

Mental Health

Relaxation, the right attitudes, and effective support systems—people who can be approached when help is needed—are all essential to improving a person's mental outlook.

Balance work and play. Take time out regularly, if only for five minutes, to relax and get away from day-to-day problems. A variety of methods can help: meditate, pray, read, listen to music, or garden, for example. The following series of steps describes a way to relax through a simple form of meditation (Benson 1975):

1. Find a quiet space where there are not likely to be any disruptions for twenty minutes.
2. Sit comfortably with eyes closed, allow every muscle to relax, and concentrate on breathing.
3. With each exhaled breath, say a word—any word at all—silently, not out loud. Concentrate on the word, and block out any and all distracting thoughts. Continue this for ten to twenty minutes.
4. When finished, count backward from five to one; the body can begin to move.
5. Repeat this twice a day for the best results.

Good life attitudes can be expressed in two simple rules. Rule 1: Don't sweat the small stuff. Rule 2: It's all small stuff. Another way to put this is simply to think positively. Other good attitudes include the following:

Manage available time realistically; do one thing at a time; learn to say no to requests that cut into available time too much.

Focus on successes.

Expect setbacks; learn from them.

Anticipate what is next—but expect the unexpected.

Don't be a perfectionist; be content to do the best possible.

Don't feel it's necessary to control everything personally.

Keep a sense of perspective and of what is important by considering whether a problem now will matter in, say, five years.

Take action; that helps self-esteem and lowers frustration.

Feel confident enough about personal skills, values, and beliefs to express opinions, but also recognize personal limitations.

View life as a challenge.

Be flexible in the face of change.

Be realistic and positive about life.

Keep a sense of humor.

Do the toughest jobs at the times when the best performance is possible.

Be patient.

An effective support system is made up of those people with whom someone can talk when feeling stressed. This might include family, friends, or others, such as members of a church group. It is also important to avoid focusing on personal ideals and how many other people fall short of them; try to be understanding and tolerant. Another way to reduce stress when talking with other people is to avoid those who are truly annoying or negative in their own attitudes.

Through training and practice, managers can learn to use these techniques and others, such as positive self-encouragement, to control stress more effectively, both on and off the job.

There are numerous ways a manager or supervisor can reduce employees' stress:

1. Treat employees as adults and with respect.
2. Be honest and open.
3. Be genuinely interested in the welfare of the employees.
4. Listen to the employees, and state agreement when possible.
5. Give feedback immediately, and make it specific.
6. Encourage good performance, and when it occurs—praise, praise, praise.
7. Let the employees participate in decision making as much as possible.
8. Communicate on a regular basis through meetings and other ways.
9. Have clear and accurate job descriptions and standards.
10. As much as possible, have one boss per employee.
11. Maintain a safe and pleasant work atmosphere.
12. Provide training for all employees; make sure employees who must deal with the public are trained to do so.
13. Keep the work schedule as consistent as possible, and keep work hours reasonable.
14. As a manager, be fair and consistent.
15. Encourage open communication between shifts.
16. Stress teamwork and cooperation; discourage gossip.

17. Encourage employees to talk to their boss about what is on their mind.

18. Try to accommodate as much as possible any employees who want to move up.

TIME MANAGEMENT

Time is a valuable resource that most managers waste without even realizing it. Time management is using or managing time efficiently. Most people first need to learn where their time is actually going before they can understand how to manage it better. This skill is fundamental to effective management on the job, and off the job as well.

The first step in successful time management is to fill out a daily time log, noting all activities and the time each requires. This step does much to start making people aware of the activities they are doing that waste time, so that they can perhaps delegate, better control, or eliminate them. Major wastes of time for managers and supervisors include the following:

- Poor organization of papers
- Poor or no delegation of tasks
- Accepting drop-in visitors
- Procrastination and indecision
- Too much socializing
- Ineffective meetings
- Lack of plans, priorities, and objectives
- Inability to say no
- Reading all junk mail
- Allowing interruptions and distractions

Regarding interruptions, it is estimated that hospitality managers are interrupted an average of once every seven to eight minutes!

At the turn of the century, the Italian sociologist Vilfredo Pareto conjectured that 80 percent of value is in 20 percent of time spent. In other words, the majority of time spent represents little achieved.

Many time management principles and techniques exist to help managers get control of their time, job, and life. First, it is essential to plan one's work and set priorities. Each day make a *"to do" list*, preferably in a calendar book along with all appointments, and refer to it frequently to stay focused. Rank each item on it, by establishing A, B, and C priorities. A priorities are the most important, and the most time should be spent on them; B priorities are medium in importance, and C items are low priority. If in doubt about the importance of a task, think, "What would happen if I didn't do this?" Plan the day, but leave time for unexpected situations, interruptions, and relaxation. Try to set aside uninterrupted blocks of time for work on more complex tasks.

While working, keep on track. Consider frequently during the day, "What is the best use of my time right now?" Don't procrastinate. Do the disliked jobs first, because they are the ones most likely to be put off indefinitely. Divide large jobs into smaller parts, in order to get started and keep moving.

Keep socializing to a minimum. Ask friends and family to call at work only if there is an emergency. Have someone else answer the telephone, if possible. Plan to return phone calls at a certain time each day. Avoid calling people at lunchtime, when they are likely to be away from their desks. Do not hesitate to have phone calls held while doing something important or when concentration is necessary. Get to the point with callers, and tell long-winded ones that there's a meeting starting right away. To cut down on outside visitors dropping in, ask them to make an appointment in advance. If this is the case, don't then break this rule by allowing casual visitors into the office when they show up with the famous line, "I was in the area so I thought I would just drop in!"

To cut down as well on the number of peers and employees who drop into the office constantly, close the door when necessary; when someone does come in, stand up and remain standing until the person is finished—this always speeds things up; and ask employees not to run in with every problem and question, but rather to save up several items to go over at one time. Also make sure the desk is in a location away from the view of others, to reduce the likelihood of frequent interruptions.

It is also important to learn to delegate work (see chapter 16). Don't waste time doing a task that an employee would like to do and can do as well—or better. Ask employees to bring solutions instead of questions.

Make meetings effective by planning and handing out an agenda in advance, starting on time, following the agenda, and making decisions as needed. Set a time for when each meeting will end, and stick to it.

Organize the work area and handle paperwork efficiently. Figure 7-3 shows an organized desk with various boxes or trays: in, out, action, pending, read, and file. Under the desk is the most important file: the wastebasket. All papers should be handled once and put into their appropriate place. When letters or notes arrive from others, handwrite an answer directly on them and mail them back. Use a tape recorder to dictate letters and memos. Carry a pad at all times to jot down ideas and things that must be done. Keep the desk clear of everything except the current task.

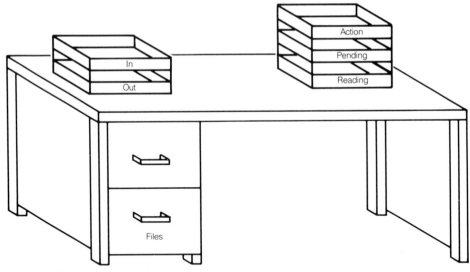

Figure 7-3.   An organized desk.

In addition, learn to say no to requests for time when they are unreasonable or unjustified. Make decisions, and do it now! Get as much sleep as is needed— and no more. Find time to exercise, relax, and be with friends and family.

Many times the difference between success and failure in business comes down to one short sentence: "I didn't have the time."

SUMMARY

Hospitality operators have legal responsibilities regarding health and safety. These are explained in the Occupational Safety and Health Act and in right-to-know and workers' compensation laws. An organization's health concerns center around physical and emotional health, and alcoholism and drug abuse. Employee assistance programs and wellness programs have been set up to respond to these health concerns. Safety programs have been established to respond to safety concerns in the workplace, involving both employees and working conditions.

In the past decade, much attention has focused on the negative health effects of stress. Unfortunately, jobs in the hospitality industry are highly stressful compared to ones in other industries. In a commercial or institutional foodservice business, for example, meals must go out in a timely fashion regardless of how many employees call in sick. Likewise, managers and employees must all try to meet the different needs of hundreds of guests every day.

Stress can be defined as the body's response to any demand made upon it; stress is not merely anxiety or nervous tension. The stressor, or force that elicits the stress reaction, can be either pleasant, such as getting married, or unpleasant, such as losing a friend. It results from two basic forces: the stress of physical activity and the stress of mental activity. Stress management is crucial to the success of hospitality managers, as stress can increase turnover and absenteeism and affect their health and their contribution to the organization's effectiveness. Stress management techniques revolve around developing sound physical and mental health habits.

Time is a valuable resource that most managers waste without even realizing it. Time management means using or managing time more efficiently, but first most people need to learn where their time is actually going before they can work out how to manage it better. This skill is fundamental to effective management, both on and off the job. Using a daily time log, managers can start to identify their time wasters and, using various techniques, become more productive.

STUDY QUESTIONS

1. Describe how a current or former employer of yours addressed your health and safety concerns. Was it adequate?
2. List ten chemicals found in a foodservice or housekeeping department that have hazardous ingredients.
3. Describe how and why workers' compensation might be abused.
4. Are hospitality operations high priority for OSHA to inspect? Why or why not?
5. As a manager, should you document that an employee has a drinking or a drug problem? Why or why not?
6. How do employees with health concerns affect an organization?
7. You are the manager in a restaurant that is just opening, and you have been asked to develop and implement a comprehensive safety program. Describe what you would do.
8. Describe how and when stress can be beneficial on the job.
9. What are the major causes of stress? There are eight factors that influence job satisfaction. Relate each of these factors to a hotel, an independent restaurant, or a hospital foodservice.

10. When comparing Type A and Type B behavior, where do you see your own?

11. Does exercise help reduce the negative effects of stress? Why or why not?

12. What is a stress that managers and supervisors have but employees do not? What stress might employees feel that managers and supervisors would not feel?

13. How might a manager act if under chronic stress?

14. What might you do, using the stress management techniques as a guide, to decrease the negative effects of stress in your life?

15. In a current or previous job, can you think of someone who managed time well? If so, how could you tell?

16. Keep a daily log of your activities to locate your time wasters. Which techniques could you use to manage your time better?

17. Speak to hospitality managers and ask them where they find problems with handling stress and time on the job. Also ask what they do to manage both situations better.

REFERENCES

Albrecht, Karl. 1979. *Stress and the Manager.* New York: Simon & Schuster.

Appelbaum, Steven H., and Barbara T. Shapiro. 1989. The ABCs of EAPs. *Personnel* 66(7):39–46.

Applied Foodservice Sanitation. 1985. New York: John Wiley & Sons.

Baker, H. Kent, and Philip Morgan. 1985. Building a professional image: Dealing with time problems. *Supervisory Management* 30(11):36–42.

Benson, Herbert. 1975. *The Relaxation Response.* New York: Avon.

Brymer, Robert A. 1982. Stress and your employees. *Cornell H.R.A. Quarterly* 22(2):61–66.

Bureau of National Affairs. 1978. *BNA Policy and Practice Series—Personnel Management.* Washington, D.C.: Bureau of National Affairs.

Cascio, Wayne F. 1986. Managing human resources. New York: McGraw-Hill Book Company.

Cerne, Frank. 1988. Hospitals not immune to high cost of stress. *Hospitals* October 5:70–71.

Dorney, Robert C. 1988. Making time to manage. *Harvard Business Review* 88(1):38–40.

Douglass, Merrill E. 1987. Do you have to suffer from all those interruptions? *Management Solutions* 32(7):40–43.

Estrin, Stephen A. 1989. Take precautions: Restaurant accidents happen. *Nation's Restaurant News* March 27:F12.

Grossman, Morton E., and Margaret Magnus. 1988. The boom in benefits. *Personnel Journal* 67(11):51–55.

Hansen, M. R. 1986. To-do lists for managers. *Supervisory Management* 31(5):37–39.

Hines, Carolyn C. W., and Wesley C. Wilson. 1986. A no-nonsense guide to being stressed. *Management Solutions* 31(10):27–29.

Hobbs, Charles R. 1987. *Time Power.* New York: Harper & Row.

Holmes, Thomas H., and R. H. Rahe. 1967. The social readjustment rating scale. *Journal of Psychosomatic Research* 11.

Hughes, Glenn H., Mark A. Pearson, and George R. Reinhart. 1984. Stress: Sources, effects, and management. *Family & Community Health* 6(5):47–58.

Jenner, Jessica Reynolds. 1986. On the way to stress resistance. *Training and Development Journal* 40(5):112–15.

Klein, Alfred. 1986. Employees under the influence—outside the law? *Personnel Journal* 65(9):57–71.

Klingeman, Harry. 1986. Fight stress from the inside out. *NRA News* 6(5):12–13.

Lawrie, John. 1985. Three steps to reducing stress. *Supervisory Management* 30(11):8–10.

Liddle, Alan. 1989. Employee assistance. *Nation's Restaurant News* May 22:F46.

Mackenzie, R. Alec. 1985. The "to do" list is obsolete. *Supervisory Management* 30(9):41–43.

Masi, Dale. 1987. Company's responses to drug abuse from AMA's nationwide survey. *Personnel* 64(3):40–46.

Morgan, Philip, and H. Kent Baker. 1985. Building a professional image: dealing with job stress. *Supervisory Management* 30(9):23–28.

Mosley, Donald C., Leon C. Megginson, and Paul H. Pietri. 1989. *Supervisory Management.* Cincinnati: South-Western Publishing Co.

National Restaurant Association. 1983. *OSHA.* Washington, D.C.: National Restaurant Association.

———. 1988. *"Right to Know."* Washington, D.C.: National Restaurant Association.

Nelson, Andre. 1985. "I won't be able to come to work today . . ." *Supervisory Management* 30(5):34–36.

Nowack, Kenneth M. 1986. Who are the hardy? *Training and Development Journal* 40(5):116–18.

Premeaux, Shane R., R. Wayne Mondy, and Arthur Sharplin. 1985. Stress and the first-line supervisor. *Supervisory Management* 30(7):36–40.

Redeker, James R., and Jonathan A. Segal. 1989. Avoiding AIDS-related liability. *Personnel* 66(8):46–50.

Schreier, James W. 1988. Combatting drugs at work. *Training and Development Journal* 42(10):56–60.

Selye, Hans. 1974. *Stress Without Distress.* New York: New American Library.

Steffen, R. James. 1982. How to stop wasting time. *Supervisory Management* 27(5):22–25.

Suojanen, W. W., and Donald R. Hudson. 1980. Coping with stress and addictive work behavior. *Business* 31(1):11.

U.S. Department of Health and Human Services. 1985. *Worksite Health Promotion and Human Resource: A Hard Look at the Data.* Baltimore: National Institutes of Health.

Voluck, Philip R. 1987. Burning legal issues of smoking in the workplace. *Personnel Journal* 66(6):140–43.

Wrich, James T. 1988. Beyond testing: Coping with drugs at work. *Harvard Business Review* 88(1):120–30.

Zauderer, Donald, and Joseph Fox. 1987. Resiliency in the face of stress. *Supervisory Management* 32(11):30–35.

Part II

Managing Staff

Chapter 8

The Nature of Management and Leadership

KEY QUESTIONS

1. What are the three sets of skills managers use, and which is most important?
2. What do management jobs have in common, and in which ways do they vary?
3. As management theory evolved, what were the different schools of thought?
4. What is a leader and the consequences of good leadership?
5. As leadership theory evolved, what were the different schools of thought?

KEY TERMS AND CONCEPTS

Technical skills

Conceptual skills

Human relations skills

Classical or traditional functions of management

PRINCESS factors

Interpersonal, informational, decision-making roles

Supervisory management

Middle management

Top management

Linking pin

Functional managers

General managers

Scientific management school

Human relations school

Hawthorne study

Division of work

Authority

Unity of command

Line of authority

Theory X and Theory Y

Theory Z

Systems management

Excellence model

Situational, or contingency, approach

Leadership

Trait theory of leadership

Behavioral theory of leadership

People-centered leader

Democratic leader

Task-centered leader

Autocratic leader

The Managerial Grid

Situational leadership

The various skills managers use in meeting their objectives include technical, conceptual, and human relations kinds. *Technical skills* have to do with things and include, for example, culinary and cost control skills. *Conceptual skills* deal with abstract thinking about the parts of an organization and how they come together. Examples include long-range planning, problem solving, and marketing.

Human relations skills are the ones most needed and most used by any hospitality manager at any level. Whereas lower-level managers use more technical skills, and upper-level managers use more conceptual skills, all levels of management need human relations skills the most. These involve the ability to interact effectively with many different people: customers, peers, subordinates, and superiors. Poor interpersonal skills represent the single biggest reason for failure, especially in the early and middle stages of a manager's career.

Managing staff using human relations skills is the topic of the remaining chapters of this book. First comes a look at the nature of management and leadership, especially how a person's management and leadership styles affect his or her ability to get along with other people.

THE NATURE OF MANAGEMENT

Management jobs in hospitality vary according to many different factors, such as the size of the operation and specific job responsibilities. Management jobs, however, do have three things in common: they share demands, constraints, and choices. Demands tell them what has to be done, such as certain specific tasks; constraints, such as budgetary or physical ones, limit what they can do; choices allow managers to select exactly what work is performed and how it gets done.

Managers also share certain functions or processes in which they are involved: planning, organizing, coordinating, leading, and controlling. Together, they are referred to as the *classical or traditional functions of management* and they provide a way to classify the many activities in which managers are engaged. Planning refers to determining what is to be done, such as positioning the operation within a competitive market. Organizing is the task of establishing the organizational chart—a hierarchy of company employees— and establishing the chain of command. Coordinating is getting the units and subunits within the organization to accomplish what has been planned. Leading is the process by which managers communicate with subordinates about getting certain plans and projects done; it also refers to how managers establish the tone, or general character, of their organization. Controlling is evaluating or comparing progress or results to objectives and standards that were decided upon earlier in the planning process, thereby linking the last step to the first step in the management cycle.

Many studies support the concept that managers spend their time fulfilling the classical management functions. One group of researchers has expanded the five managerial functions to eight: planning, representing, investigating, negotiating, coordinating, evaluating, supervising, and staffing—what the group calls the *PRINCESS factors* (Carroll and Gillen 1987). Their research also shows that managers in different jobs and at different levels spent varying amounts of time in each function.

Other areas of interest when examining managerial work include how managers distribute their time among the classical functions, other functions in which managers are involved, with whom managers interact, and the qualities of managerial work (Hales 1986). In a review of the management literature, Hales summarized the known features of managerial work as shown here (1986):

1. It combines a specialist/professional element and a general, managerial element.

2. The substantive elements involve, essentially, liaison, man-management, and responsibility for a work process, beneath which are subsumed more detailed work elements.

3. The character of work elements varies by duration, time span, recurrence, unexpectedness, and source.

4. Much time is spent in day-to-day trouble shooting and *ad hoc* problems of organization and regulation.

5. Much managerial activity consists of asking or persuading others to do things, involving the manager in face-to-face verbal communication of limited duration.

6. Patterns of communication vary in terms of what the communication is about and with whom the communication is made.

7. Little time is spent on any one particular activity and, in particular, on the conscious, systematic formulation of plans. Planning and decision making tend to take place in the course of other activity.

8. Managers spend a lot of time accounting for and explaining what they do, in informal relationships and in politicking.

9. Managerial activities are driven by contradictions, cross-pressures, and conflicts. Much managerial work involves coping with and reconciling social and technical conflict.

10. There is considerable choice in terms of what is done and how: part of managerial work is setting the boundaries of and negotiating that work itself.

Management jobs differ in terms of their level within the organizational structure. There are basically three levels: *supervisory, middle, and top man-*

agement. The number of people at each level will vary tremendously depending on the size of the organization and how many locations it operates. A small family-run restaurant may have a few supervisors, and the family functions in effect as both middle and top management. A fast-food chain with a large number of company-operated stores may have unit and assistant managers, who function as supervisory management, and various middle managers—central office support staff—all the way up the top management, including the senior staff and the chief executive officer of the company.

Supervisory management is a unique level. In some organizations, supervisors are not even seen as part of management; but when they are, they are the first on the managerial ladder. Hourly employees report to them, and the supervisor in turn reports to a manager. They are in a tough position because they have to deal with the complaints, requests, and concerns of employees; pressure from management to get tasks done; and the demands of guests to meet their service needs. Renesis Likert referred to this relationship as the *linking pin:* supervisors are the vital link between the employees and management.

Managerial jobs also differ in the extent of their responsibilities. Managers who have specialized responsibilities, such as front office manager or dining room manager, are called *functional managers.* Those with broader, multifunctional responsibilities are referred to as *general managers,* such as the ones who run hotels and restaurants.

PERSPECTIVES ON MANAGEMENT

In the early twentieth century, when writings on management began to take shape, the work of Frederick Taylor and Frank and Lillian Gilbreth focused on getting tasks done as efficiently as possible. Their work was done at a time when labor was in short supply. They founded the *scientific management school,* which used such procedures as analyzing through time studies how work is done, determining the most efficient way to do a task, creating performance standards, selecting and training workers to perform the task, and finally setting pay rates and incentives. Taylor and the Gilbreths realized good results: less worker exhaustion and higher productivity and earnings. The scientific management school held that workers have a natural tendency to take it easy but are motivated by money; therefore, financial incentives and piecework—payment per item or task completed—were used to increase productivity.

The next such management step was the *human relations school,* which Elton Mayo, Fritz Roethlisberger, and William Dickson dominated in the 1920s and 1930s. This theoretical school examined the emotional and social side of people at work, which the scientific management school neglected. The *Hawthorne study,* the most well known research of the human relations school, found that when workers were given a lot of attention it improved both morale and productivity.

According to this school of thought, managers need to look at the psychological and social needs of people at work in order to get worker cooperation and, with it, increased productivity. Workers are also motivated by more complex needs than money. This school attributed worker apathy to poor work conditions, such as management practices that were too controlling. Mayo felt good enough about human nature to write that managers can trust employees, and that letting groups of employees make some of their own decisions will increase both morale and productivity. Because of Mayo, focus was put more on people management skills rather than technical ones.

Also during the early 1900s, Henri Fayol, a Frenchman, worked on identifying the functions of an organization. He broke down an organization's activities into six functions: technical (such as production), commercial (such as buying and selling), security, financial, accounting, and managerial. Within the activities of management he identified and described the functions—planning, organizing, commanding, coordinating, and controlling—that became known as the classic or traditional functions of management. He outlined other concepts of management, many of which are still in use today, such as the following:

Division of work: A worker who has to perform fewer tasks can improve performance.

Authority: The right to give orders and reward or punish the person who does or doesn't carry them out correctly.

Unity of command: Each employee shall have one boss.

Subordination of individual interests to general interest: If managers supervise fairly and firmly and set a good example, they can get individuals to serve the organization's interests.

Compensation: Remuneration should be fair in terms of reflecting economic conditions and rewarding efforts.

Line of authority: The chain of command should be respected.

Employee initiative: Managers should stimulate employees to carry out some plans themselves.

Team spirit: Managers should build teamwork, as it helps the organization and its employees.

Fayol's greatest contribution was distinguishing managerial work from the other functions performed within the organization.

Douglas McGregor elaborated on the contrasting beliefs of the scientific management and the human relations schools in his own work, published in 1960, which he called *Theory X and Theory Y*. Each theory explains basic assumptions of human nature that managers hold about the way employees view work, and also about how they can be motivated. Table 8-1 shows the major assumptions of each theory. Theory X managers tend to be more autocratic, while Theory Y managers tend to be more participative. McGregor felt Theory Y is not the answer to all of a manager's problems, but is a basis for improved management and organizational performance.

Taking off from Theory Y, William Ouchi in 1981 published a new ap-

Table 8-1.   Major assumptions of Theory X and Theory Y

Theory X	*Theory Y*
The average human being has an inherent dislike of work and will avoid it if possible.	The expenditure of physical and mental effort in work is as natural as play or rest.
Because of this human characteristic, most people must be coerced, controlled, directed, and threatened with punishment to get them to make an adequate effort toward the achievement of organizational objectives.	External control and the threat of punishment are not the only means of bringing about effort toward organizational objectives. People will exercise self-direction and self-control in the service of objectives to which they are committed.
The average human being prefers to be directed, wishes to avoid responsibility, has relatively little ambition, and wants security above all.	Commitment to objectives is a function of the rewards associated with their achievement.
	The average human being learns, under proper conditions, not only to accept but also to seek responsibility.
	The capacity to exercise a relatively high degree of imagination, ingenuity, and creativity in solving organizational problems is widely, not narrowly, distributed in the population.
	Under the conditions of modern industrial life, the intellectual potentialities of the average human being are only partially utilized.

Source: McGregor, Douglas. 1960. *The Human Side of Enterprise.* New York: McGraw-Hill. Reprinted by permission.

proach, *Theory Z,* based on his study of Japanese organizations. Theory Z basically proposes that employees who are involved are the key to increased productivity. Other Japanese-inspired Theory Z characteristics that can improve productivity and quality include fewer explicit rules and team decision making and responsibility. The validity of Theory Z has not been proved; however, it provides some stimulating ideas for managers.

During the 1960s and 1970s, various models of foodservice systems were published. An organization is really a system composed of interdependent parts, some unrelated, and designed to accomplish certain objectives. *Systems management* involves the coordination of all parts of the organization to meet stated objectives. A systems manager realizes that when he or she intervenes in a system of interrelated parts and processes, those actions may affect many parts or subsystems.

Of current interest is the *excellence model,* derived in large part from *In Search of Excellence* (1982) by Thomas J. Peters and Robert H. Waterman. In their best-selling book, the authors listed eight attributes of well-run American companies:

- Action-oriented
- Close to the customer
- Autonomous and entrepreneurial
- Productive through convincing employees that their best efforts are necessary, and rewarding them
- Organized around hands-on, value-driven managers
- Committed to the business they know best
- Structured with few administrative layers and lean upper management
- Simultaneously centralized and decentralized

Although not all the companies displayed all eight principles to the same degree, the principles were visible in all of them. Some of the authors' conclusions are especially applicable to the hospitality industry; for example, that managers have to get back to basics such as quality service to customers, innovations, and the need to create commitment in organizations. The employee-oriented part of the excellence model is also relevant in an industry in which keeping employee morale high is difficult due to low pay, a hectic pace, and often less-than-ideal working conditions.

In the sequel, *A Passion for Excellence,* Peters and coauthor Nancy Austin emphasize how organizational pride and enthusiasm are crucial for managerial success. They feel managers need to be a combination of cheerleader, enthusiast, coach, and facilitator. In terms of starting and maintaining exceptional business performance, the authors advocate only two approaches: give the customer superior service and quality, and constantly innovate.

None of these management theories is always the right one or the best one. Research continues to tell us that given certain characteristics of people and their work, some management practices will work better than others. In other words, different management approaches work best in different situations. A *situational, or contingency, approach* to management tells us to use what works best for each particular situation.

THE NATURE OF LEADERSHIP

Although much research has been done on *leadership,* especially over the past seventy-five years, there is still no clear understanding of what distinguishes leaders from nonleaders, or effective leaders from ineffective ones. There isn't even a single definition of what leadership is; actually, hundreds have been formulated.

One function of managers is to lead. In this context, leading can be defined as the process by which managers interact with subordinates to get certain plans and projects accomplished, as well as how managers determine and maintain an organization's culture. In other words, "Leadership is what gives an organization its vision and its ability to translate that vision into reality," as Warren Bennis and Burt Nanus stated in *Leaders* (Bennis and Nanus 1985).

Good leadership may result in some of the following:

- High productivity
- More customer satisfaction and quality of service
- Enthusiastic employees
- Committed employees
- Higher trust levels
- Greater creativity

This list does not include all the potential benefits of good leadership to an organization. Depending on the situation, there are probably many more.

PERSPECTIVES ON LEADERSHIP

Several theories try to explain the key to effective leadership. The first school of thought on this compared various personal characteristics, or traits, such as intelligence or personality, of leaders and nonleaders to determine if certain traits predicted effective leadership. Research into the *trait theory of leadership* was done mostly between the 1920s and the 1950s. Although it often found certain traits, such as self-confidence and ability to influence others, in leaders, it uncovered no characteristics that could definitely predict leadership. Other traits found more in leaders were the ability to give guidance and be decisive.

Leadership research in the 1950s and 1960s examined leaders' behavior as they interacted with work groups, and how this affected performance. Research into the *behavioral theory of leadership* uncovered two types of behavior in this regard: people-centered and task-centered. The *people-centered leader* is much more sensitive to subordinates as humans and is generally considerate and concerned about people. People-centered leaders are often participative or *democratic leaders* as well: they involve the employees as much as possible in relevant job aspects, and employees participate in the decision-making process. Although people-centered leadership does not always improve productivity, it does enhance employee and group satisfaction.

The *task-centered leader,* on the other hand, is highly concerned with getting the job done, so this behavior includes assigning tasks, explaining how to do them, and stressing the importance of meeting deadlines. The task is more important than the person to the task-centered leader, who may also be an *autocratic leader.* In an autocratic style of leadership, the leader makes decisions and gives orders without any input from employees. The autocratic leader may be referred to as a dictator or authoritarian. Certain task-centered leadership behavior, such as directing and structuring, is associated with productivity; being autocratic is not. Most task-centered leadership behavior diminishes employee and group satisfaction, except in letting people know what is expected of them.

Some leaders can act in both task- and people-oriented ways. Research by Robert Blake and Jane Mouton (1985) shows that leaders who are both highly task- and people-oriented attain more productivity and employee and group satisfaction than ones who are not as highly oriented in both areas. Blake and Mouton devised *The Managerial Grid* ® (fig. 8-1), which shows the possible combinations of leadership with regard to concern for staff and concern for production. Of course, they advocate a 9,9 orientation—high in both types of concern—which they feel is the most effective in all situations.

Leaders can be not only both task- and people-oriented, but also can change between orientations depending on the situation. *Situational leadership* refers to leaders who change their orientation in order to adapt to a given situation. In the situational leadership II model, developed by Kenneth H. Blanchard, there are two dimensions of leadership behavior: task or directive and maintenance or supportive (Carew, Parisi-Carew, and Blanchard 1986). Task behaviors are used to get work done, such as telling an employee what to

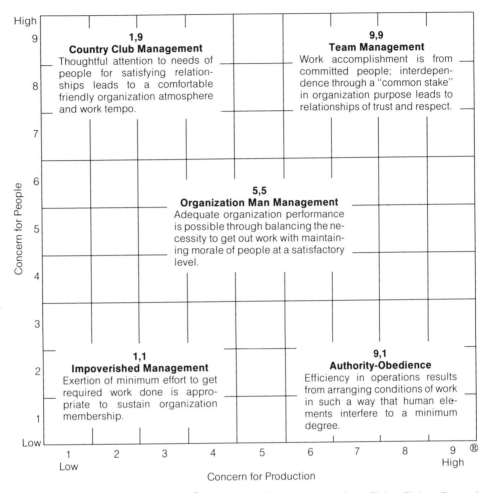

Figure 8-1. The Managerial Grid.® (Reproduced by permission from Blake, Robert R., and Mouton, Jane Srygley. *The Managerial Grid III: The Key to Leadership Excellence.* Houston: Gulf Publishing Company, Copyright © 1985, p. 12).

do and how to do it. Maintenance behaviors are supportive behaviors, such as listening and encouraging.

High or low levels of these two dimensions can form the basis for four leadership styles (fig. 8-2). Depending on the development level of the employee, a manager can determine when to use which of the four leadership styles. If an employee is enthusiastic about doing a job but not very competent, as can be the case with new hires, a directing style, emphasizing high task behavior, is appropriate. A coaching style is preferable when the employee has some competence but less enthusiasm or commitment. If employee ability is

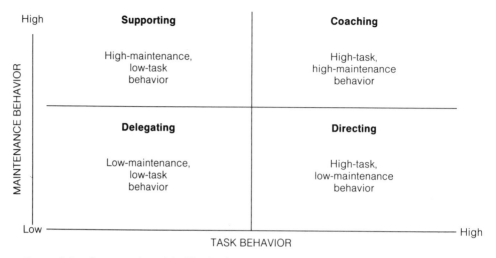

Figure 8-2. Situational model of leadership.

high, but commitment is variable, a supporting style is suitable. Lastly, when an employee is both highly competent and committed, a delegating style is appropriate.

As with management theories, there is no best leadership theory or any magic formulas. Again, situations will vary, probably requiring flexibility on the part of the leader, who needs to be aware of all the forces in each situation in order to lead in a productive manner.

SUMMARY

Managers use technical, conceptual, and human relations skills in meeting their objectives; the most important are human relations skills.

Management jobs share demands, constraints, and choices, as well as certain functions or processes: planning, organizing, coordinating, leading, and controlling, which are referred to as the classical or traditional functions of management. Another way to study management is to see what a manager's activities are throughout the day. Henry Mintzberg categorized managerial activities into three principal roles: interpersonal, informational, and decision-making roles.

Management jobs differ in terms of their level within the organizational structure. There are basically three levels: supervisory, middle, and top management. Supervisory management, which links the employees to management, is a unique and demanding position. Managerial jobs can also be classified as either functional or general.

Various perspectives or schools of thought on management have evolved: scientific management, human relations, the work of Fayol on an organization's functions, Theory X and Theory Y, the Japanese-influenced Theory Z, systems management, and the excellence model. No management theory is always the right one or the best one. Different management approaches work best in different situations. This is known as a situational, or contingency, approach.

"Leadership is what gives an organization its vision and its ability to translate that vision into reality." Several theories—trait, behavioral, and situational—try to explain the key to effective leadership. Research, although extensive, is only beginning.

STUDY QUESTIONS

1. Why are human relations skills the most important for hospitality managers at all levels? With whom does the hospitality manager interact?
2. How do management jobs vary, and how are they the same?
3. Compare and contrast the different schools of management thought.
4. Describe one application of each management theory to a hospitality operation.
5. Explain the meaning of a situational approach to either management or leadership.
6. What is a leader?
7. In a current or past job, describe in as much detail as possible someone who struck you as a real leader.
8. In general, do you see yourself more as a people-centered or task-centered leader? Explain why. Where would you fit on The Managerial Grid?
9. What are the benefits of good leadership?
10. Why does the Hersey-Blanchard model include the maturity of the employee?

REFERENCES

Bennis, Warren, and Burt Nanus. 1985. *Leaders. The Strategies for Taking Charge.* New York: Harper & Row.

Blake, Robert R., and Jane S. Mouton. 1985. *The Managerial Grid III. The Key to Leadership Excellence.* Houston: Gulf Publishing Co.

Carew, Donald K., Parisi-Carew, Eunice, and Kenneth H. Blanchard. 1986. Group development and situational leadership: A model for managing groups. *Training and Development Journal* 40(6):46–50.

Carroll, Stephen J., and Dennis J. Gillen. 1987. Are the classical management functions useful in describing managerial work? *Academy of Management Review* 12(1):38–51.

Ferguson, Dennis H., and Florence Berger. 1984. Restaurant managers: What do they really do? *Cornell H.R.A. Quarterly* 24(2):26–32.

Hales, Colin P. 1986. What do managers do? A critical review of the evidence. *Journal of Management Studies* 23(1):88–115.

Hamlin, Richard. 1986. Choosing between directive and participative management. *Supervisory Management* 31(1):14–16.

Hampton, David R. 1986. *Management.* 3d ed. New York: McGraw-Hill.

Hart, Christopher W. L., Gary S. Spizizen, and Christopher C. Muller. 1988. Management development in the foodservice industry. *Hospitality Education and Research Journal* 12(1):1–20.

Karlins, Marvin, and Edyth Hargis. 1988. Beyond leadership: The human factor in leadership. *Management Solutions* 33(8):18–21.

Lawrie, John. 1987. What is effective leadership? *Management Solutions* 32(5): 25–30.

McGregor, Douglas. 1960. *The Human Side of Enterprise.* New York: McGraw-Hill.

Meares, Larry B. 1988. What good leaders do. *Personnel* 65(9):48–52.

Mintzberg, Henry. 1980. *The Nature of Managerial Work.* Englewood Cliffs, N.J.: Prentice-Hall.

Ouchi, W. G. 1981. *Theory Z: How American Business Can Meet the Japanese Challenge.* Reading, Mass.: Addison-Wesley Publishing Co.

Peters, Tom, and Nancy Austin. 1985. *A Passion for Excellence.* New York: Warner Books.

Peters, Thomas J., and Robert H. Waterman. 1982. *In Search of Excellence.* New York: Warner Books.

Stowell, Steven J. 1988. *Training and Development Journal* 42(6):34–38.

Chapter 9

Communicating

KEY QUESTIONS

1. What is involved in the process of communication?
2. When should different communication mediums be used?
3. What barriers are there to communication?
4. How can you communicate effectively, both orally and in writing?

KEY TERMS AND CONCEPTS

Communication process	Company newsletter
Nonverbal communication	Feedback
Formal communication	Counseling
Upward communication	Lateral communication
Suggestion box	Informal communication
Management-employee meeting	Grapevine
Downward communication	Rumor
Employee handbook	Active listening

Within a hospitality organization, communication is essentially the process of passing along information and understanding from one individual or group to another. Communication takes place in a variety of ways, including verbal, nonverbal, and written, and in a number of directions, upward, downward, and lateral. It may also be formal or informal.

Of the many problems affecting any type of organization, poor communication always appears high on the list, if not at the very top. Without good communication, such serious problems as low productivity, poor service, and increased costs can occur. Lower-level managers can expect to spend at least 50 percent of their time communicating, and this percentage increases as they move up the career ladder. If the members of an organization are to achieve its goals, such as high-quality service, communication must flow freely and with understanding in all directions. This is because communication provides both the knowledge and the understanding for effort—in other words, the skill to work—and the attitudes necessary for cooperation and motivation—in other words, the will to work.

THE COMMUNICATION PROCESS

The *communication process* is a sequence of steps involving a sender, a message, and a receiver. The sender forms an idea, puts it into words, and then transmits it. During this process, the way the sender gets the message across depends greatly on the person's attitude, perceptions, communication skills, and goals, as well as the method used in sending it. The sender essentially has the responsibility of transmitting a clear message and creating understanding during this process.

Messages are conveyed using symbols such as words—either spoken or written—and *nonverbal communication*—independent of words—in the case of spoken messages. A misconception surrounding words is that they mean the same thing to all people; in fact, different people perceive the meaning of a certain word in various ways.

When communication is oral, or spoken, the message can take on entirely different meanings, depending on how it is said. Nonverbal communication includes thoughts and ideas that an individual communicates through use of not only the voice, but also the body, physical distance, or dress; it is also evident in the arrangement of the furniture in an office and the degree to which surroundings are pleasant. Body language refers specifically to body posture, facial expressions, vocal inflections, and gestures used to communicate attitudes and feelings.

The receiver gets the message, perceives and evaluates it, and then responds. The receiver, like the sender, has a perceptual filter through which messages go and possibly get misinterpreted or distorted. Understanding of the message can occur only in the receiver's mind. The communication process, or loop, is complete when the receiver responds to the sender, with what is called feedback. Feedback may express agreement or disagreement, or ask for clarification. The sender can use feedback to help determine clear understanding of the message.

TYPES OF COMMUNICATION

Communication in a hospitality organization can occur using a variety of mediums, each with its own advantages and disadvantages (table 9-1). Communication can also be formal or informal.

Formal communication between people takes place based on the lines of authority set up in an organizational chart. Formal communication can flow

Table 9-1.   Advantages and disadvantages of different communication mediums

Medium	Advantages	Disadvantages
One-on-one Discussion	Immediate feedback Can be informal Focuses message Includes nonverbal messages	Not always possible or practical Can be more time-consuming due to small talk
Telephone call	Quick Readily available Offers verbal contact with people far away	Fewer nonverbal cues
Meeting	Gets message out to many an obtain good feedback Can involve participants Gives feeling of belonging Saves time	If poorly handled, can be a waste May be impersonal
Memo or letter	Can be well thought out and organized Provides hard documentation	No feedback Time-consuming More chance for misunderstanding
Posted notice	Quick	May not be read No feedback

upward, downward, or laterally through the lines of authority. *Upward communication* refers to when employees talk to their supervisors, who in turn talk to their managers, and so on, ultimately up to the general manager. Employees may discuss concerns, grievances, suggestions about their jobs, or policies and procedures. Effective upward communication starts at the bottom of the organization and moves through the different levels to the top. The feedback that can be obtained through this type of communication is valuable in determining if what has been transmitted to employees has been received, understood, and complied with. In many organizations, unfortunately, not enough emphasis is placed on developing good channels of upward communication.

Examples of upward communication include the suggestion box, employee satisfaction survey (see fig. 10-1), open-door policy (see chapter 14), management-employee meeting, and exit interviews. The suggestion box allows employees to make written suggestions to certain problems. Some operators purposely set up management-employee meetings to allow employees to ask questions and make comments, positive and negative, about anything going on within the organization.

Downward communication involves policies and procedures, job descriptions, performance evaluations, training, and the like; it is mostly of an informative or directive nature. Communication between any superior and subordinates is downward communication. Within many organizations, goals and objectives, policies, and so forth come from top management and are communicated downward, perhaps all the way to the lowest-level employee. Downward communication helps to link the different levels of the organization together and to initiate the feedback process. Examples include employee meetings, employee handbooks, bulletin boards, company newsletters, feedback, coaching (see chapter 3), and counseling.

Employee meetings are frequently used to communicate new policies and procedures, conduct training, and improve communications. Some hospitality organizations have an employee handbook, which contains information on all rules, policies, and procedures pertinent to the employee. Often employee bulletin boards are used by operators to communicate noteworthy information, such as schedules, to employees. Company newsletters are published periodically to inform employees of developments within the company, and also to highlight employee accomplishments. Feedback is another downward communication, which managers use to discuss performance, such as in coaching, and other issues with employees. In counseling, a manager is asked to help an employee with a personal problem. Often, the employee is referred to an Employee Assistance Program for professional help (see chapter 7).

Lateral communication is among people at approximately the same level in the organization. It is important in order for employees to meet social needs and coordinate their activities.

Informal communication occurs between people independent of their organizational relationship, level of authority, or job functions. It is more commonly known as the *grapevine*, a term that arose during the Civil War when telegraph lines for intelligence reports were strung loosely from tree to tree like a grapevine. Since messages over the lines often were inaccurate or confusing, any *rumor*—unverified and usually untrue information—was said to be from the grapevine.

Since the grapevine comes out of social interaction, it is as fickle and varied as the individuals are. Features of the grapevine include its fast pace and its unusual ability to get information from the most secret of places. Some managers would prefer to ignore or cut out the grapevine, neither of which is a very wise idea. Managers can learn much from the grapevine, such as what employees are excited about, what they are griping about, and what the current rumors are. Rumors sometimes occur because by the time information is repeated several times, the story changes.

BARRIERS TO COMMUNICATION

There are many reasons managers fail to send messages effectively or receive messages correctly. In order to understand fully how to communicate effectively, it is important first to recognize possible barriers so they can be overcome or minimized. Table 9-2 lists general, upward, and downward barriers to effective communication. A major barrier lies in the differences among individuals.

Everyone comes to the workplace with different life experiences. Differences among individuals can include the following:

- Biases and prejudices
- Attitudes, values, and beliefs
- Perceptions or frames of reference
- Knowledge
- Interests
- Personalities
- Emotional orientation
- Use of verbal and nonverbal language
- Ways of interpreting communication
- Ways of listening
- Cultural background
- Appearance
- Gender
- Status
- Experiences with other jobs and bosses

It's probably a wonder that people can communicate at all.

GUIDELINES TO EFFECTIVE COMMUNICATION

Good communication is many things: sincere, personal, caring, accurate, timely, and open. Good communication is also characterized by feedback, use of appropriate channels and mediums, and listening. Listening is probably the most important part of communication, yet it is generally poorly done. When they should really be listening, many managers are instead formulating their

Table 9-2. Potential barriers to effective communication

Type	Potential Barriers
General Barriers	Differences between individuals
	Organizational climate
	Bad timing
	Poor choice of medium
	Poor choice of words
	Incongruent body language
	Lack of feedback
	Noise or distraction
	Lack of privacy
	Hidden agenda
	Lack of clarity in meaning
	Poor listening
	Failure to put some feeling into communication
	Failure to be totally honest
	Hostile or defensive attitude
Upward Barriers	Little emphasis on employee participation
	Little emphasis on listening
	Lack of concern
	Lack of trust
	Lack of sincerity
	Poor and inconsistent leadership
	Intimidation of employees
Downward Barriers	Feeling of talking down to employees
	Lack of respect for employees
	Fear or suspicion
	Mistrust
	Tendency to prejudge
	Inability to find the time
	Disorganization
	Employees' resistance to change

response. This is partly because people think about four times faster than they talk. *Active listening* is when the listener pays very close attention to the speaker.

There are many guidelines for effective communication. In general, managers need to care honestly about employees and try to understand their needs. Be sincere, knowledgeable, honest, open-minded, tactful, trusting, and responsive; mean what is being said. Show respect to employees by communicating what workers need to know. This includes the following:

The history of the organization, its goals and objectives, how it operates, its future plans, and its financial condition.

Plans for organizational change and how the employees will be affected.

The way each employee's job fits into the big picture.

All organizational policies and procedures that affect them.

Human resource policies and procedures that pertain to them, such as wage and salary administration, promotions, benefits, raises, and discipline.

How to get a hearing about complaints.

The current status of the business.

When they are performing well or poorly.

When employees leave and when new employees arrive.

Communication should always be properly timed. For instance, announcing a major change two days before it occurs is not timely; it's downright late. Time communication for when things are not too hectic. Use appropriate communication channels and mediums (see table 9-1). Keep the message simple. Always consider the receiver. And use feedback to understand a situation or person better and to make sure the message is understood properly.

When speaking, managers should think, plan, and organize what they need to communicate before they begin talking. Select the right place, one without too many distractions or others listening. In speaking, check that tone of voice and body language work with, not against, the message. Be enthusiastic and have a sense of humor. Keep emotions in line. Always explain and back up the message. Keep in mind the listener's differences.

When not actually talking, managers should use active listening, the communication skill that is used most but is taught least frequently. Concentrate on what the other person is saying. Look at the speaker. Listen for the main ideas or points. React to the ideas, not the speaker. Take into account differences with the speaker. Listen objectively. Focus on nonverbal communication as well. But focus on the content of the message, not how it is delivered. Don't jump to conclusions; instead, ask questions at the appropriate time about any unclear points. Don't turn off to information that is new, hard to understand, or complex. Restate the information to confirm understanding. Try not to be distracted. If it is necessary to take notes, do when it does not interfere with the communication process.

When writing, keep the message as concise as possible. Make sure it is perfectly clear, as writing does not allow for immediate feedback. Try to be personal in style. Identify the purpose of the communication at the beginning. Organize the contents well to increase understanding. Be positive in writing style. Always make sure written communications are neat and without misspellings or grammatical errors.

SUMMARY

Within a hospitality organization, communication is essentially the process of passing along information and understanding from one individual or group to another. The process involves a sender, message, and receiver. Communication takes place in a variety of ways, including verbal, nonverbal, and written. The most neglected aspect of verbal communication is listening. Communication also takes place in a number of directions—upward, downward, and lateral—and may be formal or informal.

In order to learn how to communicate effectively using various mediums, it is important to understand first the many barriers to communication.

STUDY QUESTIONS

1. What communication mediums are available, and when is each appropriate?
2. What barriers in communication do you find at a current or previous job?
3. List characteristics of a boss with whom you would find it easy to communicate.
4. You need to communicate a new cleaning procedure to the housekeeping staff of a large hotel. List communication guidelines.
5. How would you handle a situation in which employees are complaining about working too much overtime?

REFERENCES

Braid, Robert W. 1985. Explaining policies to subordinates. **Supervisory Management** 30(6):19–26.

Brownell, Judi. 1987. Listening: The toughest management skill. **Cornell H.R.A. Quarterly** 27(4):65–71.

Callarman, William G., and William W. McCartney. 1985. Identifying and overcoming listening problems. **Supervisory Management** 30(3):38–42.

Crapo, Raymond F. 1988. Questioning: The epitome of the art. **Training and Development Journal** 42(1):46–50.

Fielden, John S. 1988. Meaning is shaped by audience and situation. **Personnel Journal** 67(5):107–10.

Glenn, Ethel C., and Elliott A. Pood. 1989. Listening self-inventory. **Supervisory Management** 34(1):12–15.

Goddard, Robert W. 1985. Communicate: The power of one-on-one. **Management World** 14(8):8–11.

Hamilton, Cynthia, and Brian H. Kleiner. 1987. Steps to better listening. **Personnel Journal** 66(2):20–21.

Maidment, Robert. 1985. Listening—the overlooked and underdeveloped other half of talking. **Supervisory Management** 30(8):10–12.

McClelland, Valorie. 1987. Mixed signals breed mistrust. **Personnel Journal** 66(3):24–26.

Thomas, Bobbie. 1987. Better communications means smoother customer service. **Management Solutions** 32(5):31–33.

Chapter 10

Developing a Positive, Motivating Organizational Climate

KEY QUESTIONS

1. What is job satisfaction, and how can it be measured?
2. What determines job satisfaction?
3. How can you apply each of the major motivational theories?
4. What can a hospitality manager do to create a positive, motivating work climate?

KEY TERMS AND CONCEPTS

Motivation

Organizational climate

Job satisfaction

Morale

Primary needs

Secondary needs

Maslow's hierarchy of needs

Self-actualization

McClelland's secondary needs

Achievement behavior

Herzberg's two-factor theory

Satisfiers

Hygiene factors

Extrinsic motivators

Intrinsic motivators

Vroom's expectancy theory

Behaviorism

Positive reinforcement

Punishment

Negative reinforcement

Operant conditioning

Behavior modification

Consultive management

Quality circles

Suggestion programs

The benefits of having a hospitality operation with a positive, motivating work climate are numerous, including increased productivity, sales, and profitability, and excellent quality and cost control. It was once widely thought that simply paying employees enough money kept them motivated. This is no longer the case. An essential part of learning to lead staff is to understand better the conditions under which they are motivated to perform work.

What is *motivation?* It resides within an individual and helps to explain behavior. It should not be equated with behavior, however, as the causes of that are much broader than can be explained by motivation alone. Rather, motivation is a complex internal process with three components: what drives the individual to behave in certain ways, what steers the behavior, and what maintains the behavior.

Studying motivation in the workplace requires examination of the following variables: the employee, the job tasks, and the work environment. Each employee has different characteristics that affect behavior and what motivates him or her: the person's wants and needs, self-concept, attitudes, values, interests, feelings, personality, and life experiences. A manager increases the chances of motivating employees by trying to understand their beliefs, expectations, and needs.

Because motivation is a force within each person, much like desire, managers do not directly motivate individuals. The nature of motivation requires managers to take an indirect approach, by nourishing it through a positive *organizational climate*. This is the human environment within an organization, and it is made up of the business's own culture, traditions, and methods of action. Some are easygoing and personal, while others are cold. Organizational climate can be measured qualitatively by examining such dimensions as responsibility, conformity, team spirit, rewards, and standards, or it can be measured quantitatively. It is perceived at three levels: the individual, a work group, and the entire organization.

Organizational climate affects *job satisfaction* and *morale* as well as motivation. It is necessary to review the nature of job satisfaction, morale, and motivational theories before examining how to create a positive, motivating organizing climate.

JOB SATISFACTION AND MORALE

The level of satisfaction an employee derives from a job depends on what the person wants and expects from it and how this compares to what the worker actually receives. In other words, job satisfaction is the favorableness or unfavorableness with which employees view their work. It results when there is a proper fit—like two interlocking parts—between the job and the employee, and this is dynamic, or changing. Such factors as age, sex, health, personality, friends and family, and occupational and educational level influence an individual's perception of wants and needs.

Job satisfaction is reflected to an extent in employee behavior. Where there is increased job satisfaction, there is generally less absenteeism and turnover. In a study of nonmanagerial hotel workers, lower overall job satisfaction was positively related to employee intentions to leave the hotel and the hotel industry (Fernsten and Brenner, 1987). There is no definite relationship, however, between job satisfaction and performance; a high level of job satisfaction does not necessarily also mean a good performance. Some researchers have suggested that good job performance may actually lead to job satisfaction; when employees get reinforcement or reward from their job, it can be a source of satisfaction. And for some individuals, this satisfaction may lead to still more effort and effective performance. There is a consistent relationship between occupational level and job satisfaction, with higher-level occupations reporting increased satisfaction.

The little things about a job, such as availability of parking and the condition of the equipment, can be crucial to job satisfaction: such problems as a parking lot that floods whenever it rains or computer equipment that is broken more than it is fixed can become very annoying and, over time, can decrease job satisfaction if not corrected.

In a study involving entry-level employees in nine retail stores, eighty were asked to rank various factors in importance to job satisfaction. The respondents ranked them as follows, from most to least important:

- Knowledge of role (understanding of job)
- Perception of social relationships at work
- Supervisory practices
- Perceived wholeness of job (understanding of how job relates to the organization's goals)
- Satisfaction with life in general
- Management policy
- Earnings

All this suggests that management needs to monitor the level of employee job satisfaction in order to make decisions that might affect it. A typical approach is to conduct a job satisfaction survey, also known as a morale or attitude survey (fig. 10-1).

Morale and job satisfaction go hand in hand with motivation. Without good individual or group morale, a manager will have a difficult time stimulating employees. Morale is the attitude or outlook of an individual or group toward the group's purposes and goals. When morale is high, it can easily be taken for granted, but when morale is low, it is very noticeable and attention-getting. Although high morale probably enhances productivity, it doesn't always translate into high productivity. Records that may indicate employee morale concerns include turnover rate, production records, absenteeism and tardiness, grievance reports, and exit interviews.

1. Do you feel your supervisor treats you fairly?

    _____ Always   _____ Usually   _____ Seldom   _____ Never

2. Does your supervisor criticize you in front of other people?

    _____ Always   _____ Usually   _____ Seldom   _____ Never

3. Does your supervisor know and understand your job?

    _____ Always   _____ Usually   _____ Seldom   _____ Never

4. Does your supervisor express a sincere interest in your problems?

    _____ Always   _____ Usually   _____ Seldom   _____ Never

5. Do you feel free to go to your supervisor with a complaint?

    _____ Always   _____ Usually   _____ Seldom   _____ Never

6. Do you have enough time to do a good job?

    _____ Always   _____ Usually   _____ Seldom   _____ Never

7. Do you thoroughly understand how your job should be performed?

    _____ Always   _____ Usually   _____ Seldom   _____ Never

8. Did you receive adequate training in your job?

    _____ Always   _____ Usually   _____ Seldom   _____ Never

9. Do you like doing your job?

    _____ Always   _____ Usually   _____ Seldom   _____ Never

10. Do you feel your work is appreciated?

    _____ Always   _____ Usually   _____ Seldom   _____ Never

11. Do you have the equipment, supplies, and tools needed to do your work?

    _____ Always   _____ Usually   _____ Seldom   _____ Never

12. Are assignments handed out fairly by your supervisor?

    _____ Always   _____ Usually   _____ Seldom   _____ Never

13. Do you like your co-workers?

    _____ Always   _____ Usually   _____ Seldom   _____ Never

14. Do your co-workers pull their share of the load?

    _____ Always   _____ Usually   _____ Seldom   _____ Never

15. Do you feel your talents are wasted?

    _____ Always   _____ Usually   _____ Seldom   _____ Never

16. Do you have an opportunity to make suggestions to improve your job?

    _____ Always   _____ Usually   _____ Seldom   _____ Never

17. When you make suggestions, do you feel they are listened to?

    _____ Always   _____ Usually   _____ Seldom   _____ Never

18. Do you understand organizational and departmental policies and procedures?

    _____ Always   _____ Usually   _____ Seldom   _____ Never

19. Are you proud of the place you work?

    _____ Always   _____ Usually   _____ Seldom   _____ Never

20. Is your workplace safe and comfortable?

    _____ Always   _____ Usually   _____ Seldom   _____ Never

Figure 10-1. Job satisfaction survey.

MOTIVATIONAL THEORIES

Motivational theories seek to identify the factors that influence behavior. Early theories had simple approaches to the relatively uncomplicated work environment of the time, but modern theories are more complex due to today's more intricate organizations and society.

Motivational theories examine both *primary and secondary needs*. Basic physical needs essential to life are called primary needs; they include air, water, food, sleep, sex, and a reasonably comfortable temperature. They are universal among people but vary in intensity from one individual to another.

Secondary needs involve ones of the mind and spirit, such as self-esteem and a sense of belonging to a group. Secondary needs vary in type as well as intensity among different people, are often vague feelings instead of specific physical needs, can readily change within an individual, and are clearly conditioned by experience. An employee's motivation at any time may actually be a combination of several different needs. The secondary needs are those that can complicate a manager's efforts at creating a positive, motivating work climate.

Frederick Taylor and Douglas McGregor

Both Frederick Taylor and Douglas McGregor, who contributed much to management theory (see chapter 8), made important observations about motivation. Taylor, founder of the classical school of management in the early twentieth century, felt motivating employees could be achieved by a reward-and-exchange system, in which the employer exchanged the worker's time and effort for money. At that time, his theory was quite accurate. Money is probably not as powerful a motivator as it was in the early twentieth century, due in part to a much higher standard of living; it is still used quite successfully, however, as a reward for outstanding performance.

After World War II, the work environment became more complicated, and new motivational theories evolved to respond to these changes. McGregor identified psychological assumptions and generalizations about human nature and behavior that support his two styles of management: Theory X (classical) and Theory Y (participative). He endorsed the participative school of management and felt that involving the employee in the organization via decision making and other procedures would help motivate employees.

Maslow's Hierarchy of Needs

In the 1940s, Abraham Maslow developed what he called a *hierarchy of needs* theory (fig. 10-2), in which people are motivated by five types of needs:

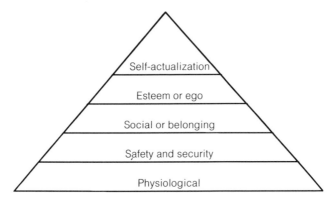

Figure 10-2   Maslow's hierarchy of needs.

physiological, safety and security, social or belonging, esteem or ego, and *self-actualization.* He said the lower, or primary, needs, physiological and safety, must be satisfied before the higher, or secondary, needs become active sources of motivation. There is no consistent sequence in which the higher needs come into operation. Examples of these needs follow:

Physiological: Food, air, water, rest, shelter

Safety and security: Order, stability, rules

Social or belonging: Affiliation, love, attention, social acceptance, family and friends, social activities

Esteem or ego: Status, respect of peers, reputation, self-respect, independence, prestige, appreciation

Self-actualization: Self-fulfillment, self-realization, achievement, growth, challenge

Self-actualization can be defined as a need to realize one's own potential and to be creative. The need for self-actualization cannot be fully satisfied, as there are always new challenges and opportunities for growth.

Maslow theorized that people are continuously in a motivational state, and as soon as one desire is satisfied, another takes its place, so people rarely reach a state of complete satisfaction except for brief moments. In other words, individuals are more enthusiastically motivated by what they are seeking (unmet needs) than by needs that have already been met. Maslow also suggested that an individual can travel down as well as up the hierarchy. A manager who is worried about possibly being laid off will start being concerned more about security needs than the esteem or ego needs he or she may have been trying to satisfy previously.

What was particularly new in Maslow's theory was that it emphasized motivation by responding to employees' unmet needs, rather than the over-used management practice of offering rewards for already satisfied needs. In spite of little experimental research that supports Maslow's theory, it is popular and has been useful in helping managers understand the diverse needs of employees. It is important to keep in mind, however, that motivating people at work requires knowledge of and response to cultural and individual differences. Secondary needs vary among people much more than the primary needs.

Table 10-1 gives some examples of what managers can do to meet each of the needs in Maslow's hierarchy.

McClelland's Three Secondary Needs

After World War II, David McClelland developed a theory of motivation based on the strength of secondary needs: affiliation, power, and achievement. Each of *McClelland's secondary needs* resembles one of Maslow's higher ones: affiliation is like social or belonging, power like ego or esteem, and achievement like self-actualization.

Beginning in 1947, McClelland investigated and wrote in depth about achievement. From his research came a profile of the characteristics of the high achiever:

- Moderate risk taking
- Need for immediate feedback
- Satisfaction with accomplishment itself
- Preoccupation with the task

He eventually studied how achievement, affiliation, and power influence managers.

Types of *achievement behavior* include setting and meeting challenging goals. Affiliation and power are involved more with interpersonal relationships. Affiliative behavior, for instance, is social in nature and includes trying to get along with others. Power behavior refers to trying to influence others through various means. These three needs affect people's behavior and have implications for success in managerial and other jobs.

Herzberg's Two-Factor Theory

In the 1950s and 1960s, Frederick Herzberg developed what he called a *two-factor theory,* which separated factors that lead to motivation, referred to

Table 10-1. What managers can do to meet
Maslow's hierarchy of needs

Hierarchy of Needs	Action by Manager
Self-actualization	Challenging work
	Participative management
Esteem or ego	Training
	Certificates of achievement
	Job rotation
	Tuition reimbursement
	Positive reinforcement
	Periodic evaluations
	Delegation of responsibility and authority
	Requests for advice
	Feedback
	Promotion
	Title
Social or belonging	Team sports
	Company newsletter
	Slogans
	Team formation
	Group meetings
	Company-sponsored events
Safety and security	On-the-job safety program
	Health insurance
	Pension plan
	Job security system
	Clear policies and procedures
	Fair evaluation system
	Fair disciplinary system
	Fair grievance system
	Unions
Physiological	Adequate wages
	Rest breaks during shift
	Clean air
	Appropriate temperature and humidity
	Meals during shift

Table 10-2.   Herzberg's two-factor theory

Satisfiers (Motivators)	Hygiene (Maintenance) Factors
Work itself	Working conditions
Achievement	Salary
Recognition	Status
Challenge	Security
Responsibility	Supervision
Advancement	Company policy and administration
	Interpersonal relations

as *satisfiers,* from those whose absence leads to job dissatisfaction, which he referred to as *hygiene factors* (table 10-2). Hygiene factors themselves do not motivate employees; but without them, employees are likely to be dissatisfied. The hygiene factors represent mostly Maslow's lower or primary needs, which our society seems to guarantee to many, so that they do not motivate but do cause dissatisfaction when absent. Herzberg probably chose the term hygiene due to his background in public health.

The satisfiers relate to Maslow's ego or esteem needs and to self-actualization. Because society does not guarantee them, the workplace can help to fulfill these needs. These are the motivators that management can use to attain employee commitment. When comparing the hygiene factors to the satisfiers, it is clear that hygiene factors are *extrinsic motivators*—outside the job—and deal with job context, while satisfiers are *intrinsic motivators* and deal with job content. Intrinsic motivators are internal rewards that an employee feels when performing a job.

Research studies differ in their support of Herzberg's theory. For some people, especially managers, the motivating factors can also be dissatisfiers if they are not present. In addition, Herzberg did not feel money was a satisfier, although it can sometimes be a motivating factor, particularly when used as a reward for outstanding performance. A strict interpretation of his theory is probably not warranted.

Vroom's Expectancy Theory

According to Victor *Vroom's expectancy theory* (1964), motivation to behave or perform in a certain way is a function of the belief the employee has about the likelihood that a particular act will yield a particular outcome, and the value the individual places on that outcome. For instance, if an employee expects that working diligently will bring about a desired promotion, he or she will be more likely to work hard. However, if an employee feels that working hard brings no other outcome than just continuing to do so, that worker may not perform so well.

Whether a certain outcome is desirable enough to motivate someone will vary from individual to individual, due to people's different needs. Whereas Maslow and Herzberg provide specific suggestions on what motivates us, expectancy theory helps to explain how motivation occurs. It tells managers to define expectations, make work assignments realistic and valuable, give regular feedback, and reward employees who meet the expectations.

Behaviorism

Behaviorism is a very simple theory compared to the ones examined up to this point. Its principal proponent, B. F. Skinner, promoted it during the 1950s and 1960s. The theory basically states that behavior depends simply on its own consequences, or reinforcement. It has no concept of motivation or of any inner needs of individuals. Whereas Maslow attempted to identify specific content factors that motivate individuals, Herzberg identified such factors in the job environment, and Vroom helped explain the process of motivation, behaviorism is not a cognitive theory like the others, because it is not based on ideas about thinking and feeling—in other words, cognition.

Behavior may result in _positive reinforcment,_ in which there are pleasant consequences, or it may be followed by _punishment,_ or unpleasant consequences. Another type of resulting action is _negative reinforcement,_ which is the removal of unpleasant consequences. The process of influencing behavior through different kinds of reinforcement is known as _operant conditioning._ _Behavior modification_ is the application of operant-conditioning techniques in a work or other situation. Although the previous theories discussed argue that internal needs influence behavior, behavior modification states that external consequences tend to determine behavior.

Positive reinforcement can be applied in an organization as follows:

1. Determine standards of behavior and performance.
2. Design positive reinforcements, such as verbal praise, when standards are met or exceeded.
3. Measure the behavior or performance.
4. Apply the positive reinforcements, and do so relatively frequently.
5. Change the program as necessary.

When behavior or performance is not up to standards, the use of any type of punishment may yield negative attitudes and avoidance or undesired behavior; therefore, punishment should be used only in unusual circumstances.

CREATING A POSITIVE, MOTIVATING CLIMATE

In a mid-1980s Gallup poll on motivation, a cross section of twelve hundred workers was asked to rank a list of forty-six motivational factors, including money. The top ten motivators selected, as worded in the poll, were working with people who respect me, interesting work, recognition for good work, chance to develop skills and abilities, opportunity to be creative, work with people who listen if you have an idea on how to make things better, seeing an end result for your effort, working for an effective manager, a job that isn't too easy, and having a mentor.

A classic study of motivation done in 1946, 1981, and 1986 (table 10-3) asked supervisors to rate various job factors in order of importance to their employees (Kovach 1987). For comparison, employees were then asked to rate the factors as well. As can be seen, the supervisors did not know very well what the employees wanted from their jobs. In both 1946 and 1986, super-

Table 10-3. Results of study on motivation

Factors	Rank Given by		
	Employees in 1946	*Employees in 1986*	*Supervisors in 1946 and 1986*
Full appreciation of work done	1	2	8
Feeling of being in on things	2	3	10
Sympathetic help with personal problems	3	10	9
Job security	4	4	2
Good wages	5	5	1
Interesting work	6	1	5
Promotion and growth in the organization	7	6	3
Personal loyalty to employees	8	8	6
Good working conditions	9	7	4
Tactful discipline	10	9	7

Source: Kovach 1987.

visors tended to think that money and job security were most important, but employees put the most emphasis in 1986 on doing interesting work, feeling involved, and being appreciated. What matters to managers is that they have much control over giving the employees what they want.

Motivational Guidelines

Numerous guidelines exist to help create a positive and motivating work climate. They are centered around treating employees as the organization's most valuable asset, managing performance properly, communicating and listening, being a good leader, recognizing employees, and involving the employees.

First, managers should treat employees as the most important company asset. By investing in the staff, managers end up with workers who will take care of that investment. Here are some ways managers can achieve this:

Maintain a safe and pleasant physical working environment.

Do not cause excessive fatigue, boredom, stress, or frustration.

Post position openings, and promote as much as possible from within.

Set in place a career ladder.

Catch people doing things right.

Treat employees the same way one personally would want to be treated.

Arrange opportunities for socializing, such as trips and company teams.

One way managers can treat employees well is by managing performance properly. The guidelines for this include the following:

Design jobs to enhance performance, achievement, and a sense of purpose.

Match the appropriate candidate to the job.

Orient and train employees so they know what is expected. Consider cross-training.

Be sure all employees know and understand their job descriptions, the standards of performance, and the evaluation forms by which their performance is measured.

Give employees what they need to do the job.

Do not overwork employees.

Let employees know what they stand to gain by performing at a certain level.

Make sure job pressures are reasonable.

Provide immediate and relevant feedback. Support employees as much as possible.

When counseling, criticize the problem behavior, not the employee.

Use positive forms of discipline.

Recognize good performance, and praise, praise, praise.

Provide flexibility, choice, and challenge, as appropriate.

Delegate to provide challenges.

When delegating, include responsibility and authority.

Evaluate and promote based on performance.

Encourage employees to set some of their own goals.

Communicating and listening are also vital ways of creating a desirable work climate. Here are some guidelines for doing these things well:

Maintain close communication between management and employees, both upward and downward.

Communicate all expectations, including those concerning performance, discipline, evaluation, rewards, and organizational goals, policies, and procedures.

Communicate to each employee where his or her job and tasks fit into the organization.

Communicate the importance of quality and service to guests.

Tell employees about changes in advance, and explain why they are being made.

Provide a means for employees to express their opinions and complaints, and to get a response.

A good manager must also be a good leader. Here are some ways this can be achieved:

Have a clear-cut organizational philosophy, values, and goals; communicate and support them.

Have reasonable and relevant controls and structure.

Set a good example; demonstrate personal motivation through personal behavior.

Cultivate and demonstrate honesty, trust, sincerity, caring, fairness, decisiveness, and consistency.

Be proud of the employees, and have confidence in them.

Individualize managerial supervision.

Manage by wandering around. Be visible and approachable.

Guidelines for recognizing employees include the following:

Set standards, and measure and reward behavior that meets or exceeds the standards.

Let employees participate in developing the organization's recognition-and-award system. Tie rewards to needs.

Adapt rewards to the situation.

Make sure rewards are fairly given, of appropriate worth, and attainable.

Give rewards sincerely and fairly.

Give rewards promptly, with appropriate fanfare, enthusiasm, and meaningful presentation.

Promote and communicate rewards, but don't oversell them.

Make some awards exclusive.

Create work situations in which employees succeed and feel good.

Review and periodically update recognition and award programs.

The final set of guidelines centers around making employees feel involved in the organization:

Allow employees to be included in relevant decision making.

Actively solicit constructive suggestions.

Use any of a variety of participative programs, such as consultation, work committees, or employee profit-sharing plans.

The last two sets of guidelines, employee recognition and employee participation, warrant detailed examination here.

Employee Recognition

Employee recognition, in the form of praise, incentives, rewards, or awards, really works in service organizations to reinforce employee commitment to service goals. Recognizing employees for meeting standards and rewarding those who exceed them lets the workers know that delivering high-quality service is the norm within the organization. Employees who believe that their efforts will be rewarded are likely to be productive and stay productive.

Studies of both executives and employees show that when pay is tied to performance, employee satisfaction, motivation, and productivity increase. For some people, increased pay uplifts their self-esteem, pride, and prestige. One study of four hundred companies (Zemke 1988) found that when work was measured and feedback given, productivity increased an average of 43 percent; when, in addition, incentives were used, productivity rose an average of 64 percent. This study points to the importance of recognizing and rewarding competent and outstanding performance. Unfortunately, only 19 percent of service companies use performance incentive systems, according to a study by the American Compensation Association and the American Productivity Center. The most successful techniques are productivity gain-sharing, pay-for-knowledge, and small-group incentives (Zemke 1988). Gain-sharing plans are programs designed to improve productivity through sharing the financial gains of the organization with employees; profit sharing is an example.

There are many examples of positive reinforcement:

Social:

- Verbal praise
- Pat on the back
- Company social events
- Letter of thanks, birthday cards
- Recognition in front of work group, in ceremony
- Picture or article or both in organization newsletter

Material:

- Cash bonus
- Pay raise
- Award
- Plaque or certificate
- Service pin or company jewelry
- Gift certificate or gift selected from a catalog
- Larger or nicer office
- Free tickets to events
- Chances to win a prize
- Points toward prizes or merchandise
- Free room or dinner
- Vacation trips

Special privileges:

- Time off with pay
- Training
- Special parking spot

Miscellaneous:

- Special job title
- Performance evaluation rating

For instance, Domino's Pizza and Pizza Hut both bring award winners to national meetings to praise their achievements. Some restaurants use sales figures, cover counts, and simple managerial judgment to give bonuses to employees in almost all job categories. For example, if the number of meals served in the dining room surpasses a certain number, the kitchen staff will receive bonus hours of pay; servers who exceed the average sales for a shift also receive bonuses. Other areas that can be acknowledged in recognition programs include good attendance, length of service, safety, training, quality of service, and teamwork.

Figure 10-3 is a questionnaire to help in determining if a recognition or service award program is needed in an organization. Appendix E contains information on where to get help for recognition or award programs.

Employee Participation

A late 1980s Gallup poll of a cross section of employees from different industries showed that "84 percent of the interviewed employees said they would work harder and do a better job if they were involved in decisions affecting their work" (Denton 1987). Participation is a sharing process that involves the following elements: the giving of responsibility by the manager, a group's acceptance of it, and the mental involvement of the group. Potential benefits of participative management include higher productivity, improved morale, and better decisions. Participative managers share responsibility with those who perform the work, although of course the manager always assumes ultimate responsibility.

In order for participation to succeed, certain conditions need to be considered. What is selected for participation must be relevant and of interest to the employees, and they should be able to communicate adequately with one another. Neither the manager nor the employees should feel that participation threatens the position of either. Employees need to feel that they can freely give opinions and suggestions, without any negative consequences. The possible

Chances are, you already suspect that your company might benefit from a service award program.

You have an underlying, "gut" feeling that management/employee relations . . . or employee commitment . . . or dedication to company goals . . . can be improved. But you can't quite put your finger on the problem or how to solve it.

To find out how accurate that feeling is, take this short quiz.

1. Does your company have a *systematic* way of letting people know that you value their contributions?

   Yes _____   No _____

2. Does your company publicly single out those people who do something right, rather than those who do something wrong?

   Yes _____   No _____

3. Has your company established one, or at most two, fundamental attributes (e.g., pride of workmanship, dedication to customer needs) to be best at—and continually reinforced that goal?

   Yes _____   No _____

4. Does management believe your company's assets are primarily its machines, product, or money, rather than its people?

   Yes _____   No _____

5. Do you encourage performance competition among workers in a way that is non-threatening?

   Yes _____   No _____

6. Do you offer rewards that are strictly monetary (salaries, bonuses) but fail to provide symbolic awards as well?

   Yes _____   No _____

7. Is management as totally committed to its people and their well-being as they wish their employees to be toward the company and its goals?

   Yes _____   No _____

8. Is top management visibly involved in the recognition of employee achievement *at all levels*?

   Yes _____   No _____

9. Does management recognize and reward only the few very top performers and ignore the remaining 80 or 90 percent?

   Yes _____   No _____

10. Has management tried various incentive programs in the past, but given them up because they "just don't seem to work"?

    Yes _____   No _____

Scoring: Check your answers and assign the number of points shown for each, then add up your total points.

1.	Yes 2	-	No	0
2.	Yes 4	-	No	0
3.	Yes 2	-	No	0
4.	Yes 0	-	No	5
5.	Yes 3	-	No	0
6.	Yes 0	-	No	4
7.	Yes 4	-	No	0
8.	Yes 3	-	No	0
9.	Yes 0	-	No	2
10.	Yes 0	-	No	1

26–30: Your management understands the needs of its people and is actively pursuing a policy to fulfill those needs. Taking this quiz may point up one or two areas for improvement, but basically your workers know you care.

18–25: You've tried to institute some system of rewards, but management's lack of commitment has caused inconsistency and only sporadic positive reinforcement for workers. A renewed commitment will increase effectiveness.

9–17: Management's attitude toward any reward system is one of looking for a "quick fix" for a problem or of focusing only on a few very highly motivated individuals. This basic misunderstanding of how, and why, to institute an award program must be corrected at the management level, and the system revised to reflect this change.

0–8: People are a means to an end— to be used and discarded or ignored at management's discretion. Workers know it— and act accordingly. You've taken this quiz because you're ready to change things for the better. Let's get started!

Figure 10-3. How to determine if you need a service award program. (Courtesy Bulova Corporation.)

benefits of participation also should be greater than its costs, especially including the time commitment.

There are many kinds of participative programs, such as *consultive management,* work committees or *quality circles, suggestion programs,* employee ownership or profit-sharing plans, and team building (see chapter 12). Consultive management refers to when managers consult with employees, asking them to think about and contribute ideas on certain situations before management makes a decision. This consultation is done informally.

Work committees, also known as quality circles, involve groups of workers who meet regularly on company time to identify and analyze job problems and develop possible solutions, which then go to management for evaluation and implementation. The problems may concern quality, productivity, safety, job structure, or work conditions. Groups usually consist of eight to ten employees from the same work area. Groups often choose their own leader to facilitate discussions or have a supervisory person do so. The leader needs formal training in working with such groups. Quality circles can work well, because employees who can generate their own solutions take ownership of them and are much more likely to support and implement them.

Suggestion programs are formal programs that ask employees to write down or otherwise express any suggestions they have to improve work methods or any other aspect of their job. A response rate in a suggestion program is typically about 15 percent, of which about one-quarter of the responses are implemented. Suggestion programs very often revolve around topics such as how to save money in an area or how to reduce accidents.

Employee ownership or profit-sharing plans allow employees to enjoy part of the company profits. These types of participative plans may generate motivation for employees to do a good job as well. In general, worker participation programs that are tied directly to financial incentives have increased productivity.

Worker participation programs will not succeed if the organization does not fully support them. Sure ways to kill these programs include poor managerial responses to employee suggestions, managers who are not trained to facilitate group discussions, insufficient time commitment, and no incentives for employees to contribute.

SUMMARY

The benefits of having a hospitality operation with a positive, motivating work climate are numerous, including increases in productivity, sales, and profitability, and excellent quality and cost control. It was once thought that simply paying employees enough money kept them motivated. This is no longer the case. An essential part of learning to manage staff is to understand better the conditions under which they are motivated to perform work. The nature of motivation requires managers to take an indirect approach by nourishing it through a positive organizational climate. Organizational climate, therefore, affects motivation, along with job satisfaction and morale.

Various theories provide insights into motivation. Major contributors to this area include Frederick Taylor, Douglas McGregor, Abraham Maslow, David McClelland, Victor Vroom, and B. F. Skinner.

Guidelines for creating a positive and motivating organizational climate focus on treating employees as the organization's most valuable asset, managing performance properly, communicating and listening, being a good leader, giving positive reinforcement, and involving the employees.

STUDY QUESTIONS

1. Describe a current or previous job in which the organizational climate either encouraged or discouraged you to perform well. Which factors motivated you or made you feel less motivated?

2. Which needs, as described in Maslow's hierarchy, do you feel you are trying to satisfy? Which are already satisfied?

3. In Herzberg's two-factor theory, are any of the satisfiers really motivators for you personally? Do the motivators really reflect what you think would stimulate you to perform on the job?

4. What are determinants of job satisfaction and morale?

5. What is positive reinforcement, and how is it used in hospitality operations to result in better service and productivity?

6. What is behavior modification? Give an example of its use in a restaurant.

7. What are the benefits of participative management?

8. How can employees be involved in the management of their areas?

9. Name five areas in which a hotel front office manager can use specific techniques to motivate the staff. Give an example of each.

REFERENCES

Bodek, Norman. 1985. The unifying theory of productivity (UTOP): How to manage human resources. **Supervisory Management** 30(5):17–26.

Brown, Abby. 1986. Today's employees choose their own recognition award. *Personnel Administrator* 31(8):51–58.

Crosby, Bob. 1986. Employee involvement: Why it fails, what it takes to succeed. *Personnel Administrator* 31(2):95–106.

Davis, Keith, and John W. Newstrom. 1985. *Human Behavior at Work: Organizational Behavior.* New York: McGraw-Hill.

DeCotiis, Thomas A., and J. Michael Jenkins. 1986. Employee commitment: Money in the bank. *Cornell H.R.A. Quarterly* 26(4):70–75.

Denton, D. Keith. 1987. Getting employee commitment. *Management Solutions* 32(10):17–24.

Elliott, Travis. 1983. *Profitable Foodservice Management Through Worker Motivation.* Washington, D.C.: National Restaurant Association.

Fernsten, Jeffrey A., and O. C. Brenner. 1987. Coping with turnover: A strategic approach. *Hospitality Education and Research Journal.* 11(3):85–94.

Ginsburg, Sigmund G. 1987. Getting hourly employees to work. *Management Solutions* 32(6):11–14.

Gooch, Bill G., and Betty J. McDowell. 1988. Use anxiety to motivate. *Personnel Journal* 67(4):51–54.

Grant, Philip C. 1988a. Rewards: The pizzazz is the package, not the prize. *Personnel Journal* 67(3):76–81.

———. 1988b. The dos and don'ts for getting top performance. *Management Solutions* 33(5):22–26.

Herzberg, Frederick. 1987. One more time: How do you motivate employees? *Harvard Business Review* 87(5):109–20.

Kovach, Kenneth A. 1987. What motivates employees? Workers and supervisors give different answers. *Business Horizons* 30(5):58–65.

Maslow, A. 1970. *Motivation and Personality.* 2d ed. New York: Harper and Row.

McAfee, R. Bruce, and Myron Glassman. 1988. Job satisfaction: It's the little things that count. *Management Solutions* 33(8):32–37.

Merchant, John E. 1988. Motivating entry-level service employees. *Management Solutions* 33(3):43–45.

Mill, Robert C. 1985. Upping the organization: Enhancing employee performance through an improved work climate. *Cornell H.R.A. Quarterly* 25(4):30–37.

Nelson, Andre. 1988. The need for recognition. *Management Solutions* 33(4):32–36.

Niehouse, Oliver L. 1986. Job satisfaction: How to motivate today's workers. *Supervisory Management* 31(2):8–11.

Nordstrom, Rodney, and R. Vance Hall. 1986a. How to develop and implement an employee incentive program. *Management Solutions* 31(9):40–43.

————. 1986b. The platinum rule. *Training and Development Journal* 40(9):57–58.

Patrellis, A. J. 1985. Producing results: Using power with your employees. *Supervisory Management* 30(3):32–37.

Quick, Thomas L. 1988. Expectancy theory in five simple steps. *Training and Development Journal* 42(7):30–32.

Roarty, Carroll J. 1987. A party crashes the communication barrier. *Personnel Administrator* 32(11):67–69.

Rinke, Wolf J. 1988. Maximizing management potential by building self-esteem. *Management Solutions* 33(3):11–16.

Ruffner, Esther R. 1987. When a circle is not a circle. *SAM Advanced Management Journal* 52(2):9–15.

Schuman, Gary. 1987. New motivational strategies to pursue. *Management Solutions* 32(1):32–34.

Sherwood, Andrew. 1987. A baker's dozen of ways to motivate people. *Management Solutions* 32(5):14–16.

Smith, Jason P. 1986. Bonuses: A little extra can make a big difference for hourly employees. *Restaurants USA* 6(7):28–30.

Wayne, Sandy J., Ricky W. Griffin, and Thomas S. Bateman. 1986. Improving the effectiveness of quality circles. *Personnel Administrator* 31(3):79–88.

Wilkinson, Harry E., Charles D. Orth, and Robert C. Benfari. 1986. Motivation theories: An integrated operational model. *SAM Advanced Management Journal* 51(4):24–31.

Woodruff, David M. 1989. Seven steps to better employee relations. *Supervisory Management* 34(1):35–38.

Zemke, Ron. 1988. Reward and recognition: Yes, they really work. *Training* 25(11):49–53.

Chapter 11

Managing a Diverse Work Force

KEY QUESTIONS

1. In what ways is the American work force going to change in the future?
2. What are the characteristics of a multicultural organization?
3. What skills are needed to manage a multicultural work force?
4. How can a manager be trained to work successfully with different cultures and ethnic groups?
5. Who is in protected groups, and what should be kept in mind when managing them?

KEY TERMS AND CONCEPTS

Diversity	Multicultural awareness
Melting pot	Protected groups
Cultural pluralism	OUCH test
Monocultural organization	Sexual harassment
Nondiscriminatory organization	Grampies
Multicultural organization	Reasonable accommodation

The U.S. Department of Labor forecasts that within the next few years, 75 percent of those entering the work force will comprise minority members and women. For the first time, white males are already in the minority, making up only 46 percent of the work force (Copeland 1988). This trend will continue, due to the combination of a declining and older white American population and a younger, growing minority population.

Diversity in today's work force refers to the special contributions and needs of blacks, Asian-Americans, Mexican-Americans, Native Americans, women, and the physically handicapped, to mention a few groups. Managing a multicultural work force takes into consideration the cultural differences of these various groups.

It was once thought that the United States is a *melting pot,* in which people from various cultures lose much of their heritage as they become American. It is now widely believed that American society is based on *cultural pluralism,* in which each component culture maintains much of its own unique heritage while also functioning in and contributing to American culture. Unfortunately, most traditional models of management methods and motivation reflect the assumptions and attitudes of a homogeneous white male work force. These methods often do not work, and even backfire, when applied to minorities such as blacks, Hispanics, or Asians. For example, patting someone on the back as a way to say thank you or motivate someone may be appropriate for white males but not for Asian employees, who generally hate being touched.

The hospitality industry has traditionally hired people from many different cultural and ethnic backgrounds, as well as women. Particularly within hotel and restaurant companies with international operations, managers have had to deal with cultural diversity in the work force and among guests. Yet even in domestic companies, members of various ethnic and cultural groups are at work in the different departments, as any walking tour demonstrates. It is obvious that effective managing of this diversity is a requirement at all levels of a hospitality organization, and that the companies in the forefront of managing diversity will have a competitive edge. How to manage diversity in the work force requires careful examination. Of related interest are selected aspects of managing certain groups that are specially protected under the law, such as senior citizens and the handicapped.

DEVELOPMENT OF THE MULTICULTURAL WORKPLACE

Not that long ago, the workplace was designed to protect itself from cultural diversity, particularly women and blacks. The majority of the work force was composed of white males, who dominated all aspects of management. Some organizations are still at this stage of development. Research in this area describes organizations as being in one of three developmental stages: monocultural, nondiscriminatory, and multicultural (Foster, Jackson, Cross, Jackson, and Hardiman 1988).

Monocultural organizations are dominated by white males, who set the pace for everything that happens within the organization. Women, minorities, and other socially oppressed groups are either not hired at all or must abide by the system set in place.

The *nondiscriminatory organization* has a genuine desire to get rid of the majority group's unfair advantage; however, this is done without significantly changing the system. With the civil rights movement of the 1960s and resulting Equal Employment Opportunity legislation, the struggle was to eliminate racism and prejudice through ignoring differences. Equality of the races was translated to mean sameness. Many civil rights advocates at that time downplayed the cultural heritage of the blacks.

The problem with the nondiscriminatory stage is that although an organization may hire more minority members and want to promote an unbiased atmosphere, the majority culture is still seen as the standard to which everyone, regardless of differences, must conform. For example, when women entered the work force in large numbers fairly recently, many felt they had to become like men in order to find a place in and measure up to the white male standards; they started wearing dark suits, talked about sports, and became more competitive and assertive (some men preferred to call it aggressive). In brief, women were seeking equality by being viewed as the same as men.

The final stage of development is the *multicultural organization*. This type is not blind to differences among cultural groups, but rather acknowledges and builds on them. Management values such diversity and seeks to derive the benefits of these differences. Power is shared, and different cultural groups in the organization contribute to its goals. An organization at this stage also recognizes that there is much diversity within a group as well.

MANAGING THE MULTICULTURAL WORK FORCE

Many Americans have already become aware of different cultures through eating or working at ethnically oriented foodservices, whose numbers have recently been increasing; they include, for example, Mexican, Japanese, and Vietnamese cooking. *Multicultural awareness* is the first step to becoming culturally effective and thus better able to communicate and motivate across different races, genders, cultures, ages, and life-styles. Mistakes due to cultural fumbles, whether in human resource management, customer service, or wherever, are costly to a company in terms of lost business, managers who leave, and poor morale.

To increase awareness of other cultures, a manager must first acknowledge and understand the effects of his or her own culture. We are all culture-bound to some extent, and our culture is so ingrained in us that we think our way of talking, perceiving, thinking, valuing, and behaving are normal and right. For example, when we hear someone talking with an accent, we are likely to think how strange it sounds, or even how wrong or abnormal it is. How many of us realize that each of us has an accent, which probably sounds really strange to those from a different background? As a matter of fact, someone else may even have difficulty understanding what we are saying and also misinterpret our nonverbal language—communication other than with words—due to cultural differences.

After becoming aware of one's own culture, the next step is to learn various facets of others. It is important for the manager to see other cultures as objectively as possible, by realizing personal cultural biases and not passing judgment. It is also important to stress the value of diversity and an appreciation of it. By learning about another culture, it is hoped that the manager will be able to understand people from this culture better, as well as to be understood better in turn. Learning an increased awareness of another culture may include some or all of the following topics:

- Myths and stereotypes of the culture
- Linguistic differences
- Nonverbal language differences
- Values and customs
- Food likes and dislikes
- Work habits and attitude toward work

A danger in learning about any culture is that the information may be overgeneralized, thereby promoting stereotypes. It is important to keep in mind that regardless of cultural background, a person is still an individual and needs to be treated as someone with a unique personality, wants, and needs.

A manager who has become aware of other cultures is ready to practice various skills designed for interacting with individuals from another culture. These skills might include either sending and receiving or interpreting both verbal and nonverbal communication, such as handing out work assignments or listening to employees. Such multicultural management skills include the following:

Self-awareness: The recognition of one's own values, assumptions, needs, and limitations.

Culture reading: The ability to find and trace the inherent logic in each culture.

Multiple perspective: The ability to suspend judgment, remove one's own cultural filters, and see through others' eyes, or perspectives.

Intercultural communication skills: The ability to send and interpret both verbal and nonverbal messages accurately across different cultures.

Gear shifting: The ability to readjust expectations, modify plans, try out new approaches, and rebound from setbacks.

Culture shock savvy: The ability to monitor one's own adjustment to a new culture.

Relationship-building skills: The ability to relate to and inspire confidence in all kinds of people and to maintain a support system.

Intercultural facilitation skills: The ability to manage cultural differences and use them to the operation's benefit.

Teaching methods such as role playing, simulations, or case studies can be used to increase multicultural awareness and develop skills for dealing successfully in multicultural situations.

A list of tips for working effectively in a multicultural organization follows (from Shames 1986):

- Learn how people are addressed in their own language. Be aware that in other cultures the order in which names are written or spoken is different. Some cultures give one, several, or multiple names.

- Before telling a joke, consider if the joke or how it is told could offend anyone. Humor sometimes uses satire, ridicule, or stereotyping, all of which may be offensive to people from other cultures. Seemingly harmless teasing may be completely misread by other cultural groups.

- Be patient with people who do not speak your language fluently, and do not judge how they speak. It is only natural that people from other cultures will have accents, choose different words, and speak with a different tone, rhythm, and pace.

- Be aware that other cultures may handle disagreement differently. In some cultures saying "No" is frowned upon, and other signals may be used to indicate disagreement.

- Realize that other cultures may put a different value on speaking directly or expressively. For instance, in some cultures it is considered impolite to complain or admit to not understanding something.

- Get different cultural groups to work together on projects. This is an excellent way to promote understanding and friendship.

- Be cautious about the use and interpretation of gestures. Gestures, such as thumbs up, and body postures are by no means universal. For example, in the United States, a customer may gesture "one" to a server in a restaurant by putting up an index finger. In some European countries, this gesture means "two." If you misinterpret someone's gesture, apologize and ask for the meaning. Be aware that body postures, such as how you sit or stand, may have specific meanings to people in other cultures.

- Watch other people's reactions to use of space, and refrain from touching anyone until you understand the use of touching in their culture.

MANAGING PROTECTED GROUPS

Protected groups are those employees who have been given special legal considerations derived from civil rights legislation or Equal Employment Opportunity regulations (see table 1-1). Some of the protected groups are racial or ethnic minorities, women, older people (over forty years old), and the handicapped.

A myth concerning protected groups is that it is illegal to discipline or terminate them. This is incorrect. Protected groups must simply be treated on an equal basis with other employees in these matters. A manager should apply the so-called *OUCH test* when taking any type of disciplinary action:

O = Objective
U = Uniform in application
C = Consistently applied
H = Have job relatedness

This will help prevent any discriminatory actions against protected group members—and others as well.

Racial or Ethnic Minorities

In addition to previous observations about taking note of cultural diversity, some additional techniques can help to facilitate communication with employees for whom English is a second language:

1. Be simple and specific when speaking. Do not talk for too long, and encourage two-way communication. Avoid slang and figures of speech, as they may be confusing. Speak slowly and clearly. Summarize the conversation.
2. Ask for feedback. Don't ask yes or no questions, as these words are used differently in other cultures; for example, some Asians avoid the word *no*. Ask open-ended questions so the employee has to verbalize his or her understanding of the matter.
3. Provide employees with written communications before and after meetings. This technique should help to minimize misunderstandings.

Women

A legal issue related to the supervision of women is *sexual harassment*. The Equal Employment Opportunity Commission issued guidelines in 1980 on sexual harassment, indicating that it is a form of sex discrimination under Title VII of the 1964 Civil Rights Act. The EEOC defines sexual harassment as follows:

> Unwelcome sexual advances, requests for sexual favors, and other verbal or physical conduct of a sexual nature constitute sexual harassment when (1) submission to such conduct is made either explicitly or implicitly a term or condition of an individual's employment, (2) submission to or rejection of such conduct by an individual is used as the basis for employment decisions affecting such individual, or (3) such conduct has the purpose or effect of unreasonably interfering with an individual's work performance or creating an intimidating, hostile, or offensive working environment.

Any employer who knows about or should have known about such misconduct and fails to correct it is considered guilty of sexual harassment. The employer is basically responsible for guarding against sexual harassment of both female and male employees. In cases where a supervisor commits sexual harassment, the employer is guilty regardless of whether it was known or should have been known. Of interest to the hospitality manager is that employers are also guilty if they allow nonemployees, such as guests or individuals making deliveries, to harass employees sexually without immediately taking corrective action.

If the employer genuinely did not know that sexual harassment took place, liability can be averted if the company has an adequate sexual harassment policy, if the employee did not use existing grievance procedures, and if the situation is corrected immediately. If found guilty, the employer may be liable to reinstate the employee and pay back wages, lost benefits, interest, and legal fees.

Research indicates that perhaps half the women in the work force experience sexual harassment at some time. One study of the tourism industry demonstrated that sexual harassment is clearly a problem: 46 percent of the respondents reported having been subjected several times to "unwanted teasing, jokes, remarks, or questions of a sexual nature" (Fernsten, Lowry, Enghagen, and Hott 1988). If a hospitality operator wants to avoid being charged with sexual harassment, it is best to develop and implement a specific sexual harassment policy, which should include the following:

- An easy-to-understand definition of sexual harassment including the right of all employees not to be sexually harassed

- Clear-cut disciplinary guidelines for those found guilty, with flexibility for different degrees of harassment
- A formal complaint procedure, with provisions for speedy resolution
- A statement assuring protection for those who make charges, and barring any retaliatory action

Once a policy is formulated, it needs to be publicized to all employees. In particular, managers should receive in-depth training on what constitutes sexual harassment, how to prevent it, and how to investigate it when charges are made. An organization's human resource department is normally very involved in this entire process.

Older Employees

The Age Discrimination in Employment Act of 1967 allows older employees to work as long as they want to in most occupations. Older employees now represent a new labor source for hospitality operators; fast-food restaurants are actively recruiting older individuals to work part-time (see chapter 1). However, this is hardly the case in the hotel industry, where due to negative stereotypes, there is little interest in hiring employees over age sixty-five. Myths associated with older employees involve lowered productivity, higher health insurance costs, higher rates of absenteeism, and a lessened ability to train.

Following are some tips for supervising what some people call *Grampies:* Growing number over sixty who are Retired, Active, Monied People In an Excellent State (Odiorne 1988).

1. Let older employees know what is expected and how well they are performing. Note that they prefer consistency in terms of job requirements and work schedules, and generally prefer part-time hours.
2. Make them feel like part of a team, perhaps by pairing with a younger worker for training. Involve them in decision making when possible. These efforts will probably yield excellent results, as these workers need to feel accepted in the workplace and may feel inadequate compared to younger workers.
3. Recognize performance, to motivate older employees.
4. Older employees may be better matched to jobs in which the ability to work without close supervision and reliability is important, rather than in high-stress or hazardous working conditions such as unloading trucks or working on wet floors.

5. Discuss with older employees any performance or other problems. Don't have higher expectations for this group than others. Offer assistance to help resolve any problems, such as training—which is key to this group.

6. Don't patronize your older employees. Treat them with dignity and respect.

Many of the tips for supervising older employees are simply good supervisory techniques.

Handicapped Employees

A handicapped person is defined as someone with a physical or mental impairment that significantly limits one or more of life's major activities. The Rehabilitation Act of 1973 only requires federal contractors, not private employers, to hire the physically or mentally handicapped.

Another legal issue with regard to handicapped employees deals with *reasonable accommodation* which also applies to other protected groups. This refers to making adjustments, without undue hardship to the employer, in the work situation so that someone who is handicapped can satisfactorily perform a useful task. Handicapped employees do generally require more training than normal, but once trained, they tend to be very dependable and reliable.

SUMMARY

Within the next few years, according to U.S. Department of Labor forecasts, 75 percent of those entering the work force will comprise members of minorities and women. For the first time, white males are currently a minority, making up only 46 percent of the work force. This trend will continue, due to the combination of a declining and older white American population and a younger, growing minority population.

The hospitality industry has traditionally hired people from different cultural and ethnic backgrounds, as well as women. Particularly within hotel and restaurant companies with international operations, managers have had to deal with cultural diversity in the work force and among guests. Yet even in domestic companies, various ethnic and cultural groups are represented in the different departments, as can be seen in any walking tour. It is obvious that effective managing of this diversity is a requirement at all levels of a hospitality organization, and that the companies in the forefront of managing diversity will have a competitive edge.

Not that long ago, the workplace was designed to protect itself from cultural diversity, particularly women and blacks. The majority of the work force was composed of white males, who dominated all aspects of management. Some organizations are still at this stage of development. Research in this area describes organizations as being in one of three developmental stages: monocultural, nondiscriminatory, and multicultural.

To increase awareness of other cultures, a manager must first acknowledge and understand the effects of his or her own culture, then learn about other cultures, and finally practice skills needed to work with people from other cultures, such as successful communication.

Protected groups are those employees who have been given special legal considerations derived from civil rights legislation and Equal Employment Opportunity regulations (see table 1-1). Protected groups include racial or ethnic minorities, women, older people (over forty), and the handicapped. Hospitality managers need to be familiar with issues involving management of these groups.

STUDY QUESTIONS

1. Why is the composition of the work force going to change? How is it going to change?
2. What skills will be important to a manager working in a multicultural environment?
3. If you were being transferred to a hotel in Saudi Arabia, what type of training might you expect to receive?
4. Why aren't hotels keen on hiring employees over sixty-five?
5. If, after prolonged training, a handicapped employee simply can't handle food preparation in a large kitchen, what should the employer do?
6. Describe two situations that would be classified as sexual harassment.
7. Does sexual harassment involve only women?
8. What is meant by the issue of comparable worth?
9. What supervisory techniques are especially crucial to use with Grampies?
10. If you are a human resource director, how would you write and implement a sexual harassment policy?

REFERENCES

Copeland, Lennie. 1988. Learning to manage a multicultural work force. *Training* 25(5):49–56.

Fernsten, Jeffrey A., Linda L. Lowry, Linda K. Enghagen, and David D. Hott. 1988. Female managers: Perspectives on sexual harassment and career development. *Hospitality Education and Research Journal* 12(2):185–96.

Foster, Badi G., Gerald Jackson, William E. Cross, Bailey Jackson, and Rita Hardiman. 1988. Workforce diversity and business. *Training and Development Journal* 42(4):38–42.

Haimann, Theo, and Raymond L. Hilgert. 1987. *Supervision: Concepts and Practices of Management.* 4th ed. Cincinnati: South-Western Publishing Co.

Kohl, John P., and Paul S. Greenlaw. 1981. Sexual harassment and the hospitality industry. *Cornell H.R.A. Quarterly* 21(4):54–68.

McCool, Audrey C. 1988. Older workers: Understanding, reaching and using this important labor resource effectively in the hospitality industry. *Hospitality Education and Research Journal* 12(2):365–76.

Meyer, Robert, and Gerald C. Meyer. 1988. Older workers: Are they a viable labor force for the hotel community? *Hospitality Education and Research Journal* 12(2):361–64.

Odiorne, George S. 1988. Managing Grampies. *Training* 25(6):37–40.

Shames, Germaine. 1986. Training for the multicultural workplace. *Cornell H.R.A. Quarterly* 26(4):25–31.

Simons, Dr. George. 1989. *Working Together: How to Become More Effective in a Multicultural Organization.* Los Altos: Crisp Publications Inc.

Stull, James B. 1988. Giving feedback to foreign-born employees. *Management Solutions* 33(7):42–45.

Welch, Trish, and Harvey Welch, Jr. 1987. Hospitality management in a multicultural environment. *Hospitality Education and Research Journal* 11(3):159–62.

Welch, Trish, Mary Tanke, and Gerald Glover. 1988. Multicultural human resource management. *Hospitality Education and Research Journal* 12(2):337–45.

Zaccarelli, Herman E. 1987. *Checklist for Management Success in a Multi-Ethnic Business-Institutional Environment.* Winona, Minn.: Saint Mary's College of Minnesota.

Chapter 12

Building a Team

KEY QUESTIONS

1. What are teamwork and team building?
2. What are characteristics and benefits of high-performing teams?
3. How do you decide if a team approach would be beneficial?
4. How do you develop a team?
5. What skills does a team leader need to lead a team effectively?

KEY TERMS AND CONCEPTS

Teamwork

Team building

Process team

Goal team

Sequential team

Plan of action

SWOT analysis

Esprit de corps

The service economy has changed the way we work. A new work culture is centered around such objectives as more employee participation, high service standards, increased communication within an organization, and more emphasis on quality of work life. *Teamwork* fits right in with this new work culture, as it helps meet these objectives.

Teamwork can be seen, for better or for worse, in professional sports teams, families, Boy and Girl Scout troops, musical groups, and some work units. It is both complex and dynamic, or changing. In general, team members work together with an emphasis on cooperation toward reaching team goals. They understand that goals are best accomplished with mutual support. In other words, teams are interdependent working units. A team must of course have more than one individual; a group of six to ten people is often found to be a good size. Teamwork does not necessarily mean that members are physically working together; sometimes they work apart. The most noteworthy aspect of teamwork is that the results are often greater than if each person was working separately. In other words, one plus one can equal three.

Team building is a process that refers to deliberate action taken to identify and remove obstacles in order to allow for teamwork and superior performance. It is crucial in hospitality organizations, in which employees from different departments often understand their own needs and interests but not those of other departments or the operation as a whole. A department may spend much time protecting its own turf and meanwhile forget about the overall purpose of serving the guest. For example, housekeeping and maintenance are both responsible for keeping rooms in good shape, yet when a manager or guest finds a room that is not up to standards, each department tends to blame the other. Even within a department, it seems at least one shift is always complaining that an earlier shift left jobs undone. These types of problems result in poorer-quality service than if everyone worked together as a team to meet the organization's overall purpose of serving the guest.

Team building can lessen tensions between departments and improve the quality of service; there are other benefits as well.

CHARACTERISTICS AND BENEFITS OF HIGH-PERFORMING TEAMS

High-performing teams share all or most of the following characteristics:

- Productivity that is greater than the individual efforts of each member
- Shared understanding of purpose and goals
- High energy level
- Open and supportive environment in which participation is valued
- Mutual respect, trust, and warmth
- Employees involved in goal-setting and problem-solving
- High morale, group cohesiveness, and flexibility
- Examination of problems in terms of "how can we do better," not "who or what can we blame this on"

The performance of teams is evaluated periodically to make sure they are functioning at a desired level and toward stated goals.

When teams are performing well, the organization derives certain benefits. Potential benefits include increased productivity, employees with higher levels of satisfaction and motivation, and better service. In addition, communication normally increases within an organization, tensions between different work groups decrease, less supervision of employees is necessary, and management receives more employee input on various issues.

DEVELOPING A TEAM

Three different types of teams can be developed. In a *process team,* each employee applies different skills toward the team's goal. For example, in a dining room, consider the different skills that the host or hostess, server, and cook all use to give the customer a good meal. In a *goal team,* each member works independently on the same task to meet a goal. At a hotel front desk, for instance, the clerks handle similar transactions aimed at satisfactorily checking guests in and out. In a *sequential team,* each employee depends in turn on another member's performing a particular function. For instance, in a fast-food restaurant, the counter worker must wait for the grill cook to prepare the food before filling the customer's order.

Symptom of situations in which team building may be beneficial include the following:

- Poor productivity
- Increase in customer complaints
- Increase in employee complaints
- Evidence of conflicts among employees
- Confusion about assignments, roles, and goals
- Apathy and lack of involvement of employees
- Low participation in employee meetings
- Increased costs
- Defensive climate, guarded communication

When a team already exists, most of these situations result from difficulties between team members or between members and leaders. Team members may not get along, as evidenced by frequent arguments, complaints, low participation, or development of cliques; there is much disagreement, with no attempt to reach some kind of truce. Team leaders may also exhibit behavior that does not encourage teamwork, such as being insensitive, aloof, or over-managing, or not inviting employee participation.

If it is felt that team building is required, a program can be undertaken. Steps include diagnosis of team functioning, introduction of the team building concept, discussion of current team functioning (including problem-solving), and implementation/follow-up. Keep in mind that team building takes time and organizational support is essential. It also requires the leader to allow and promote employee participation and team rewards.

Diagnosis of Team Functioning

The first step entails identifying and analyzing the problem. If it is possible to see symptoms of a problem, such as a group of employees who are barely talking to one another, then the causes behind the symptoms must be uncovered. Surveys and interviews can be used to answer the following questions:

1. Does each member of the group have the same conception of its goals?
2. To what degree are the members working toward the goals?
3. To what degree is there conflict among members over how to reach the goals?
4. Why are team members having difficulty reaching the goals?
5. How well coordinated are the activities of the different members to achieve the goals?
6. To what degree are necessary resources available to the group, and are they being used?
7. Do the team's goals mesh with the organizational goals?
8. Do members have an accurate understanding of each other's roles?
9. Do members feel their roles are valued and recognized?
10. How do members feel about each other's roles?
11. Is there anyone on the team who acts as an informal leader?
12. How effective are any team leaders?
13. Are team leaders respected?
14. Do team leaders respect individuals?
15. What leadership styles are used? Are they appropriate for the team?
16. To what degree are group members encouraged to participate in discussion and made to feel that their contributions are significant and appreciated?
17. To what degree are group members encouraged to participate in decision making?
18. Do all members participate?
19. Is there a need for members to respect and listen to each other more?
20. How many members of the team do not participate?
21. Why don't they participate?
22. How sound are the team's decisions?
23. Are decisions implemented and followed up?
24. Do team members want to take responsibility for decisions?
25. How is conflict handled within the team?
26. Is there any predominant style of conflict management?

27. Does the trust level of the team help or hinder the way conflict is managed?
28. Does anyone facilitate conflict resolution?
29. To what extent is there an open, supportive, caring, and trusting environment?
30. Do the members really want to belong to the team?
31. Is there a team standard or many individual standards?
32. Where is the team's standard in relationship to the organizational goals?
33. Is there much team concern over meeting standards?

The survey is probably the most nonthreatening way to get honest input from employees. It is also very useful to collect information from a survey for subsequent use in an employee meeting, because then the leader has an idea beforehand of where the conflicts and difficulties lie. If, for instance, some of the problems employees see involve the leader, that person will be better able to respond to them after some thought.

Either the leader or a consultant can conduct interviews, mostly one-on-one, with employees and other managers. If the team leader is considered a large part of the problem, a consultant can get more honest information and participation from the employees.

Introduction of the Team Building Concept

Arrange for a meeting of all team members in a comfortable place where distractions are unlikely, and stress to team members the importance of attending the meeting. First explain the reason why the meeting was called. Next, explain what a team is and the purposes of team building. Emphasize that you want to help the group assess how it is functioning and make it function more like a team, but only if the group wants to, and then only in a manner approved by the group.

Introduce some of the topics the group could discuss, such as the clarity of the team's goals and individual roles, team leadership, participation in decision making, conflict management, group cohesiveness, and group standards. Explain that discussion on these topics may bring up concerns that the team could resolve through such problem-solving techniques as brainstorming and SWOT analysis.

Also explain ground rules to the employees. These should include no blaming or poking fun at anyone and no talking about people who are not present. Explain the importance of team members showing courtesy and respect to each other at all times.

Lastly, ask employees for their ideas on how often to meet, when, and for how long.

Discussion of Current Team Functioning

Acting as a facilitator, you need to get members to discuss the topics of importance to team functioning: the clarity of the team's goals and individual roles, team leadership, participation in decision making, conflict management, group cohesiveness, and group standards. The questions listed earlier can serve as a guideline. In each area, brainstorming and/or SWOT analyis can be used as problem-solving techniques.

In brainstorming, team members are asked to suggest solutions, all of which someone writes down. As ideas are generated, members are asked not to make judgments or comments about them; later, the ideas will be examined individually and analyzed.

SWOT analysis (fig. 12-1) examines suggested solutions for internal strengths and weaknesses and external opportunities and threats—thus the acronym SWOT. Strengths and opportunities include factors that contribute to the development of the possible solution; weaknesses and threats are barriers to its development. To perform SWOT analysis, team members need to identify a suggestion's positive strengths and opportunities, then rank them from strong to weak. Next, they do the same for weaknesses and threats. After analyzing various possibilities in this way, the team decides on a plan of action for the possibility of its choice.

Implementation

In this step the team puts into place the agreed-upon plan of action. It is crucial that everyone understands his or her role in the plan and is ready to assume it. Follow-up refers to how a team keeps score. Follow-up team sessions and/or one-on-one interviewing to assess problem resolution is the key to securing and maintaining high team performance. If goals are being met consistently, the team should be rewarded.

	Positive Forces (Advantages)	Negative Forces (Barriers)
Internal	Strengths	Weaknesses
External	Opportunities	Threats

Figure 12-1. SWOT analysis.

TEAM LEADERSHIP SKILLS

A team leader needs a number of skills in order to work effectively with the group members. Participatory skills are very important. The leader must genuinely want to listen to the employees and let them have a say in how things are run. The leader still retains as much or as little authority in the situation as desired. In many cases, a leader asks for and listens to opinion and other feedback, then lets the group decide on a course of action as long as it is within reason. The leader needs to encourage an open expression of views by asking for and drawing out opinions from all members, not just the ones who always have something to say. At the same time, the leader needs to refrain from expressing personal opinions, so as not to influence what the members say. With some hospitality teams, it takes time to get members to speak freely, because sometime in the past someone told them it was better to keep quiet and never asked them to participate, or interrupted them or made fun of their ideas when they did speak up.

Another skill a leader needs is to develop an *esprit de corps* among team members. This can be defined as a spirit of enthusiasm and commitment among group members for one another, their group, and its purposes. Esprit de corps makes a free expression of opinions, support, helpfulness, and respect among team members more likely. Within a group, the abilities of different team members will always vary, so each member ends up assuming a different work load. If the group is committed to working together, members will help each other get the job done instead of complaining to one another and the supervisor that, for example, "If Susie can't get her job done, why do I have to do it?" In a group with esprit de corps, each member does his or her best, which means some do more work than others—but this is not done grudgingly, because the team members are more concerned with having the group function well than with keeping score or keeping tabs on each member.

How does a leader build esprit de corps? There are various techniques:

Reward and praise teamwork.

Show courtesy, trust, and respect for all team members.

Have a clear team purpose, and remind members constantly of that purpose.

Encourage participation by not poking fun at what is said or interrupting when someone is talking; thank people sincerely for their involvement in the group.

Communicate openly and honestly, and listen fully.

Blend in with the group as much as possible.

Table 12-1. Interpersonal skills of a team leader

Skill Name	Skill Description	Examples
Supporting	Backing a member's right to speak and give opinions	"Thank you for your comments." "Let's look at and discuss that last comment."
Blending	Finding areas of agreement between two or more members' difference of opinion	"Let's start from where both of you agree. You do agree that . . ."
Accessing	Making sure all members are able to take part in the discussion	"Bob looks as though he has been trying to get a word in here. Let's hear from him." "Sally, you've discussed several interesting ideas. Could we get some opinions from others now?"
Confronting	Getting the group to discuss a topic it seems to be avoiding Opposing others' offensive behavior such as putting someone down, dominating a discussion, interrupting, or being negative about an idea before it is fully discussed	"Nick brought up a topic ten minutes ago that seems to be ignored." "That type of behavior makes me very uncomfortable as part of this team."
Clarifying	Stepping in to clear up the positions of two or more members disputing a topic	"I am not sure I understand what Rich and Abbey are discussing. I seem to be hearing from Rich that . . ."
Summarizing	Summing up main points, particularly when many ideas are brought up at once	"Let's state the major discussion points up to now."
Processing	Making a statement to get a discussion back on track by calling attention to what is going on	"It appears to me that no one has been able to state more than a few sentences without being interrupted by someone else."
Consensus testing	Checking with members for agreement on an issue	"Does everyone agree that . . ."

Get the team together for other events, such as social activities, sports teams, or birthday parties; start a team scrapbook and develop a team logo, to be put on T-shirts and coffee mugs. Get to know team members as individuals.

Write into job descriptions the important role of team commitment and on-the-job participation.

When meeting with the team, have ground rules set up, use an agenda, and follow other meeting guidelines (see chapter 9).

Keep commitments and expect the same from team members.

Mention periodically how highly teamwork is regarded.

Table 12-1 lists several specific interpersonal skills that a team leader needs to use.

SUMMARY

The service economy has changed the way we work. A new work culture is centered around such objectives as more employee participation, high service standards, increased communication within an organization, and more emphasis on quality of work life. Teamwork fits right in with this new work culture, as it helps meet these objectives.

Team building is a process that refers to deliberate action taken to identify and remove obstacles in order to permit teamwork and superior performance. It is crucial in hospitality organizations, in which employees from different departments often understand their own needs and interests but not those of other departments or the operation as a whole.

High-performing teams share certain characteristics, such as mutual respect and employees who are involved. When teams are performing well, the organization derives certain benefits, such as increased productivity and motivated, satisfied employees.

Team building may be beneficial in solving certain undesirable situations. There are four steps in the team-building process: diagnosis of team functioning, introduction of the team building concept, discussion of current team functioning, and implementation/follow-up. Employee involvement is vital at each stage, and increases commitment. Team building also requires certain skills of the team leader, such as those that build employee participation and esprit de corps.

STUDY QUESTIONS

1. Describe a situation in a current or past job when team building was needed.

2. How would you go about integrating new members into a housekeeping team that already exists?

3. As leader of a fast-food team, describe at least five skills you would be using.

4. What characteristics distinguish a poorly functioning team from a high-performing one?

5. As a hospitality manager, what benefits are there to you and your organization from team-building efforts?

REFERENCES

Berger, Florence, and Rachel Vanger. 1986. Building your hospitality team. *Cornell H.R.A. Quarterly* 26(4):82–90.

Blake, Robert R., Jane S. Mouton, and Robert L. Allen. 1987. *Spectacular Teamwork.* New York: John Wiley & Sons.

Buller, Paul F., and Cecil H. Bell. 1986. Effects of team building and goal setting on productivity: A field experiment. *Academy of Management Journal* 29(2): 305–328.

Cooper, Colleen R., and Mary L. Ploor. 1986. The challenges that make or break a group. *Training and Development Journal* 40(4):31–33.

Davidson, Jeffrey P. 1986. A way to work in concert. *Management World* 15(3):8–10.

Dershimer, George. 1986. Keep teams turned on. *Management World* 15(3):10–12.

Dyer, William G. 1987. *Team Building, Issues and Alternatives.* Reading, Mass.: Addison-Wesley Publishing Co.

George, Paul S. 1987. Team building without tears. *Personnel Journal* 66(11): 122–29.

Hardaker, Maurice, and Bryan K. Ward. 1987. How to make a team work. *Harvard Business Review* 65(6):112–19.

Harris, Philip R. 1986. Building a high-performance team. *Training and Development Journal* 40(4):28–29.

Johnson, Cynthia Reedy. 1986. An outline for team building. *Training* 23(1):48–52.

Maddux, Robert B. 1988. *Team Building: An Exercise in Leadership.* Los Altos: Crisp Publications, Inc.

Mossop, Mary Walsh. 1988. Total teamwork: how to be a leader, how to be a member. *Management Solutions* 33(8):3–9.

Palleschi, Patricia, and Patricia Heim. 1980. The hidden barriers to team-building. *Training and Development Journal* 34(7):14–18.

Roberts, Leonard H. 1988. Building a winning team spirit. *Restaurants USA* 8(10):15–18.

Chapter 13

Managing Change and Resolving Conflicts

KEY QUESTIONS

1. During change, what are the stages an individual goes through?
2. What are the stages of the change process within an organization?
3. How can a hospitality manager best manage change?
4. How can a hospitality manager best manage conflict?

KEY TERMS AND CONCEPTS

Organization development (OD)   Competition

Change process   Compromise

Avoidance   Collaboration

Accommodation   Confrontation

Change within any hospitality organization is a constant, a given. In order to keep up with conditions both outside and inside the organization and be competitive, change is essential. Rosabeth Moss Kanter, a Yale University professor and management consultant, wrote a book called *The Change Masters* in 1983 in which she described her research on change and innovation in over one hundred American companies. She identified those companies that are more—and less—innovative and described their characteristics. She identified the change masters as ''those people and organizations adept at the art of anticipating the need for, and of leading, productive change.''

Hospitality organizations are made up of groups of individuals, each with a personal set of needs, values, goals, and ways of doing things. Conflict originates when individuals or groups disagree over defining goals and their relative importance, or in deciding how to reach goals. In most conflicts, someone or some group feels that certain needs have been denied. As with change, conflict is inevitable; it often occurs due to change.

Conflict is often seen as destructive, which it can be when it deteriorates trust, cooperation, motivation, and productivity. Conflict is not always destructive, however, and can in fact be constructive, depending upon how it is managed. When conflict is well managed, it can be beneficial—for instance, when it leads to improved results and increased understanding.

Sources of conflict within an organization may include personality differences or clashes, the sharing of resources, differing information, the reaching of goals, and contrasting perceptions, attitudes, and points of view. Conflicts may be within an individual, between two or more individuals, between individuals and groups, or between groups. Symptoms of conflict include tensions, poor communication, unfinished work, falling productivity, poor morale, increasing costs, and more frequent accidents. Conflict may be expressed openly or suppressed; the latter creates a greater problem for the organization.

Organization development (OD) refers to a contemporary approach to helping groups operate more skillfully, such as during times of change and conflict. OD programs are intended to bring about the reduction of conflict and increased ability to respond to the fast pace of change.

THE CHANGE CYCLE

People pass through four phases when they are faced with change: fear, resistance, exploration or resignation, and commitment (fig. 13-1). How quickly and easily certain employees go through this process depends on their readiness for change, evaluation of the benefits and efforts it will require, and ability to adapt.

Fear is often the first reaction to an announcement of change, particularly when the change is unexpected or unexplained. Employees may have a fear of the unknown (such as when a new owner or manager takes over), of losing the routine and familiar and having to do something differently (such as when a new menu is instituted), or of possible incompetence (such as when the front desk switches from a manual to a computerized operation).

The second phase sees resistance to change. Besides the fears just mentioned, common causes for resistance include

- Misunderstanding and lack of trust (often due to poor communication)
- Time and effort required to adjust to change
- Self-interest or group interest
- Differing assessments or perspectives on the situation

Figure 13-1. Change cycle.

It is worth noting that an employee may have difficulty explaining resistance to a change and being totally honest about it. For example, an employee upset about the time and effort required to learn a new procedure might say only that the procedure is going to take longer. A common refrain heard during this phase is, "But we've always done it this way."

In the third phase, employees either explore the change further or resign themselves to it. By now, some time has passed, during which they have had to make adjustments. People start to realize the changes are here to stay and there doesn't seem to be any going back to the old ways. Resistance significantly decreases; however, this should not be interpreted universally as acceptance, because some people intend only grudging compliance. During this stage, these individuals often do no more than what they absolutely must—frequently while looking for other employment. Other individuals, meanwhile, actively explore the nature of the change and experience a transition to the final stage of the change cycle.

In the fourth and final phase, employees start to commit themselves to the change. As time goes on, the change becomes more routine. Employees will naturally move to this stage at different times. This phase is marked by a lack of complaining or longing about the old ways. Employees become able to identify with and refocus their efforts on the new set of expectations.

GUIDELINES FOR MANAGING CHANGE

In order to increase the possibility of implementing change successfully, it is best to organize the *change process* into three stages: preliminary, transitional, and consolidating. Only necessary and useful changes should be made in an organization, and change should be by gradual evolution, not sudden revolution. There are specific guidelines for handling each stage.

Preliminary Stage

This stage occurs after there has been a realization that some type of change needs to occur, and before an actual change is implemented. The key in this stage is to build support for the change; there are several other important guidelines as well:

1. Gain the support of key people who have influence in the areas likely to be affected.

2. Create an awareness for the need to change. Discuss with employees the need for, and reasons behind, the change.

3. Communicate the need for change—well in advance of the implementation date—with the expectation that it will succeed and will improve a situation. Acknowledge both the benefits—such as improved customer service or procedures that require less time—and short-term difficulties involved in making the change.

4. Ask employees to participate to the furthest extent possible in the decision about how the change will be made. This stimulates employees to discuss, make suggestions, and think positively about the change, discourages resistance, and encourages employee commitment to the change rather than mere compliance.

5. Help employees see how the proposed change will affect them, both directly and indirectly.

6. Make sure there is some kind of reward available for employees involved in the change; for example, recognition from management, training in new skills, or emotional support. The question from employees that sounds like "What's in it for me?" needs to be addressed ahead of time. Having rewards tells the employees that management acknowledges the difficulties of the transition phase, and gives them a sense of progress.

7. Allow employees to air their feelings about the change. If employees are not allowed to complain openly, they will gripe to their co-workers, which will affect morale.

During this stage, frequent meetings of small groups of employees are essential to good communication. A final plan should also be drawn up, detailing exactly how the change will occur, including an activity plan that describes who does what, when, where, and how. This plan should be communicated in training sessions and visibly posted. Adequate training is crucial to the next stage.

Transitional Stage

During this stage, two processes occur at the same time: the operation continues to serve guests and operate normally, while at the same time, change is introduced into one or more areas that potentially could disrupt normal activities. To maneuver successfully through this stage, follow these guidelines:

1. Keep employees fully informed of everything going on, through periodic progress reports.

2. Continue to ask employees for advice and help when appropriate.

3. Managers should be very visible in leading the change effort and very supportive of both the change and the employees' own efforts. Let them know how important their work is and how much it is appreciated. Use rewards.

4. Continue to remind the employees of the need for change and its benefits.

5. Constantly monitor and evaluate how things are going.

During this phase, resistance is commonly felt. Table 13-1 reviews methods for dealing with resistance to change.

Consolidating Phase

At this point, the change has been implemented, but there are certainly still bugs to be worked out. New procedures written out on paper don't always survive the test of being used day-in and day-out in operations. The original plan most likely needs to be modified in places, with employee input.

In this stage, it is appropriate to evaluate the change by answering several questions, including the following:

1. Did the change solve the problems it was meant to?

2. What did the change fail to accomplish, and why?

3. Are the benefits of this change still worth the costs involved?

4. How has this change affected the employees involved?

5. What bugs still need to be worked out?

A final question to ask during this stage is if the employees were adequately involved and rewarded, through forms of positive reinforcement (see chapter 10).

GUIDELINES FOR MANAGING CONFLICT

Robert Blake and Jane Mouton have described five methods of handling conflict: *avoidance, accommodation, competition, compromise,* and *collaboration*. According to this model, an employee who has a conflict with someone will react in one of these five ways.

In avoidance, the employee either withdraws from the conflict or refuses to take a position in the matter. The employee does not try to understand the nature of the conflict, and if asked about it may deny it exists.

Table 13-1. Methods for dealing with resistance to change

Approach	When Used	Advantages	Drawbacks
Education and communication	Where there is inaccurate information and analysis or a lack of information.	Once persuaded, people will often help with the implementation of the change.	Can be very time-consuming if lots of people are involved.
Participation and involvement	Where the initiators do not have all the information they need to design the change, and where others have considerable power to resist.	People who participate will be committed to implementing change, and any relevant information they have will be integrated into the change plan.	Can be very time-consuming if participators design an inappropriate change.
Facilitation and support	Where people are resisting because of adjustment problems.	No other approach works as well with adjustment problems.	Can be time-consuming, expensive, and still fail.
Negotiation and agreement	Where someone or some group will clearly lose out in a change, and where that group has considerable power to resist.	Sometimes it is a relatively easy way to avoid major resistance.	Can be too expensive in many cases if it alerts others to negotiate for compliance.
Manipulation and co-optation	Where other tactics will not work, or are too expensive.	It can be a relatively quick and inexpensive solution to resistance problems.	Can lead to future problems if people feel manipulated.
Explicit and implicit coercion	Where speed is essential, and the change initiators possess considerable power.	It is speedy, and can overcome any kind of resistance.	Can be risky if it leaves people mad at the initiators.

Source: Reprinted by permission of *Harvard Business Review.* An exhibit from "Methods for dealing with resistance to change" by John P. Kotter and Leonard A. Schlesinger, March/April 1979. Copyright © 1979 by the President and Fellows of Harvard College; all rights reserved.

In accommodation, the employee again does not confront the issue, but instead disregards personal concerns and simply allows the other party to succeed. Differences are either not brought up or are downplayed so as to reach an agreement. Accommodation may take the form of obeying a manager's instructions.

Competition is the typical win-lose approach, in which each party comes out fighting to win and wants the other to lose. Compromise is not possible, and winning is all right even if it is at the expense of the other party.

Compromise can occur when each party is willing to give in to some extent about personal objectives. The solution may not fully satisfy both parties, but everyone agrees it is the best way to resolve the conflict.

In collaboration, there is a mutual tackling of the problem, and each party understands and accepts the other's objectives as both work together so they can both win. This method requires a good deal of maturity, trust, and honesty.

Table 13-2 describes various situations in which to use one of the five conflict-handling methods.

When dealing with conflict, the hospitality manager often needs to facilitate a resolution. Following are six steps in a typical confrontation:

1. *Becoming aware:* One of the parties (Party A) learns of a conflict.

2. *Deciding to confront:* Party A decides not to avoid the problem, but to confront the other party (Party B) with it.

3. *Confronting:* Party A confronts Party B. At this point, Party B may use any of the five methods of handling conflict. The conflict is often resolved at this step. The manager needs to be sure that both parties are really satisfied with the outcome. If the problem is not resolved, further steps are usually taken.

4. *Determining the nature and causes of the conflict:* At this stage, both parties need to discuss in detail what is going on, including their perceptions, feelings, and fears about the situation. This needs to be done without criticism or finger pointing. The confrontation will have failed if both parties cannot agree on what the problem is and why it is happening.

5. *Problem solving:* Both parties now can work on how to fix the problem.

6. *Following through:* To be sure that each party did what was agreed to, the manager should check to confirm that agreements are being kept.

If the manager has to step in to help resolve the conflict, he or she should follow certain guidelines:

1. Establish ground rules. For example: no hostility; one person speaks at a time; treat each other with respect; keep to the topic at hand and don't

Table 13-2.   Situations in which to use one of the five conflict-handling modes

Conflict Mode	Situation
Avoidance	When an issue is trivial, or more important issues are pressing
	When one perceives no chance of satisfying personal concerns
	When potential disruption outweighs the benefits of resolution
	To let people cool off and regain perspective
	When gathering information supersedes immediate decision
	When others can resolve the conflict more effectively
Accommodation	When one finds he or she is wrong—to allow a better position to be heard, to learn, and to show reasonableness
	When issues prove to be more important to others—to satisfy them and maintain cooperation
	To build social credits for later issues
	To minimize loss when outmatched and failing
	When harmony and stability are especially important
	To allow subordinates to develop by learning from mistakes
Competition	When quick, decisive action is vital, such as emergencies
	On important issues where unpopular actions need implementing, such as cost cutting, enforcing unpopular rules, discipline
	On issues vital to company welfare when one knows he or she is right
	Against people who take advantage of noncompetitive behavior
Compromise	When goals are important, but not worth the effort
	When opponents with equal power are committed to mutually exclusive goals
	To achieve temporary settlements of complex issues
	To arrive at an expedient solution under time pressure
	As a backup when collaboration or competition is unsuccessful
Collaboration	To find an integrative solution when both sets of concerns are too important to be compromised
	When the objective is to learn
	To merge insights from people with different perspectives
	To gain commitment by incorporating concerns into a consensus
	To work through feelings that have interfered with a relationship

Source: Thomas, Kenneth W. 1977. Toward multidimensional values in teaching: the example of conflict behavior. Academy of Management Review 2(3):487.

bring up past problems; no finger pointing, or attempting to blame anyone; this is not a win-lose situation; focus on issues and not on personalities; listen.

2. Create a supportive environment in which employees are encouraged to express themselves and participate. This will only enhance problem resolution. Emphasize operational goals, teamwork, and areas of agreement.

3. Control discussions and maintain order. Act as a moderator to help the employees find and agree upon a reasonable solution. Don't take sides. Avoid ordering a solution.

4. Allow the expression of anger and frustration in a constructive way so tensions lessen.

5. Direct but don't evaluate the quality of a party's efforts at resolving the conflict.

6. When there are deadlocks, suggest ways to break it.

7. Separate issues into their components, and deal with one at a time.

8. Check that each group totally understands what the other is saying.

9. Avoid premature resolutions.

10. Follow up to see that the resolution has been implemented correctly.

For the manager to create and maintain employees' trust, he or she must make sure that each party lives up to the resolution. This can best be done by documenting solutions and evaluating outcomes.

Although conflict resolution skills are important, time should be more efficiently used to prevent conflicts from occurring. Techniques of conflict prevention include good communication, flexibility, clarity about organizational objectives and job roles, and development of a positive, motivating organizational climate.

SUMMARY

Change within any hospitality organization is a constant, a given. In order to keep up with conditions both outside and inside the organization and be competitive, change is essential. Hospitality organizations are made up of groups of individuals, each with a personal set of needs, values, goals, and ways of doing things. Conflict originates when individuals or groups disagree over defining goals and their relative importance or deciding how to reach goals. In most conflicts, someone or some group feels that specific needs have been denied. As with change, conflict is inevitable, and it often occurs due to change.

People pass through four phases when they are faced with change: fear, resistance, exploration or resignation, and commitment. How quickly and easily certain employees go through this process depends on their readiness for change, evaluation of the benefits and efforts it will require, and ability to adapt.

In order to increase the possibility of change being implemented successfully, it is best to organize the change process into three stages: preliminary, transitional, and consolidating. Only necessary and useful changes should be made in an organization, and change should be by evolution, not revolution. There are guidelines for handling each stage.

Robert Blake and Jane Mouton have described five methods of handling conflict: avoidance, accommodation, competition, compromise, and collaboration. Following this model, when an employee has a conflict with someone, he or she will react in one of these five ways. Managers need to learn how to move individuals or groups through the conflict process, and also how to facilitate this when there is a problem.

STUDY QUESTIONS

1. Describe how changes have occurred in a current or previous job. Were they handled properly?
2. Describe the stages of change.
3. What can you do as a manager to implement this change with the least disruption of service and with attention to your employees' needs: the front desk of a hotel is going to be converted from a manual to a computerized system; in other words, all the transactions previously completed by hand will now need to be entered into the computer. Include how you would handle resistance to this change.
4. When faced with conflict, what are each of the five methods you may use to deal with it?
5. What can you do as a hospitality manager to facilitate conflict resolution?

REFERENCES

Ackerman, Linda S. 1986. Change management: Basics for training. *Training and Development Journal* 40(4):67–68.

Baker, H. Kent, and Philip Morgan. 1986. Building a professional image: Handling conflict. *Supervisory Management* 31(2):24–29.

Broadwell, Martin M. ed. 1985. *Supervisory Handbook.* New York: John Wiley & Sons.

Bryant, Jeff D. 1987. How to manage employee conflict. *Restaurants USA* 7(9): 16–19.

Davis, Keith, and John W. Newstrom. 1985. *Human Behavior at Work: Organizational Behavior.* New York: McGraw-Hill.

Gordon, Bonnie. 1988. Settling conflicts among your workers. **Nation's Business** 76(3):70–71.

Hampton, David R. 1986. **Management.** New York: McGraw-Hill.

Johnson, Homer H., and Alan J. Fredian. 1986. Simple rules for complex change. **Training and Development Journal** 40(8):47–49.

Kanter, Rosabeth Moss. 1983. **The Change Masters: Innovation for Productivity in the American Corporation.** New York: Simon and Schuster.

Kindler, Herbert S. 1988. **Managing Disagreement Constructively.** Los Altos: Crisp Publications, Inc.

Kirkpatrick, Donald L. 1987. **How to Manage Change Effectively.** San Francisco: Jossey-Bass Publishing.

Kotter, John P., and Leonard A. Schlesinger. 1979. Choosing strategies for change. **Harvard Business Review** 57(2):106–14.

Miller, J. Thomas. 1988. Change: Getting them to meet you half way. **Supervisory Management** 33(7):37–41.

Muniz, Peter, and Robert Chasnoff. 1986. Assessing the causes of conflicts—and confronting the real issues. **Supervisory Management** 31(3):34–39.

Oromaner, David S. 1985. Winning employee cooperation for change. **Supervisory Management** 30(12):18–23.

Scott, Cynthia D., and Dennis T. Jaffee. 1988. Survive and thrive in times of change. **Training and Development Journal** 42(4):25–27.

Stamatis, D. H. 1987. Conflict: You've got to accentuate the positive. **Personnel** 64(12):47–50.

Thomas, K. W. 1977. Toward multi-dimensional values in teaching: The example of conflict behaviors. **Academy of Management Review** 2(3):484–90.

Walton, Richard E. 1987. **Managing Conflict.** Reading, Mass.: Addison-Wesley Publishing Co.

Wilcox, James R., Ethel M. Wilcox, and Karen M. Cowan. 1986. Communicating creatively in conflict situations. **Supervisory Management** 31(10):18–25.

Chapter 14

Disciplining Employees

KEY QUESTIONS

1. What is the nature and purpose of discipline?
2. Why don't employees do what they are supposed to do?
3. What are the steps in the process of discipline and how is each performed?
4. What is employment-at-will and just cause, and how do they relate to termination?
5. What is the manager's role in discipline?
6. How does positive discipline differ from negative discipline?

KEY TERMS AND CONCEPTS

Negative discipline

Positive discipline

Minor infractions

Major infractions

Disciplinary guidelines

Progressive discipline

Grievances

Open-door policy

Documentation

Employment-at-will doctrine

Just cause

Employee discipline is one of the more undesirable and difficult tasks managers have, but though it may not be easy, it is crucial to good management. Discipline is a process that aims to clarify, correct, and improve inappropriate job-related conduct and behavior through rewards and sometimes penalties. In addition, a discipline system should include praise for employees' performance. A healthy discipline system can actually create employee commitment to the organization and its goals.

Discipline can be approached in both negative and positive ways. *Negative discipline* means a manager uses punishment to discourage an employee from making another mistake. In addition to written disciplinary warnings and suspensions from work, other punitive approaches used include reprimands, sarcasm, and threats of firing.

Disadvantages of punishment include that it tends to produce only a short-term change in behavior, it does little to point out or strengthen desirable behavior, and it can create fear and frustration, which may be transformed into aggressive behavior and withdrawal. The threat of punishment also must always be present for the employee to keep in line, and punishment may be ineffective with some employees. Does an employee who returns from a three-day suspension without pay usually feel great about the organization and endeavor to do a great job? Actually, employees frequently feel that once they've endured their punishment, the score is even and nothing more needs to be done.

On the other hand, *positive discipline* tries to create an organizational climate in which employees willingly abide by policies and procedures. Positive discipline uses encouragement instead of punishment and reminders rather than reprimands. It is based on the idea that the employee is responsible for his or her own conduct.

Many of the methods used to deal with problem employee performance can be viewed as either negative or positive, depending upon the intent and how it is carried out. If the intent is punishment, it is viewed as negative. If the intent is to help the employee change behavior, it is viewed as positive. A positive approach is preferable, although there are certainly situations when punishment is appropriate.

WHY EMPLOYEES DO NOT DO WHAT THEY SHOULD

It is important to remember that many times when employees make mistakes, it is not their fault. Why don't employees do what they should? Here are some common reasons:

They don't know what to do: Their training was perhaps poor or nonexistent, or performance standards were not made clear. Before asking an employee to perform a job well and follow the organization's rules, the manager must communicate all expectations and check that the employer actually does understand them. A well-written job description is a start.

They don't know how they are performing: Employees need feedback while they are working in order to understand what constitutes appropriate and inappropriate behavior. A performance management system that includes strong informal review goes a long way toward making employees aware of their conduct. Positive reinforcement, such as praise, increases the chances of their repeating the right behavior. When managers ignore problem behavior, they are allowing incompetence, which is really their fault.

They don't know why they are doing it: If employees understand why a certain task has to be done, or why it should be done a certain way, they are much more likely to do it right.

Expectations are unrealistic and unreasonable: At times, due to job design or lack of supplies or equipment, managers ask employees to perform jobs that simply can't be done. For instance, banquet cooks may be asked to prepare a meal that requires more oven space than the facility has; when there are complaints of cold food from a few guests, it is blamed on the cooking staff. It is unrealistic to expect an employee to accomplish more than can reasonably be done or to work under poor conditions.

There is a mismatch between the employee and the job: The employee may be overqualified or underqualified for the job, resulting in poor performance in either case. In the hospitality field, sometimes an employee who prefers to work alone is hired to work directly with guests. This problem will come out soon and may be blamed on the employee, rather than the selection of the wrong employee for the position.

They are not properly motivated: The reasons for this can range from being lazy to being bored and not seeing any chance of growth. In some cases, managers can do much to improve an employee's motivational level; in other cases, very little (see chapter 10).

In almost all these situations, management can do much to correct the problems.

THE PROCESS OF DISCIPLINE

Discipline is a process involving a number of steps: establishing what constitutes problem behavior, formulating disciplinary guidelines for handling each problem, and communicating these expectations to the employees; when a problem occurs, investigating the problem, interviewing the employee, deciding on the appropriate action and implementing it, and documenting the process; and finally, follow-up is of course crucial. Each of these steps requires more detailed examination.

Establish Nature of Problem Behavior

Problem behavior runs the gamut from excessive tardiness to theft of the employer's property. Besides attendance problems, there are typically concerns about performance and honesty. Some organizations categorize disciplinary problems as *minor infractions, major infractions,* and causes for immediate discharge. Minor infractions do little harm to the operation but can be serious if they occur frequently or together with another infraction. Examples include unexcused absences or latenesses, leaving the work area without permission, or taking long breaks. Major infractions interfere substantially with operations; they might include discourtesy to customers or refusal to do something. Causes for immediate discharge may be actions that are illegal or put someone in danger, such as theft or possession of drugs on company property.

Set Disciplinary Guidelines

Disciplinary guidelines stating how to handle each problem or each category of offenses (table 14-1) should be written in unambiguous language for managers and employees alike to read and use. They should also be fair, realistic, and reasonably related to the safe and efficient operation of the business. It is unlikely that any set of guidelines can cover all circumstances that may arise; on the other hand, they should not be too general.

When establishing disciplinary guidelines, most employers use a *progressive discipline* system. Progressive discipline applies corrective measures, such as counseling, in increasing degrees or steps. In other words, an employee is rarely terminated for a first offense; instead, the worker is given several opportunities to correct the behavior before anything like suspension or termination would occur.

The purpose of progressive discipline is to get the employee to correct behavior voluntarily. An example of a progressive discipline system is to use first oral warnings or counseling in response to problem behavior, then a written warning, suspension, and finally termination. At each step in the progressive discipline, the intent is to help the employee get back on track.

Any system of disciplinary guidelines must include a procedure so that an employee can appeal a disciplinary decision. Appeals are also called *grievances,* a term used more frequently in unionized organizations (see chapter 5). Managers, particularly supervisory ones, need training in how to handle grievances. They also need to encourage the use of an appeal process when an employee does not feel he or she has been treated fairly, as well as to assure employees that there will be no retaliation for making an appeal.

Some organizations attempt to resolve grievances through what is called an *open-door policy,* in which managers above the immediate supervisor are identified as the people whom employees may contact with a grievance. The purpose of an open-door policy is to increase communication and give employees the feeling that they can resolve problems at work even when the supervisor is not supportive. Unfortunately, this policy frequently has problems with it, because either managers don't really keep their doors open or the employees feel awkward using it; members of the management team also may be inconsis-

Table 14-1. Disciplinary guidelines

Type of Problem and Discipline	Examples
Minor infractions: will result in oral counseling and, if repeated, will lead to written warnings, suspension, and finally termination	Excessive absenteeism Excessive lateness Poor job performance Failure to report a work-related injury or accident promptly Improper use of company telephones Abuse of break times and meal periods Leaving assigned work area without supervisor's permission Violation or neglect of safety rules or contributing to hazardous conditions
Major infractions: will result in a written warning and possibly immediate suspension or termination	Refusal to carry out reasonable assignments from an authorized supervisor Discourteous treatment of guests or other employees, including harassing, coercing, threatening, or intimidating others Physical altercations Intoxication or incapacity on duty due to the use of alcohol or drugs Negligence that results in injury to oneself, another employee, or a guest Sleeping while on duty Fighting on company property
Causes for immediate discharge	Knowingly falsifying employment records such as time-worked records Unauthorized destruction or removal of company property Unauthorized punching of another employee's time card Possession, display, or use of firearms or other dangerous weapons while on company property Possession of alcohol or drugs while on company property

tent in giving decisions, which employees might then use to their advantage. In order for an open-door policy to work, there must be managers who support the policy and are consistent, fair, and open-minded.

Communicate Disciplinary Guidelines

Employees need to know what is expected of them in order to function appropriately on the job. A manager's expectations of an employee generally encompass the following: an honest day's work for an honest day's pay, punctuality, respect for authority, and cooperation with others to get the job done.

In order to communicate disciplinary guidelines adequately, it is a good idea to start with new employees, who need to be acquainted with the expectations of both their jobs and the organization. Job expectations are communicated through the job description and standards of performance (see chapter 2). Disciplinary guidelines should be reviewed during orientation and a copy inserted into the employee handbook given to all new employees. Guidelines should be reviewed with all employees at least annually, both as a general reminder and to allow for employees' questions. The reason for each guideline should be explained. Employees are much more likely to follow rules when they know why those rules are important.

Investigation

The purpose of an investigation is to get the facts, not to draw conclusions; that will come later. Remember, an employee should be considered innocent until proven guilty. An investigation into misconduct should be addressed as soon after the fact as possible, obtaining information from anyone who can provide any.

Review the person's employment record, including recent performance evaluations and documentation of any prior problems. Discuss this person's performance and work record with any former managers and human resource managers. Consider an employee's overall employee record and contributions to the employer.

Interview

Before going into an interview, an employee may ask to bring a representative along. Both union and nonunion employees have the right to have a representative present for an investigatory interview if it may result in discipline. Of course, this is necessary only if the employee requests it.

Of key importance in this process is to sit down with an open mind and discuss the situation with the employee. This should be done in a timely manner, as it is not fair to inform an employee that there was a concern, say, three months ago. But if the situation was somewhat emotional and, for instance, tempers flared, it is best to wait until everything has cooled down. The steps in the interview process are to state the problem, listen to the employee, reach agreement on the problem, derive a solution to which all parties agree, and set a follow-up date.

When opening the interview, try to create an informal and nonthreatening atmosphere. Remember to criticize not the person but the behavior, and always work on maintaining the employee's self-esteem. Also keep emotions under control, don't argue, and stick to the subject matter at hand. Be sure to preface the statement of the problem with an explanation that the employee will get to tell his or her side next. Present the problem and any pertinent facts in a nonjudgmental fashion, and explain how the problem relates to the expectation of the employee; for example, "Are you aware that we have found an unusually high number of errors in your night audit over the past few weeks?"

Next, ask the employee to give his or her side, or view of the problem and its causes. The manager needs to sit back and listen with an open mind, asking open-ended questions to clarify as needed, such as "What are the circumstances that may be contributing to this?" Discuss the reasons for the problem and factors that affect it, trying constantly to reach an agreement. Employees may mention personal reasons as causes; if so, refer the worker to an employee assistance program counselor, if one is available (see chapter 7). If not, and the problem is minor, such as the employee is late due to a car that's in the shop for a few weeks, the manager may be able to help.

If there is no agreement on the nature of the problem, such as employee rudeness to guests, the manager will have to end the meeting, reach a decision about what to do, and get back to the employee. Even if there is agreement, the manager may want some time to decide how to handle this situation. The manager may also decide to continue with the discussion and assist the employee in thinking of possible solutions. The primary responsibility for this is on the employee, who needs to show commitment during this phase to resolve the problem. This includes developing a plan of action, including how and when follow-up will be done, with the manager again assisting the employee in the process. Before ending the meeting, it is a good idea to ask the employee to state his or her understanding of the problem and the plan of action. This helps reinforce ownership of, or responsibility for, the problem. If no agreement is possible on a plan of action, the manager will have to decide what to do.

Decision Making

Before making a decision, the manager should thoroughly discuss the situation with other managers, including a human resource manager if possible, to ensure that any actions are consistent, fair, and appropriate within the organization. If decisions are not applied consistently, employees will be uncertain about what types of behavior are unacceptable. Inconsistency and excessive discipline also weaken employees' trust in the fairness of the manager and commitment to the organization.

Also consider whether the employee has been adequately forewarned about the consequences of such behavior. Especially in the case of termination, if the employee was not forewarned, the termination would probably be reversed in court. Additionally, if employees are surprised by disciplinary measures, it creates distrust and sometimes fear.

Extenuating circumstances need to be examined as well. Perhaps a manager or another worker provoked an employee's behavior, for instance. Also consider to what extent the behavior varies from desired performance and how significant such behavior is.

When making an employee aware of the decision, the manager should explain the reasons for it, too. The manager also must always invite the employee to use the appeal procedure, and explain how to do so.

Documentation

Documentation of the entire disciplinary process is a vital managerial function. Adequate documentation is needed in order to terminate an employee and make it hold up in court, if necessary. Documentation is also essential for a successful performance appraisal system. Following are tips on how to document:

1. Document performance as quickly as possible and date it.
2. Be specific about what the employee did and the circumstances under which the behavior occurred. Be accurate and behavior-oriented. Document thoroughly and include who, when, where, and how. Only include relevant information.
3. Opinions and hearsay have no place in documentation; note only facts, behavior, and direct observations, not inferences or impressions. Strive to be objective and clear.
4. Be consistent by recording both positive and negative performance, and by documenting in the same manner for all employees.
5. Describe the significance of the behavior as compared to expected performance.
6. Document all information revealed in the investigation as well as obtained from the employee during the interview.
7. Document any disciplinary action or action the employee must take, as well as consequences if improvement is not made. Make note of a follow-up date.
8. Employees should be encouraged to make written comments on all written disciplinary notices.

TERMINATION

Termination refers to an employee leaving his or her job. There are five types of termination: Voluntary termination, such as quitting or retiring; termination due to employee's failure to meet expectations; firing or immediate dismissal; layoff; and position elimination. In a layoff, an employee may be recalled to work. In a position elimination, a recall will not occur.

The relationship between employer and employee has long followed the *employment-at-will doctrine*. This doctrine states that either the employer or the employee is free to sever the employment relationship at any time, without notice or reason, as long as there is no employment contract requiring a specific duration of employment.

The courts have made judgments fairly recently that erode the employment-at-will doctrine. The courts have supported employees who were dismissed for refusing to behave illegally or for acting in the public interest. Employees have also found support when they were terminated in spite of an implied contract between employer and employee that employment was to continue unless there was a just or reasonable cause or when termination was motivated by bad faith or unfair dealing.

Some employers are trying to protect their at-will prerogative by asking employees to sign at-will statements on their employment application form. Such a statement may take this form:

> In consideration of my employment, I agree to conform to the rules and regulations of ABC Hotels, and my employment and compensation can be terminated, with or without cause, and with or without notice, at any time, at the option of either ABC Hotels or myself.

Some human resource specialists feel that this type of statement will be outlawed in the future as a condition of employment. In any case, it is probably sufficient for an employer to state clearly in personnel policies and procedures that a contract between employer and employee is not implied and that the company has the right to change its policies at any time.

Other employers prefer to apply and uphold a *just cause* standard in their discipline and discharge policies. This approach is certainly the best for the employee. It is also the best approach for the hospitality employer, who is sure to lose applicants if they are required to sign at-will statements or are told that their jobs can be terminated at any time. Remember, too, that the objective of a disciplinary procedure is to retain the employee, because it is expensive to hire and train workers. Termination should be used only when the employee has destroyed his or her ability to contribute to the organization.

The courts have never denied the right to dismiss an employee for just cause. When doing so, the manager needs to be able to answer yes to each of the following questions:

1. Considering the employee's past record and any possible extenuating circumstances, does termination fit the infraction?
2. Did the employee have advance notice of the rules, and was he or she forewarned of the consequences of violating them?
3. Were management's expectations of the employee reasonable?
4. Did management make a reasonable effort to help the employee resolve the problem before termination, and is there proof of this?
5. Was management's investigation of the final offense made in a fair and objective manner, and did it involve someone other than the employee's direct supervisor?
6. Has this employee been treated like others in similar circumstances?

Another thing to consider before terminating an employee is to look at other alternatives; these might include transfer to another position or demotion. Some employees may do very well either in a different position, which may even be in another location, or in a less demanding and stressful job.

If, however, termination proves necessary, the manager should follow these guidelines for conducting an effective termination meeting:

1. Hold the meeting in a private place where there will be no interruptions. Such privacy is unlikely in one's office, so choose another room.
2. Check the timing of the meeting. Don't have the meeting on a holiday, the employee's birthday, or any other special occasion. Also avoid termination when the employee has recently been involved in union organizing, has filed a complaint with the EEOC, or is able to become eligible for a company-sponsored benefit, such as becoming vested in a pension plan. Although Friday seems to be a favorite day for terminations, probably a better time is earlier in the week, to allow the employee the opportunity to get right to the task of finding another job. Choosing a time at the end of the day is probably best, as it allows the employee to get belongings together without undue attention from peers.
3. Before having the meeting, be sure there is confirmation for the action from top management, and probably human resources. Be sure all the paperwork for employees leaving the company, such as benefit continuance forms, is completed.

4. Plan to have another manager or human resource person present as a witness during the meeting. Keep news of the impending termination as private as possible.

5. State directly the decision to terminate and the reasons for it. Be firm yet tactful. Discuss some of the employee's good qualities and skills. Make it clear this decision is final. Explain when it is effective.

6. Expect the employee to be upset, emotional, and irrational. Let the employee vent some anger, and listen. Answer any of the questions the employee may have. Treat the employee with respect.

7. Explain how reference inquiries will be handled and give the employee the opportunity to speak to someone in human resources or a supervisor, if the individual so desires.

8. Explain when any benefits will run out and the terms, if applicable, of any severance pay. Keys must be turned in and so forth. It may be best at this point to let someone from human resources handle the situation.

9. Management may want the employee escorted out, by someone from human resources, for example, if it is felt the individual may cause problems.

Some managers also feel it is a good idea after terminating someone to let other employees know informally that it occurred and why. This will clear the air and offset rumors.

THE MANAGER'S ROLE IN DISCIPLINE

The manager plays a most pivotal role in administering discipline fairly and consistently. Unfortunately, many managers don't want to discipline, for example, the server who comes in late several times a week or the maintenance person who never seems to get anything fixed, yet uses excessive overtime. Managers often want to be a "good guy," and think that the employees will dislike them if they follow the disciplinary guidelines. It is also difficult for many managers to confront an employee with a problem, and because many managers have been unable to do so in the past, that only makes it harder for one to do so in the present. Managers may also feel inadequate about how to handle disciplinary problems if they have had little training in this area.

Managers, particularly supervisory ones, can do much to reduce disciplinary problems. Here are some managerial techniques that can help prevent disciplinary problems from happening:

1. Be thorough in the selection process (see chapter 1) to ensure hiring the right people. Use techniques that make the process more foolproof: longer interviews, multiple interviews and interviewers, early-morning interviews (if the applicant is late, forget about that person), and thorough reference checking.

2. Be sure to have a probationary period for new employees, in which either party can terminate the relationship for any reason during a specified period of time, usually the first sixty to ninety days. Use the probationary period to weed out employees whose performance is borderline or worse. If in doubt, extend the probationary period.

3. Be visible and build a positive atmosphere. Be friendly and approachable, and talk to all employees as equals.

4. Respect the employees and treat them like adults. Don't have favorites.

5. Make sure all expectations and standards are known and are in writing. Also be sure consequences are communicated.

6. Give plenty of praise. Always praise in public and criticize in private.

7. Communicate on a regular basis to all employees.

8. Set a good example.

9. Orient and train all employees adequately. Give employees the opportunity to learn more and better themselves in the organization.

10. Have strong supervisory managers who practice fair and consistent management and are not afraid to confront problem performance and behavior.

POSITIVE DISCIPLINE

Positive discipline is based on the idea that employees are responsible for their own conduct, including correcting it when appropriate. In other words, employees are treated as adults. This type of discipline has been used with professionals as well as nonsupervisory employees. Instead of threats and punishment, it relies on encouragement, and instead of reprimands, it uses reminders. It also means praising employees when they do something right. With negative discipline, employees do things mainly because they have to, and the organization loses the benefits of individual commitment and acceptance of personal responsibility.

Positive discipline is also progressive in nature. The first step involves a counseling session between the employee and the manager to identify the problem and find a solution. The manager does not reprimand the employee or threaten further disciplinary action. Instead, the emphasis is on confronting the employee in a mature and supportive manner with the need to change, by reminding the worker that appropriate performance and behavior are his or her responsibility. A note of this meeting is put in the manager's file. Upon follow-up, if the problem is not resolved, there is a second counseling session, in which the manager mentions again that improvement is the employee's responsibility, then helps to work on a solution. The manager draws up a written solution and gives it to the employee.

After the second conference, if the problem is still not resolved or at least improved, the employee is allowed a decision-making leave of one or more days with pay. The purpose of such a leave is to remove any hostility and show the individual that the organization wants to help. The employee is given the time off to decide if he or she is willing to meet the standards. Upon return from the leave, the employee is asked to advise the supervisor of a decision—either to try to meet the standards or to resign. If the employee stays but problems continue, termination is the next step. Because positive discipline has a just cause focus, such terminations will stand up in court.

Organizations using a positive discipline system have received certain benefits as a result. There are fewer disciplinary discussions, problem situations get addressed and resolved faster, and managers report less immature and emotional behavior when confronting employees as mature adults. Because these managers are no longer required to be punitive and judgmental, they tend to deal with problems more quickly. In general, unions support the idea of employees being responsible for their own actions. Employees also like being treated as adults and being recognized for good performance. Perhaps most important, because the emphasis is on building commitment rather than mere compliance to rules, employees are more committed to high performance and achieving the goals of the organization.

SUMMARY

Employee discipline is one of the more undesirable and difficult tasks of managers, but though it may not be easy, it is crucial to good management. Discipline is a process that aims to clarify, correct, and improve inappropriate job-related conduct and behavior through rewards and sometimes penalties. A discipline system should also include praise for employees' performance. A healthy discipline system, relying mostly on positive rather than negative discipline, can actually create employee commitment to the organization and its goals.

It is necessary to consider why employees don't do what they're supposed to do. For instance, they may not actually know what is expected, or know how well they are or are not doing.

Discipline is a process involving a number of steps. It is essential first to establish what constitutes problem behavior, set disciplinary guidelines, and communicate these expectations to the employees. When a problem occurs, the steps include investigating and interviewing the employee, deciding on the appropriate action, implementing this action, and documenting it. Follow-up is of course crucial.

With regard to termination, the employment-at-will doctrine has been severely eroded, and it is now legally, as well as managerially, preferable to use just cause in discipline and discharge policies. Alternatives to termination include transfer or demotion.

The manager plays a most pivotal role in administering discipline fairly and consistently. Unfortunately, many managers find it difficult to confront employees with their concerns. Managers, particularly supervisory ones, can do much to reduce disciplinary problems.

STUDY QUESTIONS

1. In a past or current job, was there a predominantly positive or negative discipline system in place? Describe why it was mostly positive or negative. Did you like or dislike the system? Why?

2. Describe three different reasons an employee may be unintentionally doing a job incorrectly.

3. What are the steps in the disciplinary process? Describe each one.

4. What is the purpose of discipline?

5. Why is documentation of employees' performance so important? How is it accomplished?

6. If you were considering terminating someone, what questions should you ask yourself first?

7. Why is just cause a more appropriate approach to discipline and termination in the hospitality industry than at-will employment?

8. A reservations clerk has to be terminated for a problem with repeated absences that management dealt with appropriately. How would you conduct the termination procedure?

9. You are a manager in a small independent restaurant. What would you be doing to prevent disciplinary problems from occurring?

10. What are the benefits of positive discipline? Can it work in a hospitality operation? Why or why not?

REFERENCES

Bockanic, William N., and J. Benjamin Forbes. 1986. The erosion of employment-at-will: Managerial implications. *SAM Advanced Management Journal* 51(3):16–21.

Boyle, Kathy. 1987. Effective employee discipline requires keeping in close touch. *Restaurants USA* 7(10):26–28.

Brown, Maurice. 1986. Counseling skills. *SAM Advanced Management Journal* 51(1):32–35.

Buckman, Steve. 1986. To fire or not to fire? *Supervisory Management* 31(2):30–33.

Connolly, Paul M. 1986. Clearing the deadwood. *Training and Development Journal* 40(1):58–60.

Corbett, Laurence P. 1986. Avoiding wrongful discharge suits. *Management Solutions* 31(6):19–23.

Fournies, Ferdinand F. 1988. *Why Employees Don't Do What They're Supposed to Do.* Blue Ridge Summit, Pa.: Liberty House.

Griffith, T. J. 1987. Want job improvement? Try counseling. *Management Solutions* 32(9):13–19.

Harvey, Eric L. 1987. Discipline vs. punishment. *Management Review* 76(3):25–29.

Hilgert, Raymond L. 1988. How at-will statements hurt employers. *Personnel Journal* 67(2):75–76.

Humphreys, L. Wade, and Neil J. Humphreys. 1988. The proper use of discipline. *Management Solutions* 33(5):5–10.

Jesseph, Steven A. 1989. Employee termination, 2: Some do's and don'ts. *Personnel* 66(2):36–38.

Madsen, Roger B., and Barbara Knudson-Fields. 1987. Productive progressive discipline procedures. *Management Solutions* 32(5):17–24.

Matejka, J. Kenneth, D. Neil Ashworth, and Diane Dodd-McCue. 1986. Discipline without guilt. *Supervisory Management* 31(5):34–36.

Milbourn, Gene. 1986. The case against employee punishment. *Management Solutions* 31(11):40–43.

Pulich, Marcia Ann. 1986. What to do with incompetent employees. *Supervisory Management* 31(3):10–16.

Recker, W. A. 1987. The ten commandments of firing. *Management Solutions* 32(5):42–43.

Rothman, Miriam. 1989. Employee termination, 1: A four-step procedure. *Personnel* 66(2):31–35.

Schuster, Karolyn. 1988. Wyse's company manners, the touch management jobs: How to criticize and fire with style. *Food Management* 23(6):210.

Seltzer, Joseph. 1987. Discipline with a clear sense of purpose. *Management Solutions* 32(2):32–37.

Sherman, Clayton. 1987. Eight steps to preventing problem employees. *Personnel* 64(6):38–48.

Shideler, Daniel M. 1989. Documenting disciplinary situations. Supervisory Management 10(2):15–20.

Steiner, Julius. 1988. Good supervision: The best defense against wrongful discharge claims. *Management Solutions* 33(7):28–31.

Veglahn, Peter A. 1987. The five steps in practicing effective discipline. *Management Solutions* 32(11):24–35.

Chapter 15

Delegation

KEY QUESTIONS

1. What is delegation?
2. What are the benefits of delegation?
3. Why do managers avoid delegation?
4. How do managers delegate effectively?
5. What is reverse delegation, and how is it avoided?

KEY TERMS AND CONCEPTS

Levels of delegation   Delegating authority

Delegation discussion   Responsibility

Monitoring   Accountability

Evaluation   Reverse delegation

Delegation refers to the managerial process of assigning to employees the completion of specific tasks. In other words, the manager gets work done through other people. The job description has formally delegated tasks; however, delegation usually refers to assigned tasks that are not in the job description. Delegation is actually a form of participative management that gives the manager more time to do his or her own important work and gives the employees opportunities to build knowledge, skills, confidence, and job satisfaction.

Delegation is tough for some managers to do. For example, Timothy W. Firnstahl, founder and chief executive of Restaurant Services Inc., a Seattle company that operates five restaurants and a wholesale fish company, has written of the difficulties of delegating the operations of his growing business to others so he can function as its leader (Firnstahl 1986). To be a leader, it is vital to delegate those jobs that someone else can do either better or as well. This can be an agonizing process for an entrepreneur who has built up a business to the point where he or she cannot run it single-handedly anymore.

LEVELS OF DELEGATION

There are various *levels of delegation,* each with a differing amount of authority given to the employee, as follows:

1. Ask the employee only for fact-finding.
2. Ask the employee to come up with possible solutions to a problem and to describe the advantages and disadvantages of each solution.
3. Ask the employee to figure out what to do with a given situation and then to seek approval prior to implementation.
4. Ask the employee to determine and implement a plan of action and then either inform the manager about the results, inform the manager only if there are problems, or don't bother reporting back to the manager.

BENEFITS OF DELEGATION

Why delegate at all? A measure of a manager's effectiveness lies in the ability to get work done through other people. By delegating, a manager is freed up from certain, often routine, functions, which allows more time for important managerial activities such as planning and organizing. A manager can therefore improve efficiency and achieve more by delegating. In addition, the department is more likely to continue to run smoothly during a manager's absence. Managers who delegate successfully end up being more likely to obtain promotions and good raises.

When a manager delegates correctly he or she is also training, developing, and assessing employees. Workers often find it very motivating to perform one of the manager's routine tasks, such as a physical inventory. As the manager develops their skills, the employees become more confident, skilled, versatile, valuable, and promotable. In brief, delegation improves performance of both the manager and the employees because the human resources of the organization are being more fully utilized.

WHY MANAGERS DO NOT DELEGATE

Managers can state many reasons for not delegating:

My employees won't do the job right.

I can do the job faster and better.

If I ask someone to do this job and the person goofs up, it could be costly and I'm still responsible anyway.

My employees do not have the time; they are too busy.

My employees do not have as much clout as I do to get things done around here.

My employees don't know enough about my job to do any of it, and that's just the way it is.

Underneath the myriad of excuses for not delegating lie some managerial attitudes that need redirection.

Managers who do not want to delegate may lack trust and confidence in their employees to complete a delegated assignment. They may be perfectionists who feel only they can do the job right. They may be insecure and do not want to delegate due to a fear that the employee will do either a better job or a poor one for which the manager will be responsible. Some egotistical managers will not delegate because they do not want to share their authority with anyone and they think they are indispensable to the operation. Managers who are not very well organized are less likely to delegate, as the first step in delegating is determining which tasks can be delegated and organizing these tasks. This type of manager is likely to spend the day reacting to problems, often called fighting fires, rather than delegating.

In order to get a good start at delegating, a manager needs to be

- Trusting of subordinates
- Willing to let others make mistakes
- Willing to turn over tasks
- Receptive to someone else's ideas about how to handle situations
- Willing to invest the time in training employees to take over various tasks

HOW TO DELEGATE

Delegation actually comprises four steps: preparation, the *delegation discussion, monitoring,* and *evaluation.*

Preparation

Before actually delegating, a manager needs to decide what to delegate, and to whom. A manager's job can be divided into three categories: work that only the manager can perform, work that can be delegated right away, and work that can be delegated as soon as someone else is trained to do it. Only the manager should perform certain tasks, such as discipline, counseling, performance evaluation, complex activities, and confidential or sensitive situations. Tasks that could be delegated include routine ones, fact-finding, and attendance at meetings.

When selecting someone to accept a delegated task, look for an employee who has both the skill—or the ability to be trained—and the time to do the new task. If a manager gives someone an assignment and the employee does poorly at it, the employee will not be likely to want to do so ever again. It is preferable to delegate both to the lowest possible level of employee who can perform the task and to just one employee. By giving a task over to one person, the manager has more control and this lessens any confusion; at times, of course, a team of people may be needed. Having the time to do a task is also important. There is a tendency to delegate to a select group of employees who can be relied on to do the job well; as a result, they are often overburdened with work and may resent the added pressure when others have time to spare. Delegated tasks should be distributed as evenly as possible among those people who want the challenge. Further, don't delegate just undesirable tasks; delegate whenever possible in order to give employees interesting, challenging work.

The Delegation Discussion

Now it is time for the manager and the selected employee to discuss the delegated task. This discussion should include all details of the task, the amount of authority and resources available, the activities and results expected, controls such as progress reports and deadlines, and how results will be evaluated and recognized. Effective delegation does not mean telling someone what to do, but rather mutually discussing and agreeing on a plan of action. Both parties should agree on what is to be accomplished and how it is to be monitored and evaluated.

Much has been written about *delegating authority, responsibility,* and *accountability.* Authority means the employee is given the right and power to act and make decisions, within certain predetermined limits. For example, authority may include spending money or speaking to certain people inside and outside the organization. Frequently employees are asked to do certain functions but can't get them done because they were not given enough authority. It is crucial to delegate enough authority in order to get the job accomplished, but not so much that it could be abused.

Responsibility refers to the obligation of the employee to perform the task; accountability means answering to the manager for the results. Although managers may think they are delegating full responsibility and accountability to a subordinate, however, in reality managers retain both. In other words, the manager still is ultimately responsible and accountable to superiors for the task.

Monitoring

Once a task is delegated, it needs to be monitored to evaluate progress and give any needed feedback. All parties need to agree on the degree of monitoring and the deadline dates during the delegation discussion. Monitoring techniques might include personal follow-up or written progress reports. An assignment can be either tightly or loosely monitored, depending on the task, the employee involved, and the desired results. Tight controls reduce the chances of confusion or error, but also reduce the authority of the employee; loose controls allow the employee more initiative and creativity. Whether controls are tight or loose, it is imperative to follow up on schedule, to show the employee that this project is important, and give support as needed.

While monitoring, the manager may find that progress is poor or even nonexistent. One of two things can happen at this time; either do more training to get things back on track, or reassign the project. In order to become a good delegator, it is vital to delegate as well the right to be wrong—in other words, to be tolerant toward others' mistakes. The best option is to give some help in hopes of getting things moving in the right direction. In some circumstances, however, it is necessary to reassign the task, which in many cases could have been avoided if the proper employee had been chosen initially to do the job.

Evaluation

Assess the completed task by comparing it with the results agreed upon at the beginning of this process. More than methods, results need to be evaluated. Managers need to realize that there are many ways besides their own to achieve results. Discussion should be a two-way exchange, with any criticism stated constructively. Emphasize what could have been done to prevent mistakes so they do not recur in the future; that way the employee remains motivated to take on new assignments. Most important, be sure to recognize and reward the work accomplished.

REVERSE DELEGATION

Here's a common situation: A manager asks an employee to take on a project. The employee understands what to do and agrees. After a week, the employee confronts the boss and says, "We've got a problem." The worker explains many reasons why he or she can't complete the project. In essence, the employee is trying to dump the assignment back onto the superior—which is referred to as *reverse delegation.* The employee may be doing this because he or she lacks confidence, doesn't really know enough to do the job, is afraid of making a mistake and being criticized for it, or simply does not want to take on the added responsibility.

What should the superior do? The manager should listen and discuss the dilemma, but make it perfectly clear that the task is still the employee's responsibility to complete. To encourage the employee to think through his or her own problems, the manager can ask, "What do you recommend?" It is also a good idea to train the employee to do some homework before bringing up problems, through encouragement to determine exactly what the problem is, why it occurs, and how it can be resolved.

If a manager takes back incomplete work, it fosters dependence. Some managers want to feel needed, so they may accept it when an employee delegates in reverse. It is important, however, to change any mental attitudes that interfere with effective *forward* delegation. The best way to handle reverse delegation can be summed up in a statement: "Don't bring me problems; bring me solutions."

SUMMARY

Delegation refers to the managerial process of assigning to employees the completion of specific tasks. In other words, the manager gets work done through other people. Delegation improves performance of both the manager and the employees because the human resources of the organization are being more fully utilized. In order to delegate effectively, managers need to be trusting of subordinates, willing to let others make mistakes, willing to turn over tasks, receptive to someone else's ideas about how to handle situations, and willing to invest the time in training employees to take over various tasks.

Delegation comprises four steps: preparation, the delegation discussion, monitoring, and evaluation. Before actually delegating, a manager needs to decide what to delegate, and to whom. The discussion should include all details of the task, the amount of authority and resources available, the activities and results expected, controls such as progress reports and deadlines, and how results will be evaluated and recognized. Effective delegation does not mean telling someone what to do, but rather mutually discussing and agreeing on a plan of action. Both parties should agree on what is to be accomplished and how it is to be monitored and evaluated. Once a task is delegated, it needs to be monitored to evaluate progress and give any needed feedback. Evaluation should focus primarily on results and not so heavily on the process.

Reverse delegation occurs when the employee tries to dump the delegated task back onto the superior, usually by saying that there is a problem. The manager should not accept the job back, but rather needs to encourage the employee to search for solutions to the problem before consulting the manager.

STUDY QUESTIONS

1. As a hotel general manager, why would you delegate? What mental attitudes would you need to delegate effectively?

2. Explain why a manager, such as one overseeing a dining room, may be reluctant to delegate.

3. In a current or previous position, think of a specific supervisor and describe the person's managerial style toward delegation.

4. What is meant by delegation of authority and responsibility?

5. If an employee attempts reverse delegation, what would you do?

6. As an executive chef, you plan to delegate to a subordinate a major portion of the purchasing of food. Describe how you would go through the four steps in delegation.

REFERENCES

Broadwell, Martin M. 1986. *Supervising Today: A Guide for Positive Leadership.* 2d ed. New York: John Wiley & Sons.

Callarman, William G., and William W. McCartney. 1988. Reversing reverse delegation. *Management Solutions* 33(7):11–15.

Firnstahl, Timothy W. 1986. Letting go. *Cornell H.R.A. Quarterly* 27(3):16–19.

Haimann, Theo, and Raymond L. Hilgert. 1987. *Supervision: Concepts and Practices of Management.* 4th ed. Cincinnati: South-Western Publishing Co.

Johnson, Raymond C. 1987. *The Achievers.* New York: E. P. Dutton.

McConnell, Charles R. 1987. A new look at delegation: The supervisor's personal approach. *Health Care Supervisor* 5(3):77–89.

Nelson, Robert B. 1988. *Delegation: The Power of Letting Go.* Glenview, Ill.: Scott, Foresman and Co.

Pringle, Charles D. 1986. Seven reasons why managers don't delegate. *Management Solutions* 31(11):26–30.

Savary, Suzanne. 1985. Ineffective delegation—symptom or problem? *Supervisory Management* 30(6):27–33.

Schwartz, Andrew E. 1987. The why, what, and to whom of delegation. *Management Solutions* 32(6):31–38.

Vinton, Donna. 1987. Delegation for employee development. *Training and Development Journal* 41(1):65–67.

White, James. 1986. *Successful Supervision.* 2d ed. London: McGraw-Hill Book Co. (UK) Ltd.

Chapter 16

Managing Service

KEY QUESTIONS

1. What is the size and nature of service industries?
2. What are the components of service?
3. What characteristics do successful service organizations share?
4. How do you manage service in the hospitality industry?

KEY TERMS AND CONCEPTS

Service industries	Comment cards
Moment of truth	Hot lines
Empathy	Focus groups
Mission statement	Mystery shoppers
Service audits	Complaint logs
Customer surveys	

Service industries and service jobs are growing fast, with hospitality and data processing jobs leading the way. Such industries also encompass trade, communications, transportation, financial and medical services, education, government, and technical services for industry. The United States has shifted from a manufacturing economy, based on producing goods, to one based on producing services, as seen in these 1986 statistics from the U.S. Department of Commerce:

- About 75 percent of workers in the nonagricultural private sector have service-producing jobs
- The other 25 percent work in goods-producing jobs
- About 70 percent of the national income comes from service industries

In addition, services have absorbed most of the influx of women and minority members into the work force, as well as fueled all recent economic recoveries.

Service is as different from the production of goods as factories are to the farms that preceded them. The primary output of a service is not a product or a construction. Instead, the output is consumed when produced, and value is added to the output in an intangible way, such as added convenience. A service can't be kept in inventory and the person receiving it is left with only a service experience. Due in large part to these differences, the way service companies are structured and managed needs to be different from that of companies producing goods.

Customer service refers to satisfactorily meeting customer needs and wants with products or services. Service management is much more comprehensive and involves "a structured, systematic approach for planning, organizing, and controlling the development and delivery of a product or service that promotes superior customer satisfaction and superior results for the organization" (Albrecht, 1988b). Service management is emerging as a way for a hospitality operator to deal with competition. If service is managed properly, it can give the customer more value for his dollar.

Good service is frequently the main reason customers frequent certain hospitality operations, and poor service the major reason customers try the competition. Interestingly enough, most customers who are unhappy with service never complain to the company; they simply tell their friends and go to the competitor. A 1985 Gallup Monthly Report on Eating Out found that 83 percent of customers will not go to a restaurant if service is bad, and if service slips, 34 percent will tell a friend (Mill 1986). Three out of five customers reported in a 1984 survey being bothered most by poor service in restaurants (Tastes of America, 1984). If a customer complains, it is far cheaper and better business to try to please that customer than to find a new one.

Service management is first a philosophy, a set of values and attitudes, which must be translated into a set of methods. It can benefit from, among other things, an examination of characteristics of successful service organizations, as well as specific steps to manage service in the hospitality industry.

THE NATURE OF SERVICE

The exact nature of quality service varies according to an individual customer's needs, expectations, definition of good service, and perceptions of service. Someone's expectations of service will obviously be different if walking into a luxury hotel than into a budget facility. Expectations of restaurant customers identified in a National Restaurant survey included employees who smile when greeting customers, put customers at ease, check if the meal is fine, explain how long the meal will take to be served, and are knowledgeable about the menu and food preparation. Nevertheless, every customer defines and perceives overall good service differently. This explains why some customers appear to be very demanding; they simply may have a different definition, perception, or level of expectation for service.

The critical point of service occurs when the customer comes in contact with any aspect of an organization and is left with an impression of the quality of its service. This has been referred to by Jan Carlzon of Scandinavian Airlines as *"the moment of truth"* (Albrecht and Zemke 1985). Every service business has anywhere from one to thousands of moments of truth every day. It is at these encounters that customers are won, maintained, or lost. To the customer, the employee *is* the company, so the amount of responsibility the frontline service personnel carry is tremendous.

Service can be split into two dimensions: tangible and intangible. The tangible, or physical, aspects of service in hospitality include the meal, the hotel or motel room, any other facilities or equipment the customer can use such as a hotel pool, and the cleanliness of the operation. Despite these tangible aspects, the guest is left with nothing tangible.

The intangible dimensions of service include reliability, assurance, accuracy, responsiveness, and *empathy*. Reliability refers to the service being delivered dependably and consistently. Assurance looks at how the service employees relieve customers of any uncertainties and put them at ease; in a restaurant, for instance, servers need to assure customers when their table will be ready or when entrées will be served. Accuracy involves being attentive to details and following procedures correctly; for example, servers need to follow precisely the order of service in a dining room, as well as other procedures there. Responsiveness refers to prompt, timely service.

The last intangible dimension of service, empathy, relies on many interpersonal skills of the employee. It refers to the ability to imagine any service encounter from the customer's point of view. It encompasses a caring attitude, attentiveness, courteousness, and awareness. Some empathic skills that frontline service personnel in the hospitality industry use include the following:

Greeting customers promptly and keeping them informed as to when a service will be performed.

Giving personal attention, such as calling customers by name when appropriate, and giving undivided attention.

Being aware of and anticipating customers' needs.

Being natural, courteous, and friendly.

Being aware of how the customer views the level of service.

Explaining when there are delays or problems.

Communicating clearly through verbal and nonverbal language.

Maintaining a calm, relaxed tone of voice.

Being helpful and going beyond the call of duty.

Handling complaints in an effective and timely manner.

Many of these skills can be taught or reinforced through training.

CHARACTERISTICS OF SUCCESSFUL SERVICE ORGANIZATIONS

An appropriate example of a successful service organization is McDonald's. Built on the philosophy of quality, service, cleanliness, and good value, McDonald's is number one in the fast-food market even though other chains were in this market earlier. For McDonald's the customer comes first, and this is reflected in all its policies and procedures. At Stew Leonard's in Norwalk, Connecticut, the world's largest dairy store, the customer policy—"Our Policy: Rule 1. The customer is always right. Rule 2. If the customer is ever wrong, reread rule 1"—is chiseled in a six-thousand-pound rock at the entrance to the store.

Successful service organizations share several characteristics. First, management has formulated and supports a policy statement providing for excellent customer service. Unfortunately, some companies make profits their primary objective. When customer satisfaction is most important, profitability will follow. It is one thing to state that customer service is important, however, and another actually to put this into effect. Often parts of the organizational culture may block efforts. A certain level of teamwork, cooperation, optimism, and loyalty is necessary for success. Management also needs to be sure that sufficient steps have been taken to implement the program. In addition, management sets a model for excellent guest relations. The managers who are to implement the program are also given the appropriate authority and can change it as needed, within a certain framework.

Successful organizations design systems for the convenience of the customer, not the operator. Two examples include drive-through windows in fast-food operations and express checkout procedures in hotels. These organizations put the customers first and know their customers' needs, attitudes, values, and perceptions.

Another important characteristic is that frontline service employees are given latitude to satisfy the customer; they do not have rigid rule books detailing how to do everything, so the customer does not hear the otherwise familiar refrain "I'm sorry but that is our policy." For instance, at Stew Leonard's, when a customer realized she had no money with her to pay for groceries, the cashier simply took her name and address and asked her to pay for them the next time she came in. The customer was so shocked that she asked to see a manager before she would leave the store without paying for her groceries.

In all ways, in fact, frontline service employees are customer-oriented. How employees treat customers reflects, to an extent, how management treats the employees. If management maintains a healthy work environment, in which employees are respected, involved, and rewarded for providing quality service, good customer service is more likely. This idea is easily summed up by a statement J. Willard Marriott, Jr. makes frequently to Marriott Corporation managers: "Take care of your employees and they'll take care of your customers." Frontline service employees also receive training to support job performance in such areas as handling complaints, for which they are taught to seek out and welcome complaints in order to improve service and retain customers. In sum, management has sold its employees on the service idea and won their commitment.

STEPS TO MANAGE SERVICE IN THE HOSPITALITY INDUSTRY

The first step in managing service is to make it an important part of the *mission statement* of the company. A mission statement typically describes what kind of business the company is in, what its mission, or purpose, is, and what it believes in. For instance, the Holiday Inn chain of hotels offers convenience at a moderate price. The hotels are conveniently located near airports or city centers and either have a restaurant or are near eating places; the rooms are clean and comfortable. Implicit in its mission are various service objectives. In order to develop a mission statement and service objectives, the organization must be sure to know and understand its customers.

Once the mission statement and service objectives are clear, a service strategy must be developed to clarify and implement them. A key part of the plan should be to establish service performance standards. Performance standards translate work requirements into levels of acceptable or unacceptable performance, and they need to be built into job descriptions and evaluation forms. For example, these are sample performance standards for a server:

1. Customers are greeted within one minute of sitting down.
2. Customer complaints are resolved immediately, and the dining room manager is notified.
3. The server looks directly at the customers when speaking with them.
4. The server checks back with each party at least once during the meal.
5. Meals are accurately served.
6. Refills are taken care of before the customer orders them.
7. The server correctly answers all questions on the menu.
8. The server accommodates at least 80 percent of customers' special requests.

9. The server is rated as "friendly" by at least 90 percent of customers on comment cards.

10. The server is always in proper uniform.

When service standards are being established, employees should be asked to participate in the process, so they will be more likely to adhere to the standards later. In addition, new and revised standards need to be communicated to all current and new employees.

The next step in managing service concerns educating everyone in the organization about the program, especially the frontline service personnel. Because they are the ones who manage the moments of truth, it is crucial to give a lot of attention to their training, hiring, and orientation. When hiring employees who will deal directly with customers, it is important to look for empathic people who have good interpersonal relationship skills and self-esteem. They also need to be flexible in dealing with the many different situations that present themselves in hospitality and effective in communicating, both verbally and nonverbally. Preemployment testing can help determine some of these qualities. During the interview, open-ended and situational questions can be used to get an idea of the person's personality and interpersonal skills. The importance to the job of good customer relations should be stressed at this time.

During orientation and training, customer relations need to be given prominence. Training topics may include why customer relations are so important, an explanation and discussion about performance standards, and such skills as showing empathy and handling complaints and breakdowns in service. So-called smile training and attitude training, however, have not worked to build customer relation skills. If it is necessary to teach a new employee how to smile or make eye contact, perhaps the wrong person was hired; and attitude really means nothing until it is displayed in behavior and actions, which can then be observed. Useful training methods include role playing, behavior modeling, and performance tryout (see chapter 3).

In order for the hiring, orientation, and training process to pay off, the employees must be well managed. Table 16-1 shows how management actions affect employees' behavior with customers. Management needs to maintain good communication with and supervision of the frontline service personnel, reward employees when appropriate, involve them in decisions, promote from within, set a good example, clearly communicate expectations, and evaluate performance periodically. There must be a more-than-satisfactory quality of work life as well as a motivating environment. Within hospitality organizations, many frontline customer contact positions are entry-level jobs for which wages are far from outstanding, so good management is vital to good service.

Table 16-1.   What management says and what employees do

Management's Messages to Employees	Employees' Translation into Behavior with Customers
What are your problems, and how can I help solve them?	How may I be of assistance to you?
We want you to know what's happening in our organization, so here is what's going on.	I am capable of helping you because I am knowledgeable.
Each of us has a role in the company, so we will share accountability for what happens here.	I'm empowered to help you, and take pride in my ability to do so.
We treat each other with professional respect.	I have respect for you as an individual.
We stand behind each other's decisions and support each other.	You can count on me and our organization to deliver on our promises.

Source: Reprinted, by permission of publisher, from *Management Review,* October 1987 © 1987. American Management Association, New York. All rights reserved.

Performance needs to be measured and monitored to determine if the standards are being met. This can be accomplished by various methods, including *service audits,* checklists, overall supervision, and customer feedback. Service audits examine whether standards are being met, by either rating this or judging the frequency of such success. A service audit may examine, for example, the timeliness of service.

Customer surveys, comment cards (fig. 16-1), *hot lines, focus groups, mystery shoppers,* and *complaint logs* are ways to keep touch with the level of customer satisfaction and the nature of customer dissatisfaction. Customer surveys and comment cards should ask such questions as "How are we doing?" and "How can we do better?" The amount of information from customers will vary depending on the complexity of the business and size of the effort. Hot lines are phone numbers customers can dial if there is a concern. Focus groups involve a trained interviewer meeting with a small group of customers. The interviewer discusses a specific product, service, or organization, in order to gain insight into consumer thoughts and feelings. Mystery shoppers are people who, unknown to employees, are paid to be a customer and observe service in a hospitality operation. Complaint logs are written records of complaints received.

Please take a moment and let us know how we are doing.

	Excellent	Good	Average	Below Average	Poor
1. Friendliness of your server	_____	_____	_____	_____	_____
2. Helpfulness of your server	_____	_____	_____	_____	_____
3. Promptness of service	_____	_____	_____	_____	_____
4. Quality of food	_____	_____	_____	_____	_____
5. Menu variety	_____	_____	_____	_____	_____

6. Please write below any comments or suggestions so we may better serve you. _____

_____

_____

_____

Thank you for your time!

Figure 16-1. Comment card.

After measuring and monitoring performance, managers should report good results to employees, who need to be rewarded accordingly. Also discuss poor results with employees, analyzing the problems for possible causes and solutions. Then implement and monitor solutions to fit into the overall service objectives. This service management cycle is summarized in figure 16-2.

Develop overall mission statement and service objectives

Develop a service strategy, including service standards

Educate the organization personnel

Manage service to include measuring and monitoring of performance standards

Solve problems and reinforce excellence

Figure 16-2. The service cycle.

SUMMARY

Service industries and service jobs are growing fast, with hospitality and data processing jobs leading the way. The U.S. economy has shifted from one based on producing goods to one based on producing services. The output of a service industry is consumed when produced, and value is added to the output in an intangible way, such as added convenience. Customer service is emerging as a way to differentiate a service from the competition, which is ever present in the hospitality sector. Good service is frequently the main reason customers frequent certain hospitality operations, and poor service the major reason customers try the competition. Service management is first a philosophy, a set of values and attitudes, which must be translated into a set of methods.

The exact nature of quality service varies according to an individual customer's needs, expectations, and definition and perception of service. The critical point of service, the moment of truth, occurs when there is contact or an exchange between the frontline service employee and the customer. Service has both tangible and intangible dimensions. Tangible aspects include the meal, the hotel or motel room, any other facilities or equipment the customer uses, and the cleanliness of the operation. The intangible dimensions of service include reliability, assurance, accuracy, responsiveness, and empathy.

Characteristics of successful service organizations include a clearly written commitment to quality service, managers who support the program and have the appropriate authority to change it as needed, systems designed for the convenience of the customer, and customer-oriented frontline employees, who are given latitude to satisfy the customer. The service management cycle includes developing overall objectives, setting standards, hiring and training appropriate frontline personnel, and monitoring their performance in order to improve objectives as needed.

STUDY QUESTIONS

1. What distinguishes a service from a product? What services does the hospitality industry offer?
2. Name five service industries other than hospitality.
3. Do most customers complain if there is a problem?
4. How high a priority is service to restaurant customers?
5. Define *moment of truth.*
6. Discuss four variables in how customers view service.

7. Discuss the tangible and intangible dimensions of service as they relate to a hospitality operation that you frequent.

8. What characteristics set apart successful service organizations from less successful ones?

9. Discuss the steps in managing service in a hospitality operation.

10. Review with a local hospitality operator the nature of a commitment to a customer relations program.

REFERENCES

Albrecht, Karl. 1988a. *At America's Service.* Homewood, Ill.: Dow Jones–Irwin.

Albrecht, Karl. 1988b. The service imperative. *Restaurant Business* May 20:156–57.

Albrecht, Karl, and Ron Zemke. 1985. *Service America!* Homewood, Ill.: Dow Jones–Irwin.

Bell, Chip R., and Ron E. Zemke. 1987. Service breakdown: The road to recovery. *Management Review* 76(10):32–35.

Blume, Eric R. 1988. Customer service: Giving companies the competitive edge. *Training and Development Journal* 42(9):24–32.

Desatnick, Robert L. 1987. Service: A CEO's perspective. *Management Review* 76(10):41–45.

Dore, Christopher D. 1988. The interpretation of service: An anthropological view. *Hospitality Education and Research Journal* 12(1):81–91.

Feinberg, Mortimer R., and Aaron Levenstein. 1986. "It's not my job, man." *Cornell H.R.A. Quarterly* 26(4):10.

Frankovich, Jim, and L. R. Baldwin. 1988. Quality principles for service industries. *Management Solutions* 33(11):18–24.

Frumkin, Paul. 1988. Operator solutions. *Restaurant Business* May 20:142–45.

Heskett, James L. 1987. Lessons in the service sector. *Harvard Business Review* 87(2):118–26.

Kurman, Marsha. 1987. Customer relations: The personnel angle. *Personnel* 64(9):38–40.

Lash, Linda M. 1989. *The Complete Guide to Customer Service.* New York: John Wiley and Sons.

LeBoeuf, Michael. 1987. *How to Win Customers and Keep Them for Life.* New York: G. P. Putnam's Sons.

Leonard, Stew. 1987. Love that customer! *Management Review* 76(10):36–39.

Lewis, Robert C., and Susan V. Morris. 1987. The positive side of guest complaints. *Cornell H.R.A. Quarterly* 27(4):13–15.

Lieberman, Lawrence. 1988. The basis for good customer service. *Management Solutions* 33(11):25–31.

Lydecker, Toni. 1986. The crisis in service: A look at the problem. *NRA News* 6(3):13–16.

Martin, William B. 1986a. Defining what quality service is for you. *Cornell H.R.A. Quarterly* 26(4):32–38.

———. 1986b. Measuring and improving your service quality. *Cornell H.R.A. Quarterly* 27(1):80–87.

———. 1986c. *Quality Service: The Restaurant Manager's Bible.* Ithaca, N.Y.: Cornell University School of Hotel Administration.

Martin, William B. 1989. *Managing Quality Customer Service.* Los Altos: Crisp Publications Inc.

Mill, Robert C. 1986. Managing the service encounter. *Cornell H.R.A. Quarterly* 26(4):39–46.

Quinn, James Brian, and Christopher E. Gagnon. 1986. Will services follow manufacturing into decline? *Harvard Business Review* 86(6):95–103.

Schleh, Edward C. 1987. Make your executive decisions inspire service. *Management Review* 76(10):46–49.

Schlesinger, Leonard. 1988. Service fundamentals. *Restaurant Business* May 20: 154–55.

———. 1984. Tastes of America. *Restaurants and Institutions* December 4:102.

Wehrenberg, Stephen B. 1987. Front-line interpersonal skills a must in today's service economy. *Personnel Journal* 66(1):115–18.

Zemke, Ron. 1987. Health care rediscovers patients. *Training* 24(4):40–45.

Training Resources

Educational Institute of the American Hotel and Motel Association
  P.O. Box 1240
  East Lansing, MI 48826
  800-752-4567
  517-353-5527

National Restaurant Association
  1200 Seventeenth Street, N.W.
  Washington D.C. 20036-3097
  800-424-5156
  202-331-5900

Educational Foundation of the National Restaurant Association
  250 South Wacker Drive
  Chicago, IL 60606
  800-522-7578
  312-715-1010

American Management Association
  135 West 50th Street
  New York, NY 10020
  212-586-8100

American Society for Training and Development
  1630 Duke Street
  Alexandria, VA 22313
  703-683-8100

Council of Hotel and Restaurant Trainers
Call National Restaurant Association for current address information.

American Culinary Federation
P.O. Box 3466
St. Augustine, FL 32084

An Accident Prevention Guide

CUTS

Pay attention when using sharp equipment.

Know how to operate equipment before using it.

Follow directions when operating equipment.

Use guards when provided on equipment.

Use tampers to push food into equipment.

No loose sleeves, ties, or dangling jewelry near equipment.

Sweep up broken glass.

Use a special container to dispose of glass, broken dishes, and other sharp objects.

Turn equipment off before adjusting.

Carry dishes and glassware carefully.

Keep hands clear of garbage disposals.

Turn disposal on before putting garbage in.

Remove and discard nails and staples found in shipping cartons and crates.

Use knives safely.

BURNS

Pay attention when working around hot equipment.

Use dry potholders.

Keep pot handles turned in from the edge of the range.

Keep pot handles away from open flames.

Avoid overfilling containers with hot foods.

Get help lifting heavy pots of food.

Open lids of pots and doors of steamers away from you, and do so slowly.

Stir foods with long-handled spoons.

Let equipment cool before cleaning.

Don't put icy frozen foods into the fryer.

Put foods slowly into the fryer and stand back.

Warn others of hot surfaces.

Strike match before turning on gas.

Wear closed-toe and closed-heel shoes that don't absorb liquids.

Wear a cloth apron, not a plastic one.

No loose apron strings.

FIRES

Don't turn your back on hot fat.

Keep hoods and equipment free from grease buildup.

Don't set the fryer at too high a temperature.

Smoke only in designated areas.

Throw garbage out!

Store matches in a covered container away from heat.

Store fats and chemicals away from the heat.

FALLS

Wipe up spills immediately.

Wear shoes with nonskid soles and heels, such as rubber.

Keep aisles and stairs clear.

Walk, don't run.

Follow established traffic patterns.

Turn lights on to see.

Don't carry anything that blocks your vision.

Keep drawers closed.

Don't have any dangling electric cords!

Use handrails.

Use ladders properly.

ELECTRIC SHOCK

Make sure all electrical equipment is grounded.

Unplug equipment before cleaning or disassembling.

Never touch electrical equipment or outlets with wet hands or while standing in water.

Pull plugs out of the socket properly.

Report damaged and worn cords and plugs to your supervisor.

Safety Self-Inspection Form

Following on pages 304–323 is a form that hospitality managers can use to inspect the foodservice department for safety concerns. Each functional area within the foodservice operation is included in the inspection.

For each area, there are questions, which, if answered NO, indicate an unsafe condition to be corrected.

AREA: Receiving and Dry Storage **INSPECTED BY:** _____ **DATE:** _____

QUESTION	YES	NO	PROBLEM NOTED	CORRECTIONS	WHEN DONE
1. Are floors and walls in safe condition: dry, clean, no tiles missing or broken, no worn areas?					
2. Are "Wet Floor" signs available and used when needed?					
3. Is all lighting in working order and adequate?					
4. Are any tables, counters, and equipment free from sharp corners or dangerous projections?					
5. Is ventilation sufficient?					
6. Are doors and aisles kept clear of supplies?					
7. Are there sufficient waste receptacles of leakproof non-absorbent material?					
8. Are waste receptacles covered?					
9. Is the receiving dock in good repair?					
10. Are incoming supplies being inspected for damage?					

AREA: Receiving and Dry Storage **INSPECTED BY:**   **DATE:**

QUESTION	YES	NO	PROBLEM NOTED	CORRECTIONS	WHEN DONE
11. Are adequate tools such as wire cutters, cardboard carton openers, and gloves available, and being used safely?					
12. Are supplies being lifted properly using the leg muscles and not the back muscles?					
13. Are handtrucks, carts, and dollies available to transport supplies?					
14. Are handtrucks, carts, and dollies in good repair and not being overloaded?					
15. In storage areas, are dented canned goods set on a special shelf reserved for them?					
16. Are shelves strong enough to hold the load?					
17. Are storage racks in good condition and standing solidly?					
18. Are heavy items on lower shelves only?					
19. Are the most used supplies the most accessible?					
20. Are supplies stacked neatly and safely?					

AREA: <u>Receiving and Dry Storage</u> **INSPECTED BY:** _____ **DATE:** _____

QUESTION	YES	NO	PROBLEM NOTED	CORRECTIONS	WHEN DONE
21. Is a ladder available which is solid and in good working condition?					
22. Are supplies stored at least 18 to 24 inches from light bulbs and fire sprinkler heads?					
23. Is there enough storage space so that nothing is stored on the floor or in aisles?					
24. Are hazardous materials kept separate from food?					

AREA: Refrigerators/Freezers   **INSPECTED BY:**   **DATE:**

QUESTION	YES	NO	PROBLEM NOTED	CORRECTIONS	WHEN DONE
25. Are floors and walls in safe condition: dry, clean, no tiles missing or broken, no worn areas?					
26. Is all lighting in working order and adequate?					
27. Is air circulation sufficient?					
28. Are doors and aisles kept clear of supplies?					
29. Do walk-ins have an alarm bell or a handle to open the door from the inside?					
30. Are shelves strong enough to hold the load?					
31. Are shelves and equipment free from sharp corners or dangerous projections?					
32. Are storage racks in good condition and standing solidly?					
33. Are heavy items on lower shelves only?					
34. Are the most used supplies the most accessible?					

AREA: Refrigerators/Freezers   **INSPECTED BY:**   **DATE:**

QUESTION	YES	NO	PROBLEM NOTED	CORRECTIONS	WHEN DONE
35. Are supplies stacked neatly and safely?					
36. Is there enough storage space in each area so that nothing is stored on the floor or in aisles?					
37. Are blower fans clean and guarded?					
38. Are coils clean?					
39. Are freezer coats and gloves available and being used?					

AREA: Food Preparation Areas   **INSPECTED BY:**   **DATE:**

QUESTION	YES	NO	PROBLEM NOTED	CORRECTIONS	WHEN DONE
40. Are floors and walls in safe condition: dry, clean, no tiles missing or broken, no worn areas?					
41. Are "Wet Floor" signs available and used when needed?					
42. Is all lighting in working order and adequate?					
43. Are any tables, counters, and equipment free from sharp corners or dangerous projections?					
44. Is ventilation sufficient?					
45. Are doors and aisles kept clear of supplies?					
46. Are there sufficient waste receptacles of leakproof non-absorbent material?					
47. Are waste receptacles covered?					
48. Is there enough aisle space to prevent accidents?					
49. Are there enough hot pads and gloves and are they being used?					

AREA: Food Preparation Areas **INSPECTED BY:** **DATE:**

QUESTION	YES	NO	PROBLEM NOTED	CORRECTIONS	WHEN DONE
50. Are lids being lifted carefully to avoid steam burns?					
51. Do employees warn each other if carrying hot food?					
52. Are guards on equipment being used?					
53. Is all equipment working properly?					
54. Are employees using equipment instructed on using it safely?					
55. Is equipment turned off when not in use?					
56. Is electrical equipment grounded with either 3-prong plugs or pigtail adapters?					
57. Are electrical cords in good repair?					
58. Are service cords long enough so extension cords are not needed?					
59. Are all electrical outlets in good repair?					

AREA: Food Preparation Areas   **INSPECTED BY:**   **DATE:**

QUESTION	YES	NO	PROBLEM NOTED	CORRECTIONS	WHEN DONE
60. Are electrical outlets not overloaded and out of danger of splash?					
61. Are electrical switches in a place where the equipment can't be turned on accidentally, but are accessible for quick shut-off in an emergency?					
62. Is equipment unplugged before cleaning?					
63. Are equipment handles pushed in so they do not hang over the range?					
64. Are knives stored in racks or sheaths?					
65. Are knives sharp and in good repair?					
66. Are knives being used safely?					
67. Are matches for gas equipment being stored in a metal box away from gas equipment?					
68. Is area free of grease buildup? Check stoves, fryers, hoods, filters, etc.					
69. Are any stainless steel bowls and mixer attachments in good repair and free of rust?					

AREA: <u>Food Preparation Areas</u>   INSPECTED BY: _____   DATE: _____

QUESTION	YES	NO	PROBLEM NOTED	CORRECTIONS	WHEN DONE
70. Are hazardous chemicals kept separate from food?					
71. Are the shut-off valves for steam equipment in good working order?					

AREA: <u>Serving and Dining Areas</u>   **INSPECTED BY:**   **DATE:**

QUESTION	YES	NO	PROBLEM NOTED	CORRECTIONS	WHEN DONE
72. Are floors and walls in safe condition: dry, clean, no tiles missing or broken, no worn areas?					
73. Are "Wet Floor" signs available and used when needed?					
74. Is all lighting in working order and adequate?					
75. Are any tables, counters, and equipment free from sharp corners or dangerous projections?					
76. Is ventilation sufficient?					
77. Are doors and aisles kept clear of supplies?					
78. Are there sufficient waste receptacles of leakproof non-absorbent material?					
79. Are waste receptacles covered?					
80. Are lids being lifted carefully to avoid steam burns?					
81. Do employees warn each other if carrying hot food?					

AREA: <u>Serving and Dining Areas</u> **INSPECTED BY:** _____ **DATE:** _____

QUESTION	YES	NO	PROBLEM NOTED	CORRECTIONS	WHEN DONE
82. Are chipped tableware being disposed of so they are not used to serve food?					
83. Are waitstaff trays not being overloaded?					
84. Are waitstaff trays being lifted with leg and not back muscles?					
85. Are tray stands in good repair and not blocking traffic?					
86. Are service doors marked for traffic flow, and is this being observed?					
87. Are hazardous chemicals kept separate from food?					
88. Is all equipment working properly?					
89. Is equipment turned off when not in use?					
90. Is electrical equipment grounded with either 3-prong plugs or pigtail adapters?					
91. Are electrical cords in good repair?					

AREA: <u>Serving and Dining Areas</u> INSPECTED BY: DATE:

QUESTION	YES	NO	PROBLEM NOTED	CORRECTIONS	WHEN DONE
92. Are service cords long enough so extension cords are not needed?					
93. Are all electrical outlets in good repair?					
94. Is equipment unplugged before cleaning?					

AREA: Warewashing Areas   **INSPECTED BY:**   **DATE:**

QUESTION	YES	NO	PROBLEM NOTED	CORRECTIONS	WHEN DONE
95. Are floors and walls in safe condition: dry, clean, no tiles missing or broken, no worn areas?					
96. Are "Wet Floor" signs available and used when needed?					
97. Is all lighting in working order and adequate?					
98. Are any tables, counters, and equipment free from sharp corners or dangerous projections?					
99. Is ventilation sufficient?					
100. Are doors and aisles kept clear of supplies?					
101. Are there sufficient waste receptacles of leakproof non-absorbent material?					
102. Are waste receptacles covered?					
103. Is there enough aisle space to prevent accidents?					
104. Are floors that stay wet covered with floor mats?					

AREA: Warewashing Areas   **INSPECTED BY:**   **DATE:**

QUESTION	YES	NO	PROBLEM NOTED	CORRECTIONS	WHEN DONE
105. Are broken dishes and glasses being swept up promptly and disposed per policy?					
106. Are employees trained on using chemicals safely?					
107. Are employees handling chemicals safely?					
108. Is there adequate space for air drying of equipment?					
109. Are gloves available?					
110. Are racks of dishes stacked neatly?					

AREA: Waste Disposal Area   **INSPECTED BY:**   **DATE:**

QUESTION	YES	NO	PROBLEM NOTED	CORRECTIONS	WHEN DONE
111. Is the area clean and clear of debris such as broken glass and cans?					
112. Are floors and walls in safe condition: dry, clean, no tiles missing or broken, no worn areas?					
113. Are "Wet Floor" signs available and used when needed?					
114. Is all lighting in working order and adequate?					
115. Are any tables, counters, and equipment free from sharp corners or dangerous projections?					
116. Is ventilation sufficient?					
117. Are employees instructed on how to use any trash compaction devices?					
118. Do employees operate trash compactors safely?					
119. Are gloves available and being used?					
120. Is smoking forbidden in this area, and is this posted?					

AREA: <u>Hazardous Material Storage</u> **INSPECTED BY:**   **DATE:**

QUESTION	YES	NO	PROBLEM NOTED	CORRECTIONS	WHEN DONE
121. Are MSDSs available to employees?					
122. Are hazardous materials being used according to instructions on MSDSs?					
123. Are flammable hazardous materials being stored in a safe manner?					
124. Are CO_2 tanks for soft drink machines protected from falling over?					
125. Do hazardous materials have identifying labels with instructions on how to use?					

AREA: Employee Facilities   **INSPECTED BY:** _____   **DATE:** _____

QUESTION	YES	NO	PROBLEM NOTED	CORRECTIONS	WHEN DONE
126. Are floors and walls in safe condition: dry, clean, no tiles missing or broken, no worn areas?					
127. Is all lighting in working order and adequate?					
128. Is ventilation sufficient?					
129. Are doors and aisles kept clear of supplies?					
130. Are there sufficient waste receptacles of leakproof non-absorbent material?					
131. Are waste receptacles covered?					
132. Is equipment safe and in good repair?					
133. Are there safe receptacles for cigarettes?					

AREA: Employees   **INSPECTED BY:**   **DATE:**

QUESTION	YES	NO	PROBLEM NOTED	CORRECTIONS	WHEN DONE
134. Do employees wear non-absorbent shoes with nonskid soles and low heels? Nonskid soles may be made of rubber or neoprene.					
135. Do employees walk, not run?					
136. Are employees paying attention to what they are doing?					
137. Are employees wearing clothing and jewelry that will not get caught in equipment?					

AREA: General			INSPECTED BY:		DATE:	
QUESTION	**YES**	**NO**	**PROBLEM NOTED**	**CORRECTIONS**	**WHEN DONE**
138. Are fire extinguishers visible and accessible?					
139. Are fire extinguishers inspected regularly?					
140. Do employees know where to find and how to use fire extinguishers?					
141. Are fats, oils, and matches stored in closed containers away from heat?					
142. Are ceiling sprinkler systems clear of obstacles?					
143. Are exits clearly marked and accessible?					
144. Do employees know what to do in case of a fire?					
145. Do stairs have adequate lighting?					
146. Are stairways clear of obstacles?					
147. Are electrical panels accessible and labeled?					

AREA: General   **INSPECTED BY:**   **DATE:**

QUESTION	YES	NO	PROBLEM NOTED	CORRECTIONS	WHEN DONE
148. Are all hot pipes insulated?					
149. Are carts and trucks in good repair?					
150. Are no smoking rules being observed?					
151. Is ice making equipment protected from foreign objects falling accidentally into the ice?					
152. Is there a scoop available for the ice machine and is it used?					
153. Is there a fully stocked first aid kit available?					
154. Do employees know where the first aid kit is?					
155. Are emergency phone numbers posted on or by the phone?					

Basic Requirements of the Fair Labor Standards Act

The Fair Labor Standards Act (FLSA), commonly referred to as the Wage and Hour Law, establishes minimum wage, overtime pay, record keeping, and child labor standards. It applies to all hotels and restaurants with total annual revenues exceeding a certain figure (excluding sales or excise taxes). In 1987, the sales figure was $362,500. Although the law took effect in 1938, it was not fully extended to include hotel and restaurant employees until the late 1970s. The Wage and Hour Division (Wage-Hour) administers and enforces FLSA with respect to private employers and state and local government employment.

Two important terms used in FLSA are *work week* and *hours worked*. A work week is a period of 168 hours encompassing seven consecutive 24-hour periods. It may begin on any hour of any day of the week as established by the employer. Generally, for purposes of minimum wage and overtime payment, each work week stands alone; there can be no averaging of two or more work weeks. Employee coverage, compliance with wage payment requirements, and the application of most exemptions are determined on a work week basis.

Hours worked includes all time during which an employee must be on duty, or on the employer's premises, or at any other prescribed place of work. Also included is any additional time the employee must or is permitted to work. Employees must be paid for work done after the end of their shift, including cleaning the work area, attending meetings either before or after the shift, and setting up work areas. An employer can deduct time spent for a meal period if the employee is allowed thirty continuous minutes. If the employee only gets to take fifteen minutes, or has to split the thirty minutes into two separate breaks, the employer cannot deduct the thirty minutes.

FSLA-covered nonexempt workers are entitled to a minimum wage and, after forty hours of work in a work week, overtime pay at a rate of not less than 150 percent of their regular rate of pay. Wages required by FLSA are due on the regular payday for the pay period covered.

EXCEPTIONS AND QUALIFICATIONS TO THE MINIMUM WAGE

The FLSA provides for the employment of certain individuals at wage rates below the minimum wage. Such individuals include vocational education students as well as other full-time students. Also included are individuals whose earning or productive capacity is impaired by age or physical or mental deficiency or injury. Employment at less than the minimum wage is provided for in order to prevent the curtailment of employment opportunities. Such employment is permitted only under certificates issued by Wage-Hour.

The reasonable cost (defined as providing no profit to the employer) of meals, lodging, and other facilities regularly provided by the employer for the employee's benefit may be considered part of wages and used in calculating the minimum wage. Deductions made from wages for such items as cash shortages, breakage, employer-required uniforms (when they are not street clothes), and tools of the trade are not legal if they reduce the wages of employees below the minimum rate required by FLSA or reduce the amount of overtime pay due under FLSA. Deductions for missing cash or breakage, even if they do not reduce the wage below the minimum, can only be made if the employee voluntarily agrees to it without threat of being fired or similar intimidation.

Tipped employees are those who customarily and regularly receive more than thirty dollars per month in tips. A tip is payment above and beyond the bill, left voluntarily by the guest expressly for the employee. Gratuities that are tacked automatically onto guest checks, such as for a banquet, are not considered tips. The employer may consider tips as part of wages, but such a wage credit must not exceed 40 percent of the minimum wage. The same tip credit can be applied to overtime hours.

The employer who elects to use the tip credit provision must inform the employee in advance and must be able to show that the employee receives at least the minimum wage when direct wages and the tip credit allowance are combined. Also, employees must be told to retain all of their tips, notwithstanding any voluntary participation in a valid tip pooling or sharing arrangement. All tipped employees must fill out and retain Internal Revenue Service Form 4070A—Employee's Daily Record of Tips. They must also fill out Form

4070—Employee's Report of Tips to Employer, which is a monthly record of tips to be handed in to the employer on or before the tenth day of the following month.

OVERTIME

Overtime rates, equal to at least 150 percent of an employee's hourly wage rate, must be paid for all hours worked in excess of forty hours in a single work week. For example, if an employee paid $3.80 per hour works forty-four hours in a work week, he is entitled to at least 150 percent of $3.80, or $5.70, for each hour over forty. Pay for the week would be $152 for the first forty hours, plus at least $22.80 for the four hours of overtime.

The base wage rate on which the overtime rate is determined must include bonuses or incentive payments that are received during the same period. For example, if an employee's wage rate is $5.00 per hour, and he works forty-five hours in a week and receives a $90 incentive payment, the actual rate per hour is $7.00. This is calculated by dividing the $90 bonus by the forty-five hours required to earn it. The resulting figure, $2.00, is then added to the employee's wage rate of $5.00. The correct overtime rate must then be 150 percent of $7.00, or $10.50. When employees work positions in different departments and work over forty hours in a week, the overtime rate is based on 150 percent of the average earning per hour (total dollars earned divided by total hours worked).

Certain employees are exempt from both minimum wage and overtime pay: executive, administrative, professional, and outside salespeople. To be considered an executive employee, the employee must:

- Supervise two or more employees
- Be able to hire and fire employees, or make recommendations to do so that are seriously considered
- Receive a salary of at least $155 per week
- Be responsible primarily for management duties, with no more than 40 percent of the employee's work time spent performing nonexempt work
- Be able to set policy and use independent judgment and discretion

Administrative employees are typically people who work in an office, and may include positions such as purchasing directors and agents. There are very few positions in the hospitality field that meet the criteria of the professional employee category, which typically includes doctors, lawyers, and teachers, whose work is mostly intellectual and varied. The position of chef has not been recognized by Wage-Hour as professional. Outside salespeople must pursue sales away from the main office at least 90 percent of the work week to meet the criteria.

FLSA requires employers to keep records on wages, hours, and other items, as specified in Department of Labor regulations. Most of the information is generally maintained by employers in ordinary business practice and in compliance with other laws and regulations. The records do not have to be kept in any particular form, and time clocks need not be used. For employees subject to both minimum wage and overtime pay provisions, the following records must be kept:

- Personal information, including employee's name, home address, occupation, sex, and birth date (if under nineteen years of age)
- Hour and day when work week begins
- Total hours worked each work day and each work week
- Total daily or weekly straight-time earnings
- Regular hourly pay rate for any week when overtime is worked
- Total overtime pay for the work week
- Deductions from or additions to wages
- Total wages paid each pay period
- Date of payment and pay period covered

Records required for exempt employees differ from those for nonexempt workers, and special information is required for employees to whom lodging or other facilities are furnished. For tipped employees, records must also be kept of tips received and amount of tip credit taken.

The equal pay provisions of FLSA prohibit wage differentials based on sex, between men and women employed in the same establishment, and for jobs that require equal skill, effort, and responsibility and are performed under similar working conditions. These provisions are enforced by the Equal Employment Opportunity Commission.

When FLSA corresponds or overlaps with similar state and/or local requirements, the strictest set of laws applies and must be followed.

Recognition, Incentives, Awards: Where to Get Help

Ames & Rollinson Inc.
215 Park Ave.
New York, NY 10003
212-473-7000

AT&T
Corporate Education Center
P.O. Box 1000
Hopewell, NJ 08525
609-639-4509

L. G. Balfour
21 East Street
North Attleboro, MA 02760
617-222-3600

Bulova Watch Company, Inc.
75-20 Astoria Boulevard
Jackson Heights, NY 11370
718-565-4544

Bushnell/Bausch & Lomb
2828 E. Foothill Blvd.
Pasadena, CA 91107
818-577-1500

Center for Housewares Design
704 Silver Spur Road
Rolling Hills Estates, CA 90274
213-541-2448

Citizens Scholarship Foundation
P.O. Box 297
St. Peter, MN 56082
507-931-1682

Designs, implements, and manages scholarship programs and other types of student aid incentives for corporations, foundations, individuals, and trusts. Programs mainly targeted for sons and daughters of company employees, but also used as incentives for employee recruitment and retention.

Encyclopedia Britannica USA
310 South Michigan Ave.
Chicago, IL 60604
312-347-7349

The Gold Lance Co.
1920 Memorial Way
Houston, TX 77007
713-861-2311

Manufactures cast and stamped emblematic jewelry and fine jewelry accents.

Gralan Distributors
P.O. Box 45134
Baton Rouge, LA 70895
504-927-1478

Specializes in quality business and travel accessories: attachés, briefcases, portfolios, desk accessories, garment bags, totes, and eelskin products. Offers silkscreen logos, gold embossing, or embroidered monograms.

Haltom
1200 Evergreen Parkway
Fort Worth, TX 76140
800-433-2907

Hamilton Watch
941 Wheatland Ave.
Lancaster, PA 17604
800-233-0283

Supplies full line of men's and women's watches; also clocks: desk, wall, mantle, and grandfather. Can feature company logo.

Herff Jones, Inc.
226 Public Street
Providence, RI 02940
401-331-1240

J. H. Awards
7800 S.W. Barbur Blvd.
Portland, OR 97219
503-244-1165

Manufactures emblematic jewelry and supplies gift merchandise for recognition and motivation in areas of service, safety, and sales.

Jostens, Recognition Division
5501 Norman Center Drive
Minneapolis, MN 55437
612-830-3364

Supplies custom award products, including emblematic jewelry, rings, medallion timepieces, plaques, certificates, pewter, crystal, and walnut gift products.

Longines-Wittenauer Watch Co.
145 Huguenot St.
New Rochelle, NY 10802
914-576-1000

Manufactures Swiss-crafted quartz timepieces for incentives and recognition awards; also supplies Atmos Heritage clock.

McCormack Enterprises
637 So. Hayden Road
Tempe, AZ 85281
602-967-7760

Metal Decor
P.O. Box 3606
Springfield, IL 62708
217-523-4565

Manufactures custom service award desk pieces, plaques, and shadowboxes for incentives, recognition, service awards. Items personalized before leaving factory.

Howard Miller Clock Company
860 East Main Avenue
Zeeland, MI 49464
616-772-9131

Manufactures floor, wall, mantle, tabletop, and alarm clocks—traditional and modern. Can feature company logo.

Omega Watch
301 E. 57th St.
New York, NY 10022
212-753-3000

Orrefors Crystal
107 Gaither Drive
Mt. Laurel, NJ 08504
609-234-8411

Pendleton Woolen Mills
P.O. Box 1691
Portland, OR 97207
503-226-4801

Pentel of America Ltd.
2715 Columbia Street
Torrance, CA 90509
213-320-3944

Performax Systems International
12755 State Highway 55
Minneapolis, MN 55441
612-559-2322

Perma Plaque
7251 Varna Avenue
North Hollywood, CA 91605
818-764-3100

Presenta Plaque
P.O. Box 48
Ronkonkoma, NY 11779
516-563-2691

Ridgeway Clocks
P.O. Box 407
Ridgeway, VA 24148

The Robbins Company
O'Neil Boulevard
Attleboro, MA 02703
617-222-2900

Creates personalized awards programs in service, sales, performance, safety, and special corporative recognition. Supplies jewelry, emblems, gifts.

Seiko Watch Company
640 Fifth Avenue
New York, NY 10019
212-977-2820

Manufactures quartz watches and clocks ranging from $17.70 to $390.00. Offers variety of personalization services.

Clyde A. Short Company
P.O. Box 310
Shelby, NC 28150
704-482-9591

Supplies variety of items for award and recognition programs, including brand housewares, sporting goods, and tools grouped in 18 different price levels geared to fit all budgets.

Silver Reed America, Inc.
19600 South Vermont Ave.
Torrance, CA 90502
213-516-7008

Smart Jewelers
3350 West Devon Ave.
Lincolnwood, IL 60659
312-673-7500

Supplies fine timepieces for corporate awards, presentation, and retirement, including Rolex, Cartier, Baume & Mercier, and others.

O. C. Tanner
1930 South State Street
Salt Lake City, UT 84115
801-486-2430

Manufactures quality employee recognition award products for service, sales, safety, and other achievements. Complete program design and implementation backed by computerized administrative systems.

Terryberry
2033 Oak Industrial N.E.
Grand Rapids, MI 49505
616-458-1391

Specializes in service award jewelry.

The Thompson Group
17700 West Capital Drive
Brookfield, WI 53005
414-781-0150

Tiffany & Co.
727 Fifth Avenue
New York, NY 10022
212-605-4350

Offers specialized services to companies buying gifts for business purposes. Services include development and implementation of service recognition, incentive, and awards programs.

United Industries
1200 Belle Avenue
Winter Springs, FL 32708
305-699-9152

Index